Reconstruction Era
Almanac

Reconstruction Era
Almanac

Kelly King Howes
Lawrence W. Baker,
Project Editor

U·X·L
An imprint of Thomson Gale,
a part of The Thomson Corporation

THOMSON
GALE

Detroit • New York • San Francisco • San Diego • New Haven, Conn. • Waterville, Maine • London • Munich

THOMSON

GALE

Reconstruction Era: Almanac

Kelly King Howes

Project Editor
Lawrence W. Baker

Permissions
Margaret Abendroth, Denise Buckley,
Margaret Chamberlain

Imaging and Multimedia
Lezlie Light, Mike Logusz, Christine
O'Bryan, Denay Wilding, Robyn Young

Product Design
Pamela A. E. Galbreath, Kate Scheible

Composition
Evi Seoud

Manufacturing
Rita Wimberley

LIBRARY OF CONGRESS CATALOGING-IN-PUBLICATION DATA

Howes, Kelly King.
    Reconstruction era : almanac / Kelly King Howes ; Lawrence W. Baker, project editor.
        p. cm. — (Reconstruction Era reference library)
    Includes bibliographical references (p.) and index.
    ISBN 0-7876-9217-4 (alk. paper)
    1. Reconstruction (U.S. history, 1865–1877)—Juvenile literature. 2. Almanacs, American—Juvenile literature. I. Baker, Lawrence W. II. Title. III. Series.

    E668.H86 2004
    973.8'1—dc22   2004017301

This title is also available as an e-book.
ISBN 1-4144-0454-9
Contact your Thomson Gale sales representative for ordering information.

Printed in the United States of America
10 9 8 7 6 5 4 3

Contents

Reader's Guide vii

Words to Know xi

Reconstruction Era Timeline xxiii

Research and Activity Ideas xxxv

Chapter 1: The Promise of Freedom 1

Chapter 2: The Civil War Draws to a Close. 27

Chapter 3: Slavery's End Brings Both Joy
and Confusion 51

Chapter 4: The President's Plan for Reconstruction . . . 73

Chapter 5: The Radical Republicans Clash with
the President 97

Chapter 6: The Radical Republicans Move Forward
with Reconstruction 123

Chapter 7: The Reconstruction Governments. 143

Chapter 8: White Supremacists "Redeem" the South . . 167

Chapter 9: The Mixed Legacy of the
Reconstruction Era 189

Where to Learn More. 211
Index 215

Reader's Guide

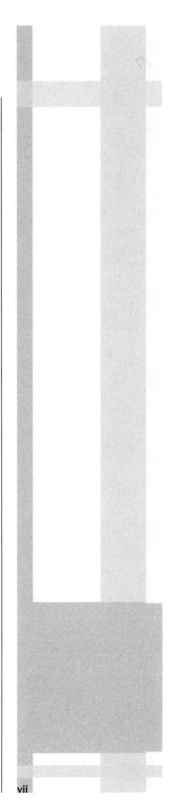

Reconstruction Era: Almanac presents a comprehensive overview of the Reconstruction era, the period stretching roughly from the end of the American Civil War in April 1865 to the inauguration of President Rutherford B. Hayes in 1877. Reconstruction was a federal policy intended to restore the relationship between the former Confederate states and the federal Union, to oversee the transition of the newly freed slaves into citizens, and to help convert the Southern economy from one based on slave labor to one based on paid labor. Reconstruction officially ended following the resolution to the controversial presidential election of 1876 in which an electoral commission declared Hayes the victor, just days before he was inaugurated in March 1877. The new president had federal troops removed from the former Confederate region in the South to bring an end to the Reconstruction era.

Coverage and features

Reconstruction Era: Almanac's nine chapters include information about the effects of freedom on black family life,

Radical Republicans, carpetbaggers and scalawags, amnesty for white Southerners, Black Codes, the impeachment of President Andrew Johnson, the rise of the Ku Klux Klan, attempts to restore the old order in the South, the disputed presidential election of 1876, and the Compromise of 1877. Each chapter contains two types of sidebars: "Words to Know" boxes, which define important terms discussed in the chapter; and boxes that describe people, events, and facts of special interest. Each chapter concludes with a list of additional sources students can go to for more information. Nearly sixty black-and-white photographs and maps help illustrate the book.

The volume begins with a "Words to Know" section that features important terms from the entire Reconstruction era; a "Reconstruction Era Timeline" that lists significant dates and events of the Reconstruction era; and a "Research and Activity Ideas" section with suggestions for study questions, group projects, and oral and dramatic presentations. The volume concludes with a general bibliography and an index so students can easily find the people, places, and events discussed throughout *Reconstruction Era: Almanac.*

U•X•L Reconstruction Era Reference Library

Reconstruction Era: Almanac is only one component of the three-part U•X•L Reconstruction Era Reference Library. The other two titles in this set are:

• *Reconstruction Era: Biographies:* This volume presents twenty-five entries covering twenty-eight people who lived during the Reconstruction era. Profiled are well-known figures such as embattled president Andrew Johnson, his political enemies Thaddeus Stevens and Charles Sumner, and African American pioneers Frederick Douglass and Hiram Revels, as well as lesser-known individuals such as chemist and home economics founder Ellen Richards, 1876 presidential election loser Samuel J. Tilden, and early baseball star Harry Wright. *Biographies* includes nearly eighty black-and-white photographs and illustrations, a timeline, and an index.

- *Reconstruction Era: Primary Sources:* This title tells the story of the Reconstruction era in the words of the people who lived and shaped it and the laws that contributed to it. Nineteen complete or excerpted documents provide a wide range of perspectives on this period of history. Included are excerpts from abolitionist Frederick Douglass's famous article about Reconstruction, Frances Butler Leigh's account of life after slavery as the daughter of a plantation owner, former slave John Paterson Green's experiences with the Ku Klux Klan, and U.S. senator Charles Sumner's argument in favor of the impeachment of President Andrew Johnson. *Primary Sources* includes nearly sixty black-and-white photographs and illustrations, a timeline, and an index.

- A cumulative index of all three titles in the U•X•L Reconstruction Era Reference Library is also available.

Acknowledgments

Thanks to copyeditor and caption writer Theresa Murray; proofreader Amy Marcaccio Keyzer; the indexers from Synapse, the Knowledge Link Corporation; and typesetter Jake Di Vita of the Graphix Group for their fine work.

Comments and suggestions

We welcome your comments on *Reconstruction Era: Almanac* and suggestions for other topics to consider. Please write: Editors, *Reconstruction Era: Almanac,* U•X•L, 27500 Drake Rd., Farmington Hills, Michigan 48331-3535; call toll free: (800) 877-4253; fax to (248) 699-8097; or send e-mail via http://www.gale.com.

Words to Know

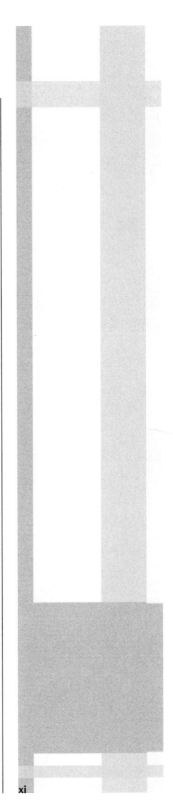

A

Abolitionism: The movement to end slavery, which gained followers as the United States grew and more people began to protest the enslavement of blacks in the South. By the time of the Civil War, its followers exerted considerable influence on public opinion in the North.

Amnesty: An official pardon for those convicted of political offenses.

B

Black Codes: Laws put in place by the Southern governments formed under the Reconstruction plan of President Andrew Johnson, which returned power to the former leaders of the Confederacy. They limited the economic options and civil rights of the former slaves through strict regulations on both their working conditions and their behavior.

Black suffrage: The right of African Americans to cast votes in elections. The Fifteenth Amendment to the Constitution, passed in 1870, guaranteed that voting rights could not be denied on the basis of race or "previous condition of servitude."

Border states: States located on the border between the North and the South (Delaware, Maryland, Kentucky, and Missouri). Although they were slave states, their citizens had voted against seceding (separating) from the Union, so they did not become part of the Confederacy.

C

Carpetbaggers: The intentionally offensive nickname for Northerners who went to the South after the Civil War to participate in Reconstruction. Although many white Southerners felt they had come to take advantage of the devastated, demoralized South (and later, racist accounts of Reconstruction reinforced this view), most were actually educated, middle-class men with good intentions. Among their number were Union army veterans, teachers, and investors.

Civil Rights Act of 1867: Legislation guaranteeing that all persons born in the United States (except for Native Americans) were to be considered U.S. citizens with full protection of "person and property" under the law.

Civil Rights Act of 1875: Legislation that was supposed to reinforce the guarantee of civil and political rights for blacks and also prohibit segregation in public places, especially public schools. It proved ineffective, though, and was struck down by the Supreme Court in 1883.

Civil rights movement: A political, civil, and social struggle that took place in the middle of the twentieth century. Seeking full citizenship and equality for African Americans, the movement challenged segregation and discrimination through such activities as protest marches, boycotts, and refusals to go along with racist laws.

Civil War: The bloody conflict that divided the United States from 1861 to 1865. It pitted the Northern Union (federal government) against the Confederacy, the eleven Southern states that had seceded, or broken away, from the United States. Initially sparked by the secession of the Confederacy and the desire to keep the Union together, the war eventually became a struggle to free the four million blacks held as slaves in the South.

Compromise of 1877: The agreement that resolved the controversy over the election of Republican Rutherford B. Hayes as president. Democrats agreed to accept Hayes's election in exchange for Home Rule in the South. The agreement allowed for the overthrow of the last three Reconstruction governments.

Confederacy: The eleven Southern states that seceded (separated themselves) from the Union, sparking the Civil War. These states, also known as the Confederate States of America, included Virginia, North Carolina, South Carolina, Georgia, Florida, Mississippi, Alabama, Arkansas, Louisiana, Tennessee, and Texas.

Contrabands: Slaves who became refugees when, as the Union army advanced through the South, they fled from their masters and sought refuge in the Union camps. The word contraband refers to property confiscated by an invading army during war.

D

Davis Bend, Mississippi: The site of a successful experiment in which blacks were given control by the Union army of their own land and labor. The setting was a large plantation confiscated from the family of Confederate president Jefferson Davis.

Democratic Party: The political party that had been dominant in the South before the Civil War and which regained control at the end of Reconstruction. Generally, Democrats were conservatives who opposed the kinds of changes advocated by the Republicans, especially those that, they felt, gave the federal government too much power.

E

Enforcement Acts: Legislation passed in 1871 that was designed to help protect African Americans' right to vote.

Exoduster movement: A migration made up of African Americans who, following the overthrow of the multiracial Reconstruction governments in the South by white supremacist "Redeemers," migrated to the new western state of Kansas. They sought a greater degree of political equality, expanded educational and economic opportunities, and an escape from racial violence.

F

Fifteenth Amendment: A constitutional amendment, passed in early 1870, that barred state governments from denying or abridging voting rights "on account of race, color, or previous condition of servitude."

Fifty-fourth Massachusetts regiment: A Union army unit formed in Boston in early 1863 that fought at Fort Wagner in South Carolina. The regiment lost the battle and sustained heavy losses (including its white commander, Robert Gould Shaw), but was honored for its valiant fighting.

First South Carolina Volunteers: The first regiment of black soldiers (formed in November 1862) to join the Union army during the Civil War. Because they were paid substantially less than white soldiers, these men refused to accept any pay at all and fought for free.

"Forty Acres and a Mule": The slogan that became a popular representation of what African Americans hoped the federal government would give them after the Civil War, in compensation for their many years of unpaid labor.

Fourteenth Amendment: A constitutional amendment, passed in 1868, that made it illegal for any state to deny equality before the law to any male citizen. Although it did not guarantee that blacks could vote, it gave an advantage to states that did allow black suffrage.

Free blacks: African Americans who had never been slaves, or who had escaped from slavery into the North.

Freedmen's Bureau: A federal agency that existed from 1865 to 1869 that assisted the former slaves in their transition to freedom. The program helped African Americans by distributing clothing, food, and fuel; handling legal cases; dispensing medical care; and setting up black schools.

Freedmen's Conventions: Meetings held by African Americans following the end of the Civil War, at which they discussed the issues facing them and drew up statements to present to white leaders.

G

Gideon's Band: A group of Northern teachers and missionaries whose abolitionist ideals inspired them to travel to the Sea Islands of South Carolina as the Civil War was ending to help the freed slaves.

H

Home Rule: Local self-government, desired by white supremacists in the South as a way to regain control of their state governments.

I

Impeachment: The process of charging an elected official with misconduct. On February 24, 1868, the House of Representatives passed a resolution to impeach President Andrew Johnson; he was specifically charged with violating the Tenure of Office Act and with bringing the office of the president into "contempt, ridicule, and disgrace." The trial results were one vote short of the two-thirds majority required to remove the president from office.

Integration: The intermixing of people or groups previously segregated (separated).

J

Jim Crow: The system of legalized segregation found in the South beginning in the 1890s that mandated the segregation of schools and other public facilities.

K

Ku Klux Klan: The most prominent of several white supremacist groups that used violence—in the form of beatings, whippings, murder, rape, and arson—to control black people and their sympathizers through fear and intimidation.

L

Liberal Republicans: Members of a reform movement who were against corruption, high taxes, and what they saw as extravagant public spending. They favored free trade, limited government, and basing the allotment of federal government jobs on examinations. They also supported Home Rule for the South as well as amnesty for former Confederates, who they considered the "natural leaders" of the South.

Lynch law: A brutal system of justice by which blacks accused of crimes but usually not formally charged or tried would be hanged by mobs of whites.

M

Militia Act: Legislation signed by President Abraham Lincoln in 1862 that guaranteed that slaves who enlisted in the Union Army would earn their freedom. The act helped open the way for African Americans to join the Union Army.

Mississippi plan: The pattern of violent disruptions of elections that would become a blueprint for the "redemption" of Southern states by Democrats and other white supremacists.

Mulattoes: People of biracial, or mixed black and white, heritage.

Mutual benefit societies: Organizations created by African Americans following the end of slavery. These societies lent strength and support to the black communities that began to thrive during the Reconstruction era and were often organized around professions or reform movements.

N

New Departure: A brief attempt by members of the Southern Democratic Party to attract black voters by downplaying its true white supremacist views and focusing on such issues as taxes, government spending, and amnesty for former Confederates.

P

Panic of 1873: A period of serious economic decline that was set off by the bankruptcy of powerful banker Jay Cooke.

Plantation: A large farm or estate on which basic crops like cotton, tobacco, sugar, and rice were grown. Before the Civil War, the Southern economy was dependent on the agricultural production of the plantations, which in turn depended on the unpaid labor of slaves.

Plessy v. Ferguson: A U.S. Supreme Court case regarding segregation of the railroads. Asserting that the Fourteenth Amendment was never intended to prevent "social" segregation, the court found that segregation was acceptable as long as black passengers were provided with "equal" accommodations.

Proclamation of Amnesty: A document issued by President Andrew Johnson soon after he took office, that established that most Southerners would be allowed to take an oath of allegiance that would offer them a complete pardon and amnesty and would restore to them any property other than slaves that the federal government had seized during the war.

Proclamation of Amnesty and Reconstruction: Also known as the Ten Per Cent Plan, a plan created by President Abraham Lincoln that would allow most Southerners who took an oath of loyalty to the United States and agreed to accept the abolition of slavery to receive a full pardon and the restoration of all rights guaranteed to U.S. citizens.

R

Race riots: Outbreaks of violence that highlighted racial tensions in both the North and South. Major riots occurred in New York, Memphis, and New Orleans.

Racism: The belief that there are characteristics or qualities specific to each race, which often results in discrimination (treating people differently based on race).

Radical Republicans: A group of senators and representatives with a history of activism in the abolitionist movement who turned their energies, during the Reconstruction era, toward trying to create a truly democratic society in the South.

Ratification: The process of both houses of the U.S. Congress or a state legislature approving and signing a bill.

Reconstruction Acts of 1867: The legislation devised by the Radical Republicans in Congress as a plan for remaking Southern society. The first act divided the ten Southern states—Tennessee had already been readmitted to the Union—into five military districts ruled by military commanders until the new state governments wrote and approved constitutions. The states had to ratify the Fourteenth Amendment as well as guarantee suffrage for all male citizens. Three subsequent Reconstruction Acts refined some of the issues brought up by the first.

Reconstruction era: The period stretching roughly from the end of the Civil War in April 1865 to the inauguration of President Rutherford B. Hayes in 1877. During Reconstruction, representatives of the U.S. government—including the president and Congress—and the military would join with both white and black Southerners to try to reorganize the political and social structure of the devastated, defeated South.

Redemption movement: The successful effort, which took place between 1869 and 1877, to overthrow or "redeem" the Republican governments and replace its leaders with men devoted to white supremacy.

Republican Party: The political party that dominated both the U.S. Congress and the new Southern governments during the Reconstruction era. Before the war, most Republicans had tended to live in the North and had favored protections for business interests, public support for internal improvements (like roads and services), and social reforms. As the Reconstruction era progressed, the Republican Party grew more conservative, and its influence in the South decreased as that of the white Southern Democrats increased.

S

Scalawags: The intentionally offensive nickname for the white Southerners who joined the Republican Party and took part in the Reconstruction governments. Some scalawags saw this submission as the best route to gaining white control of the South again, whereas others were sincerely interested in creating a new, more just society.

Sea Islands: A chain of islands located off the coasts of South Carolina and Georgia. They were the site of an early experiment in distributing confiscated land to former slaves, and the destination of Gideon's Band, a group of teachers and missionaries who helped the freed slaves.

Secession: The separation of the eleven Southern states of the Confederacy from the rest of the Union, an act that sparked the Civil War.

Second Mississippi Plan: A concerted effort by the Redeemer governments to prevent blacks from voting. Whereas the first Mississippi Plan had used terror to accomplish this goal, the second featured the inclusion of new voting laws or "suppression clauses" in state constitutions that restricted voting through literacy and property requirements, poll taxes, and "understanding clauses."

Segregation: The separation of people or groups which, in the Southern United States, was based on race.

Sharecropping: The system of labor that came to dominate the rural South in the years following the Civil War. Preferred by blacks over the old gang-labor system because it gave them some control over their time, work conditions, and families, sharecropping involved the allotment of plots of land to individual families. At harvest time, they would either give the owner a share of the crop they had raised or pay rent to him.

Slaughterhouse Cases: A series of Supreme Court cases in the 1880s in which the rulings effectively denied blacks the right to use the federal courts to fight unfair state laws, declared that the U.S. Constitution did not "confer the right of suffrage on anyone," and voided parts of the Enforcement Acts (which had guaranteed penalties for those who use violence to interfere with elections).

Slavery: The practice of making human beings the property of others and forcing them to obey. Slaves captured in Africa were brought as unpaid laborers to the Southern United States, beginning in the seventeenth century. They endured harsh living and working conditions and, often, brutal punishment. By the time of the Civil War, there were about four million slaves in the United States. The 1863 Emancipation Proclamation declared most of them free. The end of the Civil War, followed by the passage of the Thirteenth Amendment to the Constitution, brought an end to slavery.

Special Field Order #15: A document issued by Union general William T. Sherman that allowed blacks to settle on 40-acre plots located along the South Carolina and Georgia coasts. Hopes for independence were dashed when this so-called "Sherman land" was returned to its Confederate owners soon after the end of the war.

T

Thirteenth Amendment: The amendment in the U.S. Constitution, passed in 1865, that officially abolished slavery in the United States.

U

Union League: An organization, closely allied with the Republican Party, that African Americans across the South joined soon after the end of the Civil War. The group helped build schools and churches, care for the sick, assist workers in demanding fair wages and better working conditions, register black voters.

Unionists: Southerners who opposed secession and continued to support the Union throughout the Civil War.

V

Vagrancy: Being without a home or a job. Beginning in the Reconstruction era, vagrancy laws made joblessness a crime, thus forcing unemployed blacks to accept work on white Southerners' plantations.

Veto: Refuse to approve.

W

Wade-Davis Bill: Legislation that called for a majority of a Southern state's white males to sign an oath saying they had never aided the Confederacy before a new state constitution could be drawn up. Only those who signed the oath could vote on a new constitution, which had to outlaw slavery but did not have to ensure blacks the right to vote. President Abraham Lincoln opted not to sign the bill.

White supremacists: Those who hold the racist view that people of northern European or white heritage are superior to those of African and other nonwhite descent and ought to be in control of society.

Women's suffrage: A movement to win for women the right to vote.

Reconstruction Era Timeline

1622 The first African slaves are brought to the British colonies in North America, which will eventually become the United States of America.

1803 The Louisiana Purchase adds about 800,000 square miles of new territory to the United States.

1820 The Missouri Compromise allows Missouri to be admitted to the Union as a slave state, while Maine is admitted as a free state, thus maintaining the balance between states where slavery is allowed and where it is illegal. Slavery is prohibited in any of the lands of the Louisiana Purchase that are north of the Missouri border.

1848 The U.S. victory in the Mexican-American War brings a large area of new territory into the United States, including what will become the states of Texas, New Mexico, Arizona, and California.

February 28, 1854 The Republican Party is formed by politicians—most of them from the Northern states—who favor protections for business interests, public support for internal improvements (like roads and services), and social reforms, especially an end to slavery.

May 30, 1854 The Kansas-Nebraska Bill, which reverses the Missouri Compromise by allowing the status of slavery in Kansas and Nebraska to be decided by settlers, is signed into law.

May 19–20, 1856 U.S. senator Charles Sumner of Massachusetts gives his "Crime against Kansas" speech in which he insults proslavery supporters of the Kansas-Missouri bill of 1854.

August 21, 1858 Future president Abraham Lincoln and U.S. senator Stephen A. Douglas of Illinois hold the first in a series of seven debates on the issue of slavery; they take place over a period of two months.

November 6, 1860 Illinois Republican Abraham Lincoln is elected president, sending shockwaves of panic through the South, where many believe that Lincoln will immediately take steps to outlaw slavery.

February 4, 1861 Seven Southern states that have seceded (broken away) from the Federal Union form a government of their own called the Confederate States of America, or the Confederacy. They establish their capitol in Richmond, Virginia, with former U.S. senator Jefferson Davis of Mississippi as president. In April and May, four more Southern states will join the Confederacy.

April 12–13, 1861 A successful Confederate attack on the Union outpost at Fort Sumter, South Carolina, marks the beginning of the American Civil War.

May 24, 1861 Three Virginia slaves who have escaped from their plantation and fled to a Union army camp are labeled "contraband" (property confiscated during a war) by Union general Benjamin Butler.

July 21, 1861 The Confederate army defeats Union forces at the first Battle of Bull Run in Virginia, not far from Washington, D.C.

November 7, 1861 The U.S. Navy occupies the city of Port Royal in the Sea Islands off the shore of South Carolina. The white plantation owners in the area have already fled, leaving behind a large population of slaves.

February 24, 1862 The Union army takes control of Nashville, Tennessee. In early April, they will also win a victory at Shiloh, Tennessee.

March 13, 1862 Congress passes an Article of War that prohibits the Army from returning runaway slaves to their masters.

April 25, 1862 Union naval forces under Commander David Farragut capture the important southern city of New Orleans, Louisiana.

May 13, 1862 South Carolina slave Robert Smalls steals a Confederate navy ship from Charleston Harbor and turns it over to the Union forces.

July 17, 1862 President Abraham Lincoln signs the Second Confiscation Act, which declares free all slaves who escape to the Union lines.

September 17, 1862 The Union army wins a decisive victory at the Battle of Antietam near Sharpsburg, Maryland.

September 27, 1862 The First Louisiana Native Guard, made up of African Americans from New Orleans's free black community, becomes the first official black regiment to join the Union army.

1863 The Militia Act, passed on July 17, 1862, allows former slaves to enroll in the U.S. Army.

January 1, 1863 President Abraham Lincoln signs the Emancipation Proclamation, which declares forever free most of the four million slaves living in the Confederate states. Excluded are approximately 450,000 slaves in the loyal border states, the 275,000 in Union-held Tennessee, and those in the parts of Virginia and Louisiana that are under Union control.

January 25, 1863 The Fifty-fourth Massachusetts Infantry becomes the first African American regiment in the North to join the Union army.

March 1863 The group of idealistic northern missionaries and teachers known as Gideon's Band arrives in Port

Royal, South Carolina, intending to assist the large population of former slaves living there.

May 1863 The all-black Fifty-fourth Massachusetts Regiment departs from Boston for South Carolina, where the soldiers will win acclaim for their bravery during a battle at Fort Wagner.

July 1–3, 1863 At Gettysburg, Pennsylvania, the Union army wins an important victory, forcing the Confederate army to retreat into Virginia.

July 4, 1863 After an eight-week siege, Union forces under General Ulysses S. Grant defeat Confederate troops in Vicksburg, Mississippi.

July 13–16, 1863 Nearly a thousand people are killed or wounded in a bloody race riot in New York City that highlights northern opposition to the war and white hostility toward African Americans.

November 1863 At Beaufort, South Carolina, the First South Carolina Volunteers become the first Union regiments of black soldiers to be formed in the Confederate states.

December 8, 1863 President Abraham Lincoln issues his Proclamation of Amnesty and Reconstruction, also known as the Ten Per Cent Plan. The plan allows almost any Southerner who will take an oath of loyalty to the United States to receive a full pardon and all rights of a U.S. citizen. Once 10 percent of a Southern state's population have signed the oath, the state may form a new government. Lincoln's plan is criticized by several members of Congress as too lenient toward the Confederacy.

March 1864 Davis Bend, Mississippi, is the site of an experiment in which about 5,000 blacks are given control over their own land and labor. The freed people not only establish their own government but, by 1865, raise almost 2,000 bales of cotton, earning a profit of $160,000.

July 4, 1864 President Abraham Lincoln pocket-vetoes the Wade-Davis Bill, which would have allowed a Southern state to be readmitted to the Union only after 50 percent of those who voted in 1860 signed a loyalty oath.

September 2, 1864 The Southern city of Atlanta, Georgia, falls to Union forces under General William T. Sherman.

November 8, 1864 Abraham Lincoln is reelected president.

November 16, 1864 Union general William T. Sherman leaves Atlanta, Georgia, and begins his "March to the Sea," which ends on December 21 when he takes control of the coastal city of Savannah without a fight.

January 16, 1865 Union general William T. Sherman issues his Special Field Order #15, which sets aside land along the Georgia coast for settlement by African Americans.

January 31, 1865 Congress passes the Thirteenth Amendment, officially abolishing slavery in the United States.

March 3, 1865 The U.S. Department of War establishes the Freedmen's Bureau, a federal agency authorized to assist the former slaves in their transition to freedom by distributing clothing, food, fuel, and medical care and to help coordinate the establishment of black schools. Later, the agency's powers will be expanded to set up black schools and handle legal cases brought by blacks.

April 3, 1865 Union forces capture Richmond, Virginia, the Confederate capitol. The next day, President Abraham Lincoln travels down from Washington, D.C., to stroll through the city.

April 9, 1865 Confederate general Robert E. Lee formally surrenders to the Union army at Appomattox Courthouse, Virginia.

April 14, 1865 Southern actor John Wilkes Booth shoots Abraham Lincoln while the president is attending a play at Ford's Theatre in Washington, D.C. Lincoln dies the next day, and Vice President Andrew Johnson is sworn in as president.

May 29, 1865 Choosing not to wait until Congress is in session, President Andrew Johnson announces his plan for the Reconstruction of the South. His program is so lenient toward the Confederacy that it will allow most of those who dominated Southern politics before the war to return to power.

Summer 1865 The Southern states hold conventions to form state governments under President Andrew Johnson's plan. They put in place new laws called Black Codes that are meant to restrict the employment options and personal freedom of African Americans. At the same time, Southern blacks hold Freedmen's Conventions throughout the South, at which they discuss and record their views.

Fall 1865 Noted orator and writer Frederick Douglass undertakes a speaking tour in support of voting and civil rights for freedmen. The following year, Douglass speaks and writes against the policies of President Andrew Johnson, who refused to use his federal powers to pursue voting rights for freedmen or to interfere with states on civil rights issues.

December 1865 Politician and former Union general Carl Schurz reports on conditions in the South, warning that blacks need the federal government's protection from hostile white Southerners. Although President Andrew Johnson ignores the report, many Northerners are horrified by its contents.

December 6, 1865 In an address to the Thirty-ninth Congress, President Andrew Johnson announces that the reconstruction of the South has been completed. Congress disagrees, and refuses to seat the new Southern representatives and senators.

December 18, 1865 After being named House chairman of a joint congressional committee on Reconstruction, U.S. representative Thaddeus Stevens of Pennsylvania declares that it is the duty of Congress to supervise Reconstruction and demand tough terms of the former Confederate states, rejecting President Andrew Johnson's authority to define the terms of Reconstruction.

January 1866 Alexander Stephens, former vice president of the Confederate States of America, is elected to the U.S. Senate in Georgia under the Reconstruction Plan initiated by President Andrew Johnson. Congress, however, rejects the plan and does not allow Stephens to serve.

April 9, 1866 A Congress dominated by a group called the Radical Republicans passes the Civil Rights Bill over President Andrew Johnson's veto. This legislation guarantees that all persons born in the United States (except for Native Americans) are to be considered U.S. citizens with full protection of "person and property" under the law.

May 1, 1866 A three-day race riot begins in Memphis, Tennessee. When it is over, forty-six blacks will have died.

June 13, 1866 Congress approves the Fourteenth Amendment to the U.S. Constitution, which makes it illegal for any state to deny equality before the law to any male citizen.

July 16, 1866 Over President Andrew Johnson's veto, Congress passes a bill extending the life and expanding the powers of the Freedmen's Bureau.

July 30, 1866 Thirty-four blacks and three whites die in a race riot in New Orleans, Louisiana.

August 28, 1866 President Andrew Johnson embarks on what will prove to be a disastrous "swing around the circle" speaking tour.

November 1866 The Republicans win a landslide victory in the midterm elections. They are now in control of every Northern state legislature and government, and the Radicals Republicans in the U.S. Congress are at their peak of power.

March 2, 1867 Over President Andrew Johnson's veto, Congress passes the first in a series of Reconstruction Acts. This one divides the South into five military districts, to be run by military commanders until the states meet the federal requirements for forming new governments. Seeking to prevent Johnson from overriding the Republicans' Reconstruction efforts, Congress also passes the Tenure of Office Act, which limits the president from dismissing government officials who have been approved by Congress.

May 1867 Former Confederate general Nathan Bedford Forrest becomes the first Grand Wizard of the Ku Klux Klan, a white terrorist group formed a year earlier.

Fall 1867 In accordance with the Reconstruction Act, the former states of the Confederacy hold constitutional conventions. Nearly a million and a half voters are registered, including about seven hundred thousand African Americans.

February 1868 After President Andrew Johnson dismisses Secretary of War Edwin Stanton, whose political views differ from his own, Congress impeaches him on the grounds that he has violated the Tenure of Office Act and other charges.

May 1868 U.S. senator Charles Sumner of Massachusetts offers a fierce argument in favor of removing President Andrew Johnson from office.

May 16, 1868 President Andrew Johnson is acquitted of violating the Tenure of Office Act. He escapes being dismissed from office by one vote.

June 1868 The states of Alabama, Arkansas, Florida, Georgia, Louisiana, North Carolina, and South Carolina are readmitted to the Union under the Reconstruction plan developed by the Republicans in Congress.

August 11, 1868 The death of U.S. representive Thaddeus Stevens of Pennsylvania a longtime advocate for black equality, represents waning congressional advocacy concern for African American civil rights.

November 3, 1868 Civil War hero Ulysses S. Grant is elected president. The votes cast by newly enfranchised African Americans play a key role in his win.

1869 The newly formed Reconstruction governments are established.

February 26, 1869 Jefferson Davis, former president of the Confederate States of America, is released from prison following delays in his trial and a general amnesty proclamation for ex-Confederates by President Andrew Johnson.

May 1869 The National Woman Suffrage Association (NWSA) is founded by Susan B. Anthony and Elizabeth Cady Stanton.

February 25, 1870 Hiram Revels of Mississippi, the first African American to serve in the U.S. Senate, takes over the seat once occupied by former Confederate president Jefferson Davis.

March 30, 1870 The Fifteenth Amendment, which bars state governments from denying or abridging voting rights "on account of race, color, or previous condition of servitude," becomes part of the U.S. Constitution.

May 31, 1870 In response to the widespread violence that had terrorized Southern blacks, Congress passes the first of three Enforcement Acts designed to protect the civil and political rights of African Americans.

1871 Congress declares that the Indian nations are no longer sovereign, an act that will lead to the gradual relocation of all Native Americans onto reservations.

April 20, 1871 The second Enforcement Act, known as the Ku Klux Klan Act, is passed by Congress.

May 1, 1872 The Liberal Republican Party nominates New York newspaper editor Horace Greeley for president. Two months later, the Democratic Party also nominates Greeley.

November 5, 1872 President Ulysses S. Grant wins reelection.

December 11, 1872 African American P. B. S. Pinchback becomes acting governor of Louisiana, serving for a little less than one month.

September 18, 1873 The period of serious economic decline known as the Panic of 1873 begins, set off by the bankruptcy of Jay Cooke, one of the most powerful bankers in the country. More than a million people lose their jobs, thousands of businesses close, and agricultural prices and land values fall. Miners and factory workers react to wage cuts with violent strikes.

March 11, 1874 With the death of U.S. senator Charles Sumner of Massachusetts, the waning influence of the

Radical Republicans of Congress effectively ends. The Radical Republicans had controlled Reconstruction policy.

Fall 1874 To keep blacks away from the polls in the November elections in Mississippi, a program of terrorism called the "Mississippi Plan" is put into effect. Widespread violence and intimidation are successfully employed as weapons to prevent blacks from exercising their voting rights. Similar effects will be achieved by the same means in other states during the 1876 elections, leading to victories by white supremacists across the South.

November 1874 Blanche K. Bruce of Mississippi becomes the first African American to be elected to a full term to the U.S. Senate.

March 1, 1875 Congress passes the Civil Rights Act, which is meant to reinforce the government's commitment to protecting black rights. Key provisions of the act will be found unconstitutional in the Slaughterhouse Cases, which will come before the Supreme Court in the 1880s.

December 9, 1875 The Whiskey Ring corruption scandal erupts when President Ulysses S. Grant's private secretary, Orville E. Babcock, is charged with participating in fraud involving tax revenues.

November 7, 1876 The results of the presidential election in which Republican Rutherford B. Hayes narrowly beats Democrat Samuel J. Tilden are disputed. Four months later, in a compromise that will allow the Redemption movement to overthrow the southern Reconstruction governments, Democrats agree to accept Hayes's election if the government will leave the South to manage its own affairs.

April 1877 Federal troops are withdrawn from the state capitols of South Carolina and Louisiana, allowing white supremacists known as "Redeemers" to take control of these states' governments. Soon the Redemption movement will have overthrown all of the Reconstruction governments.

Summer 1877 President Rutherford B. Hayes tours the South and makes speeches announcing the end of Reconstruction.

Spring 1879 Discouraged by the overthrow of the multiracial Reconstruction governments by white supremacists, some Southern blacks migrate to the new western state of Kansas. Members of the Exoduster movement, as it is called, seek wider employment opportunities, protection of civil rights, and an escape from the anti-black violence that plagues the South.

1880 Poverty is widespread in the South, where the per capita income is only 40 percent of that of the North.

1881 Influential black leader Booker T. Washington is named principal of the Tuskegee Institute, which will soon become the leading black educational institution in the nation.

1887 The first Jim Crow law is enacted in Florida. This system of legalized segregation mandates separate schools and public facilities (such as hospitals, prisons, hotels, restaurants, parks, waiting rooms, elevators, cemeteries, and drinking fountains) for blacks and whites.

1894 W. E. B. Du Bois, who will become the leading black intellectual and founder of the Niagara Movement, earns a Ph.D. from Harvard University.

September 18, 1895 African American activist Booker T. Washington delivers his famous Atlanta Compromise Speech, in which he tells a white audience that blacks are more interested in economic advancement than political and social equality.

1896 In the *Plessy v. Ferguson* case, the Supreme Court validates the concept of "separate but equal," asserting that the Fourteenth Amendment was never intended to prevent social segregation.

January 1, 1913 African American communities across the nation hold Jubilee celebrations to commemorate the fiftieth anniversary of the signing of the Emancipation Proclamation.

1929 The stock market crash marks the onset of the Great Depression, a period of economic hardship that will last until the entrance of the United States into World War II.

1955–56 Civil rights advocates take part in the Montgomery Bus Boycott, refusing to ride on the city buses of Montgomery, Alabama, until they are integrated. Many believe that this event inaugurates the Civil Rights Movement.

1965 The passage of the Voting Rights Act marks a new era in public and government commitment to the guarantee of black civil and political rights.

Research and Activity Ideas

The following research and activity ideas are intended to offer suggestions for complementing social studies and history curricula, to trigger additional ideas for enhancing learning, and to provide cross-disciplinary projects for library and classroom use.

- **Change history:** Imagine if President Abraham Lincoln had not been assassinated, or the Redeemers had not succeeded in overthrowing the Reconstruction governments. Think about how Southern society—and U.S. history—might have turned out differently if key events had never happened. Write a series of journal entries, an exchange of letters, or a standard essay describing what life is like in this alternative world.

- **Three women from different worlds:** Imagine the voices and outlooks of three women of the Reconstruction era: the wife of a plantation owner who has lost a son in the Civil War, a former slave who is the mother of three children (one of whom was sold away to another plantation), and a northern teacher who has come South to help the freed people. What would these women have had in common, and how would their perspectives have differed? Write a play in which these three characters encounter and interact with each other, or speak through their voices in written form.

- **The land and labor problem:** Read a variety of sources to learn how and why sharecropping came to be the solution—however inadequate—to the problem of land and labor in the post–Civil War South. Can you think of a solution that might have worked better? Present your research and conclusions in report form.

- **The many voices of Reconstruction:** Hold a panel discussion on how to reconstruct the South with students playing the roles of (1) a white Northerner who has come to the South to invest in a plantation; (2) an upcountry white Southerner who has joined the Republican party; (3) a former slave who is eager to acquire an education; (4) a Radical Republican member of Congress; (5) a former Confederate soldier who has joined the Ku Klux Klan; and (6) an African American who was a free black living in the North before the war.

- **Life as a slave:** Create a large poster or mural that combines text and illustrations to show how African Americans lived during slavery and how their lives changed after the Civil War.

- **Impersonate a famous Reconstruction figure:** Research the life of a prominent Reconstruction figure (such as Frederick Douglass, Wade Hampton, Oliver Otis Howard, Andrew Johnson, John Roy Lynch, Robert Smalls, Thaddeus Stevens, or Charles Sumner) and present a monologue in which you impersonate the figure and discuss his or her life and opinions.

- **North and South: Exploring the differences:** Write a report or make a presentation—including graphs, charts and maps—about the economic, geographical, and cultural differences between the North and South, and how these influenced people's viewpoints before, during, and after Reconstruction.

- **A voice from the women's movement:** Feminist leaders like Elizabeth Cady Stanton and Susan B. Anthony were disappointed by the passage of the Fourteenth Amendment, which guaranteed civil and political rights for all male citizens, but not for women. In the voice of one of these women, write an open letter to African American leader Frederick Douglass (long an advocate of women's right) in which you criticize him for his support of the amendment.

- **Reconstruction and the arts:** Research the music, literature, art, crafts, or recreation of the Reconstruction era to determine how they were influenced by the events occurring in the United States during this period. Present your results in the form of a museum catalog that includes text and pictures.

- **A Reconstruction talk show:** Create a taped discussion structured like a radio call-in show, or a videotaped talk show, with callers or guests who express different viewpoints on Reconstruction. Represent as many backgrounds, outlooks, and emotions as possible.

The Promise of Freedom

Edisto Island must have seemed like an exotic place to Mary Ames. A native of Boston, Massachusetts, Ames had arrived in this community in the Sea Islands, located just off the shore of South Carolina, in May 1865. Mary believed that slavery (the practice of forcing human beings to work for no wages and without the prospect of freedom) was wrong. She had come to Edisto Island to give its black residents—most of them former slaves freed after the Union victory in the Civil War (1861–65)—something they had long been denied. She was here to give them an education, to teach them.

The Civil War may have ended, but great challenges lay ahead. Black and white Southerners sought to remake a society that had been shaken by four years of bloody conflict between the Northern Union (federal government) and the Confederacy, the eleven Southern states that had seceded, or broken away, from the United States. Initially sparked by the secession of the Confederacy and the desire to keep the Union together, the war eventually became a struggle to free the four million blacks held as slaves in the South. Like other Northern teachers who had traveled south to help in this ef-

Words to Know

Abolitionism: The movement to end slavery, which gained followers as the United States grew and more people began to protest the enslavement of blacks in the South. By the time of the Civil War, its followers exerted considerable influence on public opinion in the North.

Border states: States located on the border between the North and the South (Delaware, Maryland, Kentucky, and Missouri). Although they were slave states, their citizens had voted against seceding (separating) from the Union, so they did not become part of the Confederacy.

Civil War: The bloody conflict that divided the United States from 1861 to 1865. It pitted the Northern Union (federal government) against the Confederacy, the eleven Southern states that had seceded, or broken away, from the United States. Initially sparked by the secession of the Confederacy and the desire to keep the Union together, the war eventually became a struggle to free the four million blacks held as slaves in the South.

Confederacy: The eleven Southern states that seceded (separated themselves) from the Union, sparking the Civil War. These states, also known as the Confederate States of America, included Virginia, North Carolina, South Carolina, Georgia, Florida, Mississippi, Alabama, Arkansas, Louisiana, Tennessee, and Texas.

Fifty-fourth Massachusetts regiment: A Union army unit formed in Boston in early 1863 that fought at Fort Wagner in South Carolina. The regiment lost the battle and sustained heavy losses (including its white commander, Robert Gould Shaw), but was honored for its valiant fighting.

First South Carolina Volunteers: The first regiment of black soldiers (formed in November of 1862) to join the Union army during the Civil War. Because they were paid substantially less than white soldiers, these men refused to accept any pay at all and fought for free.

Militia Act: Legislation signed by President Abraham Lincoln in 1862 that guaranteed that slaves who enlisted in the Union army would earn their freedom. The act helped open the way for African Americans to join the Union army.

fort, Mary Ames was struck by the freed slaves' eagerness to learn. Students of all ages, from small children to grandparents, flocked to the brand new schools. In her diary, Ames wrote that on the first evening of class, a bent-backed old woman announced that she was "mighty anxious to know something."

Plantation: A large farm or estate on which basic crops like cotton, tobacco, sugar, and rice were grown. Before the Civil War, the Southern economy was dependent on the agricultural production of the plantations, which in turn depended on the unpaid labor of slaves.

Racism: The belief that there are characteristics or qualities specific to each race, which often results in discrimination (treating people differently based on race).

Reconstruction Acts of 1867: The legislation devised by the Radical Republicans in Congress as a plan for remaking Southern society. The first act divided the ten Southern states—Tennessee had already been readmitted to the Union—into five military districts ruled by military commanders until the new state governments wrote and approved constitutions. The states had to ratify the Fourteenth Amendment as well as guarantee suffrage for all male citizens. Three subsequent Reconstruction Acts refined some of the issues brought up by the first.

Reconstruction era: The period stretching roughly from the end of the Civil War in April 1865 to the inauguration of President Rutherford B. Hayes in 1877. During Reconstruction, representatives of the U.S. government—including the president and Congress—and the military would join with both white and black Southerners to try to reorganize the political and social structure of the devastated, defeated South.

Secession: The separation of the eleven Southern states of the Confederacy from the rest of the Union, an act that sparked the Civil War.

Slavery: The practice of making human beings the property of others and forcing them to obey. Slaves captured in Africa were brought as unpaid laborers to the Southern United States, beginning in the seventeenth century. They endured harsh living and working conditions and, often, brutal punishment. By the time of the Civil War, there were about four million slaves in the United States. The 1863 Emancipation Proclamation declared most of them free. The end of the Civil War, followed by the passage of the Thirteenth Amendment to the Constitution, brought an end to slavery.

A time of conflict, healing, and change

The desire among slaves to learn was deep and profound. This yearning extended throughout the Southern United States as African Americans adjusted not only to the strange reality of freedom but to the hopes and plans that freedom had awakened. For the next fifteen years or so, some of these hopes and plans would be realized, while others would be crushed. During the Reconstruction era, which began before the Civil War ended and lasted through the 1870s, U.S. citizens from both the North and the South took part in a process that was messy and full of setbacks yet also marked by achievement.

A deepening division

In the years following the founding of the United States of America, a division had been growing among the states and people that made up the young nation. In the Northern part of the country, the economy thrived on industry and trade, whereas in the Southern part, the states depended mostly on agriculture. Many Southern farms and plantations (large estates on which basic crops like cotton, rice, and tobacco were grown) depended, in turn, on the free labor of slaves, who had been taken against their will from their homes in Africa and brought to the shores of what to them was an unknown place.

As the nation grew, and especially as new states were added, the issue of slavery became more and more hotly debated. Many people—most of them Northerners—called for an end to this practice, which they considered immoral and inhumane. Others—most of them Southerners—asserted the racist view that black people were inferior to those with northern European ancestors, that they were not even fully human and thus undeserving of equal rights. They even claimed that slavery was good for black people, as they were not capable of taking care of themselves.

The fundamental disagreement about slavery and about whether individual states had the right to determine whether or not it should be allowed finally led to the Civil War. Eleven Southern states had seceded from the Union. President Abraham Lincoln (1809–1865; served 1861–65; see box) had declared that this could not be allowed. He had led the nation into war with the Confederacy (the name the Southern states had taken), first to preserve the Union, and eventually to free the slaves.

"With malice toward none..."

By the spring of 1865, the war was coming to an end. It was clear to both sides that the North would be the winner and that the prewar United States would survive. The Union victory brought freedom to four million enslaved African Americans, but the cost had been great: over six hundred thousand people had lost their lives, the South lay in ruins, and old hatreds had deepened. Lincoln had been reelected in the fall of 1864. In his second inaugural address, delivered on March 4, 1865, he referred to the healing that must now take place.

It would be the nation's task, Lincoln said, "to finish the work we are in; to bind up the nation's wounds; to care for him who shall have borne the battle and for his widow, and his orphan." Most important, this task must be done "with malice [spitefulness] toward none; with charity for all." Although these eloquent words have been well remembered, the intention behind them was never fully realized. The years that immediately followed the war's end were marked more by malice than by charity. Yet they were also remarkable years, and what happened during this period would have profound consequences—both good and bad—for the decades that followed.

The challenge ahead

The Reconstruction era is often described as a time of dramatic change in the United States. The entire nation was changed, in a sense, by the fact that the Union had remained intact, and the power and reach of the government had been demonstrated. But in the South, the changes were especially noticeable and immediate. Southerners had to face the challenges of reorganizing their state governments, of rebuilding their cities and farms and renewing their shattered economy, and of finding a way for blacks and whites to live together in a much different relationship than before the war.

The last change was probably the hardest, and at the end of the Reconstruction era it appeared that this goal had not been met. During the late 1860s and 1870s, Southern blacks had actually been able to vote and hold political office. The promise of integrated (open to both blacks and whites) schools and public places had seemed within reach. By the end of the century, these rights and promises had disappeared. White terrorist groups like the Ku Klux Klan kept African Americans in a stranglehold of fear and dread, while a labor system shaped by prejudice and resentment kept

Abraham Lincoln: Beloved Leader in Hard Times

One of the most beloved of U.S. presidents, Abraham Lincoln, presided over the beginning of the Reconstruction era. Historians have often wondered how things might have turned out differently if Lincoln had lived through the whole period.

Lincoln was born in a backwoods Kentucky log cabin in 1809. His parents were poor, illiterate farmers. The family moved to Indiana in 1816, and two years later his mother died. A year later, his father remarried. Lincoln received less than a year of formal schooling but, at his stepmother's encouragement, educated himself by reading every book he could find. He learned about hard work by helping his father farm, but he wanted to do something else with his own life.

In 1828, Lincoln joined a four-month expedition on a Mississippi River flatboat, which took him into the South and exposed him for the first time to the harsh realities of slavery. This experience, as well as his parents' antislavery stance, seem to have influenced his later views.

For the next six years, after his family had resettled in Illinois, Lincoln worked in a number of jobs, including general-store owner, postmaster, surveyor, and hired hand. During this period, he also served briefly in his state's militia (an army called up to help in emergencies) and was elected captain of his unit.

Lincoln taught himself law and became qualified as an attorney in 1836. He served in the Illinois state legislature from 1834 until 1841. In November 1842, he married Mary Todd (1818–1882), with whom he would have four sons: Robert, Edward, William, and Thomas. Returning to his law practice, Lincoln earned a fine reputation as an attorney.

In the meantime, the United States was embroiled in a debate about whether slavery should be allowed in the new territories of the West, which were on their way to becoming states. In 1820, the Missouri Compromise had barred the expansion of slavery, but this ruling was overturned by the Kansas-Nebraska Act of 1854. Sponsored by U.S. senator Stephen Douglas (1813–1861) of Illinois, the act allowed the individual states to decide if they would allow slavery.

In 1858, the brand new Republican Party recruited Lincoln to run for senator against Douglas. In a political event that would become one of the most famous in U.S. history, Lincoln met Douglas in a series of seven debates on the slavery issue that drew huge crowds and national attention. Lincoln lost that election, but when it came time for the Republicans to choose a candidate for the 1860 presidential election, they called upon him again.

The campaign's focus on the issue of slavery highlighted the deep divisions

President Abraham Lincoln. *The Library of Congress.*

between the Northern and Southern states. Lincoln's victory in the election caused panic among white Southerners, who feared that despite his reassurances to the contrary the new president would outlaw slavery immediately. In February 1861, eleven states that had seceded from the Union formed the Confederate States of America (also known as the Confederacy) and began gathering an army.

In April, the Confederacy captured Fort Sumter, located on the South Carolina coast, sparking the Civil War. The first years of the conflict did not go well for the North, and public confidence in Lincoln ebbed. His initial goal had not so much been to end slavery as to hold the Union together, but after the Union army started to gain ground on the battlefield, the war's focus shifted. Lincoln began to emphasize the need to end slavery, and on January 1, 1863, he signed the Emancipation Proclamation, which declared most slaves forever free.

Lincoln did not expect to win the 1864 election, and he was surprised by his victory in the fall of 1864. Following the January 1865 passage of the Thirteenth Amendment, which officially outlawed slavery, the nation's leaders began to discuss how the Southern states would be readmitted to the Union and what shape the new South would take. In a partial answer to these questions, Lincoln issued a Reconstruction program called the Ten Per Cent plan. It was considered too mild by some, because it did not include harsh punishment for former Confederates.

No one will ever known how Lincoln's ideas about Reconstruction would have developed. On April 14, he was shot by a Southern-born actor who blamed Lincoln for the South's troubles. The next day, Lincoln died. He was deeply mourned by the nation he had served, but especially by African Americans, many of whom gave the president credit for leading them out of slavery.

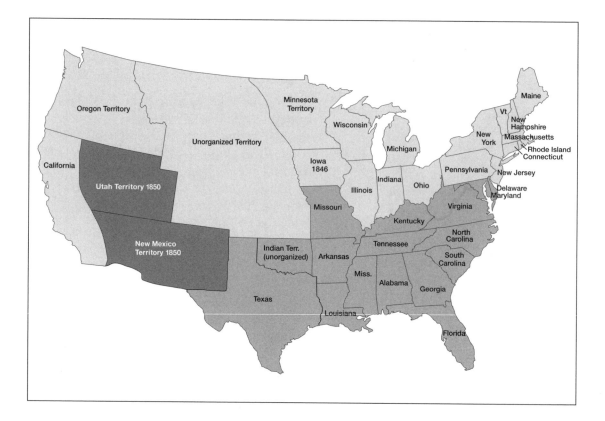

The Missouri Compromise of 1820 divided the United States into free states and territories (lightly shaded areas) banning slavery and slave states and territories (darker shaded areas) allowing the practice. In the Utah and New Mexico territories (darkest shade), voters determined the status of slavery. *Illustration by XNR Productions. Reproduced by permission of Thomson Gale.*

most of them in poverty. Southern society was fully segregated (blacks and whites were kept apart), and equality was nowhere in sight. These circumstances would not begin to change until the twentieth century, and in some ways and in some places such arrangements have lasted into the twenty-first century.

A changing view of the Reconstruction era

For many years, the popular view of the Reconstruction era focused on its effects on white Southerners. Historians who shared the prevailing view of blacks as inferior to whites claimed that African Americans had proved their incompetence to take part in politics. They portrayed the Reconstruction era governments as hopelessly corrupt, and the carpetbaggers (Northerners who came south to participate in various aspects of Reconstruction) and scalawags (white Southerners who belonged to the Republican political party, which had sponsored the Reconstruction policies) as people who took advantage of and preyed on the South. According to this view, white Southerners had been victimized by Reconstruction.

During the 1960s, however, U.S. society began to change as the civil rights movement gained strength and African Americans made advances. Historians began to put forth a different and more balanced view of the Reconstruction era. They asserted that Reconstruction had, in fact, led to some important achievements, especially the three amendments that were added to the U.S. Constitution during this period.

There is no doubt that the Reconstruction era was a troubled time. White Southerners resented the military occupation that followed their defeat in the Civil War, and even more deeply they resented the destruction of a way of life they valued. They fought the changes in every way they could, including violence. For their part, black Southerners were allowed only a brief glimpse of equality before it was snatched away. They saw their hopes for advancement die, not to be rekindled for many, many years. Although the policies of the Reconstruction era may not have been successful, this period holds important clues to later developments in U.S. history. The first of those clues may be found before the Civil War ended, or even before it began.

North and South: Two different worlds

In the years between the founding of the United States of America and the Civil War that threatened its survival, two distinct areas or regions of the nation developed. Each had its own economic system, and the residents of each region had their own way of life.

Although there were plenty of small farms in the North, this part of the country was home to several of the nation's largest and busiest cities. Most of the residents of these urban centers were laborers in factories or seaports or in other places of business and trade. Many were merchants who bought and sold the goods either being manufactured in the factories at home or imported from abroad, with customers all over the United States as well as in other countries.

The Lives of Slaves

By the time of the Civil War, nearly four million blacks were living as slaves in the Southern United States. Only about one-quarter of Southern whites owned slaves, of whom more than half lived on plantations with twenty or more slaves. About a quarter of Southern blacks lived among fifty or more slaves.

Their work and living conditions depended to some extent on where they lived and what kind of masters they had. In the states of the Deep South—such as South Carolina, Georgia, Louisiana, and Mississippi—most slaves lived on large plantations, where they worked either in labor gangs tending cash crops like cotton, tobacco, rice, and sugar, or as domestic servants in homes. In the Upper South and border states (such as Missouri and Kentucky), slaves lived on smaller farms and often worked alongside their owners, performing not only field labor but a variety of other tasks. Half a million blacks also worked in the cities and towns, serving as domestic servants or toiling in factories, lumber or cotton mills, mines, or other places of business.

Plantation owners employed white overseers, who supervised the work, care, and output of the slaves. The overseers often used harsh forms of punishment to control the slaves and were frequently hated figures, as were the drivers (many of them black) who drove the work gangs along with whips. Also hated and feared were the "pattyrollers," the slaves' name for the patrollers who roamed the neighborhood, making sure that any slaves they found had passes from their owners. The patrollers were employed to prevent slaves not only from running away but from organizing rebellions or uprisings, and they whipped any slave they caught off the plantation without a pass.

Some masters treated their slaves fairly well, even trying to keep slave families together. But most slaves endured long work hours (fifteen or sixteen hours a day during the peak seasons) as well as poor food, shelter, and clothing. They were subjected to a wide variety of punishments, including beatings, whippings, being hung by the thumbs, and branding. Worst of all was to be sold away to another plantation. This meant separation from friends and family, often permanently. Slaves were generally sold at auctions, public sales where they were put on display (sometimes stripped of clothing) for prospective buyers. Prices for slaves varied according to their sex, age, and physical condition: a young, healthy male might be sold for as much as $1,800, while babies were often sold by the pound.

Describing an 1846 scene in which slaves learned they were to be sold, a nineteenth-century writer (quoted in *Everyday Life in the 1800s*) recounted their horror:

Living conditions for plantation slaves were poor. This slave family, consisting of several generations living together, gather before their rough, one-room cabin. *The Library of Congress.*

"A shade of astonishment and affright passed over their faces, as they stared first at each other and then at the crowd of purchasers whose attention was now directed to them. When the horrible truth was revealed to their minds that they were to be sold, and nearest relations and friends parted forever, the effect was indescribably agonizing. Women snatched up their babies, and ran screaming into the huts. Children hid behind the huts and trees, and the men stood in mute despair."

Most slaves were sold at least twice, making it very difficult if not impossible to maintain family ties. In addition, slaves were not allowed to become legally married, instead taking part in a simple ritual that required a couple to jump over an extended broom, after which they were declared married. When slavery ended, many couples hurried to legalize their marriages.

Plantation slaves lived in gatherings of one-room cabins, usually referred to as slave quarters, that usually had dirt floors and lacked glass windows or furniture. On a typical work day, they would wake before sunrise to the sound of a bell or horn and, after a meager breakfast of corn cakes and perhaps a small amount of salt pork, they would be led to the fields to work until dark. Men, women (even when pregnant or nursing), and older children and teenagers worked, while the elderly often stayed behind to care for the smaller children. Slaves who worked in homes performed such duties as cooking, cleaning, and child care, often working even longer hours than the field hands.

Most slaves were not required to work on Saturday afternoon and Sunday. Saturday afternoons were for washing clothes, cleaning homes, and tending gardens. Social events were often held on Saturday nights, while on Sundays slaves attended church, fished and hunted, and socialized. Many slaves found comfort in religion, and especially in the religious songs called spirituals that they sang both in church and in the fields.

Meanwhile, in the warmer surroundings of the South, most people lived on farms where they grew such crops as tobacco, rice, and especially cotton, which was turned into fabric in the great textile mills of the North. The owners of the largest farms, called plantations, counted on the labor of their unpaid work force of slaves brought from Africa. The Northern states had outlawed slavery around the time of the American Revolution (1775–83), but the South held onto slavery as an essential part of its economy and culture.

Wealth based on slave labor

Although many Southerners did not own slaves, the region's politics were dominated by what has been called the plantation aristocracy. Traditionally, aristocrats were occupants of society's highest positions and enjoyed privileges they had gained merely through birth into particular families. In the South, the wealthiest plantation owners lived in a manner modeled after that of European aristocrats. Even though relatively few white Southerners actually could afford this lifestyle, few questioned its validity.

The South's prosperity, shown off most dramatically in the huge, richly decorated mansions of the plantation aristocracy, would not have been possible without the broken-down cabins called slave quarters that were found close to every grand mansion. Beginning in 1620, Africans had been captured and brought to the shores of North and South America on slave ships. Shackled together in the most brutal of conditions, those who survived the treacherous journey (known as the Middle Passage) were sold at public auctions. They were then forced to work for their owners, some as household servants but most as field laborers.

The majority of the slave population was concentrated in the Deep South—including such states as Mississippi, Alabama, Louisiana, and South Carolina—but many also lived in the border states in which slavery was allowed, such as Delaware, Maryland, Kentucky, and Missouri. Only about one-quarter of Southern farmers actually owned slaves, and 90 percent of these owned fewer than twenty. About ten thousand families made up the planter aristocracy, one-third of which owned more than one hundred slaves.

Conditions under slavery

Although their situations and their treatment varied, the vast majority of slaves worked long hours, ate poor food, wore tattered clothing, and lived in unfurnished, dirt-floored dwellings. Families were often separated when individuals were sold to other owners, never knowing if they would ever see each other again. Most slaves were denied any education, for it was considered dangerous to teach a slave to read and write. Those who misbehaved or tried to escape were punished harshly. Black women and girls were often forced into having sex with the white master or his sons, and the biracial children who were born of these encounters joined the ranks of the slaves.

Through all the long years of hardships, indignities, and suffering, African Americans demonstrated incredible resilience and courage. Despite their isolation, their illiteracy (inability to read), and the chains that bound them, many of them managed to keep the hope of freedom alive. By the middle of the nineteenth century, they were no longer Africans, even though traces of their heritage remained. They were African Americans. The enslavement of four million of them was in stark, brutal defiance of the supposed ideals on which the United States had been founded.

Abolitionists condemn a cruel system

Over one hundred years later, people wonder how this situation could have existed. After all, freedom was supposed to be one of the highest values of the founders of the United States, and the Declaration of Independence said that "all men are created equal." How could U.S. citizens have approved of slavery? The answer lies in both economic necessity and racism. On the one hand, slavery allowed Southerners to build a thriving agricultural economy without paying for labor; on the other hand, their belief in the inferiority of black people eased their consciences. They believed, in fact, that blacks were better off living as slaves, because they needed someone to tell them what to do and to take care of them. Because they viewed people of African descent more as property than as human beings, they did not think the words of the Declaration of Independence applied to slaves.

Abolitionist William Lloyd Garrison. *The Library of Congress.*

Of course, these opinions were held, to varying degrees, not only by white Southerners but by many other white people in all parts of the United States. Such racist thinking was a fact of life in the seventeenth through nineteenth centuries, and some of it survives into the twenty-first century. But even in the earliest days of slavery in the United States, there were individuals who fought against it. They were called abolitionists because they wanted to abolish (get rid of) slavery. Many were followers of the Quaker religion, which holds both equality and nonviolence as sacred values. As the nineteenth century progressed, the abolitionist movement began to grow in strength and influence as its members spoke out more and more against slavery. They also served as "conductors" on the Underground Railroad, the network of safe houses (places of refuge) that helped runaway slaves escape to freedom in the North.

Both free blacks (of which about 180,000 existed, most living in the North) and whites were active in the abolitionist movement. One of the leading white abolitionists was William Lloyd Garrison (1805–1879), the publisher of an antislavery newspaper called the *Liberator*. The most prominent black abolitionist, Frederick Douglass (c. 1817–1895; see box), was a former slave who, after escaping from bondage, had achieved an education and a reputation as an eloquent speaker and strong leader. While individuals like Garrison and Douglass called for an end to slavery on moral grounds, others declared that slavery was wrong because it gave the South an unfair economic advantage. Even among those who disapproved of slavery, there was disagreement about how much equality black people deserved. Eventually, a split developed between those who—like Douglass and Garrison—wanted not only freedom but full civil and political (especially voting) rights for African Americans and those who wanted only a limited equality for blacks.

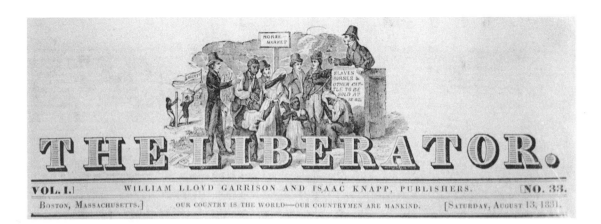

The sectional split deepens

By the middle of the nineteenth century, the United States had expanded far beyond the borders of its original thirteen colonies. Events like the Louisiana Purchase (an area of more than 800,000 square miles purchased by the United States from France in 1803) and the Mexican-American War (1846–48; a conflict that resulted in the United States gaining territory that would become California, New Mexico, Arizona, and parts of other western states) made more land available for the ever-growing U.S. population, and settlers moved west. As new states were formed and admitted to the Union, the sectional split between North and South deepened. Each state had to determine if it would allow slavery or not, and this caused political tension because it meant that either the North or the South would become more powerful. Both sides wanted to gain advantage, so each hoped to win the new western states over to its side.

The slavery question also helped to bring about a new political party in the United States. Formed in 1854, the Republican Party appealed mostly to Northerners. Its members favored business interests, public support for internal improvements (like roads and services), and social reforms. Although the party disapproved of slavery on moral grounds, its position was that the federal government should not intervene in the issue. On the other side, especially in the South, was the Democratic Party, which was opposed to the kinds of changes proposed by the Republicans. They felt that the Republicans were wealthy elites who wanted to limit in-

Masthead of the *Liberator,* an antislavery newspaper published by white abolitionist William Lloyd Garrison. *The Library of Congress.*

dividual freedom by making the federal government too strong. Democrats favored stronger state governments (giving citizens more local control) and a society in which white people were in charge and blacks kept in slavery.

The tensions between North and South were now heating up, with Southerners expressing the belief that individual states should have the right to govern themselves. Fiercely independent and proud, they felt that their very lifestyle and culture were threatened, and many believed that they should break away from the Union and form their own country. The 1860 presidential election was a crucial turning point. The winner was former U.S. representative Abraham Lincoln of Illinois, whose positions on slavery and on equality for blacks were somewhat ambiguous. He had spoken against slavery as an immoral practice, but he had also expressed the view that blacks and whites would never be able to live together peacefully in the United States. In any case, Lincoln had, during the campaign, tried to reassure Southerners that he had no intention of interfering with slavery. He did, however, promise to keep the Union together.

The Civil War begins

Soon after Lincoln's election, the slave states began to secede from the Union. In the spring of 1861, eleven Southern states joined together to form the Confederate States of America, or the Confederacy. The legislatures of the four slaveholding border states—Delaware, Maryland, Kentucky, and Missouri—voted against secession. The Confederacy established its capital in Richmond, Virginia, with former U.S. senator Jefferson Davis (1808–1889) of Mississippi as its president. The leaders of the North and South both began to gather armies. The Civil War began on April 12, 1861, when Confederate troops fired on the Union outpost of Fort Sumter on the coast of South Carolina. The federal troops defending the fort surrendered the next day.

The problem of runaway slaves

As the war got underway, the North appeared to have many advantages. The population from which soldiers could be recruited or drafted to fight (that is, white

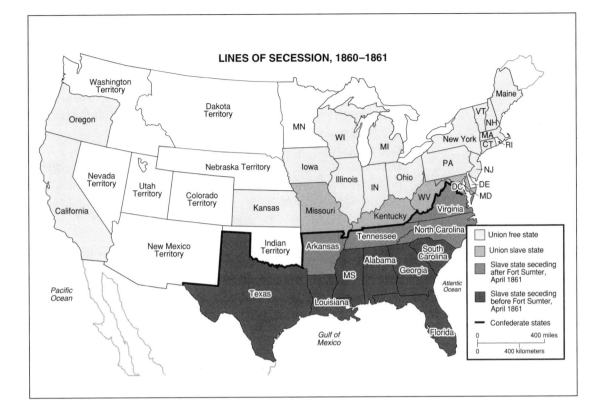

LINES OF SECESSION, 1860–1861

Washington Territory
Oregon
Nevada Territory
Utah Territory
California
New Mexico Territory
Dakota Territory
MN
WI
MI
Nebraska Territory
Colorado Territory
Kansas
Iowa
Illinois
IN
Ohio
Indian Territory
Missouri
Kentucky
Arkansas
Tennessee
MS
Alabama
Georgia
Texas
Louisiana
Maine
VT
NH
MA
CT
RI
New York
PA
NJ
DE
MD
DC
WV
Virginia
North Carolina
South Carolina
Florida
Pacific Ocean
Gulf of Mexico
Atlantic Ocean

Legend:
- Union free state
- Union slave state
- Slave state seceding after Fort Sumter, April 1861
- Slave state seceding before Fort Sumter, April 1861
- Confederate states

0   400 miles
0   400 kilometers

A map of the continental United States shows the lines of secession (1860–61) during the Civil War.
Thomson Gale.

males) was much higher, and the North had a greater industrial capability for making weapons and equipment. In addition, the Union's navy was much stronger, as was quickly demonstrated when the North blockaded the South's largest ports.

Although it was not at all clear at the beginning of the war that slavery was its central issue, the question was always present. Almost immediately, Union troops began to be approached by slaves, who, equating the Northern army with the coming of freedom, had run away from their masters and were now seeking protection. It was clear that deciding what to do with runaway or freed slaves was going to be a big problem. One solution was demonstrated at Fort Monroe, Virginia, when the Federal commander, General Benjamin Butler (1818–1893), refused the request of a Confederate officer to return to their masters three slaves who had crossed the Union line. Instead, Butler declared that the slaves were contraband, or property that could be legally confiscated during wartime. In other places, freed slaves were put to work as wage-earning army laborers or farm workers.

In March 1862, Congress passed an article of war (a special wartime law) that prohibited the Union army from returning fugitive slaves to their former owners. Soon after this, slavery was abolished in the District of Columbia and the territories (areas in the west that were not yet states, such as Colorado Territory and Utah Territory). These steps, along with the Union's seesawing fortunes in the war, paved the way for a bold move on Lincoln's part that would set the stage for the freeing of the slaves.

No quick and easy victory in sight

In the days leading up to the war, both Northern and Southern commentators had predicted a quick and easy victory for their own sides. But the first two years of combat revealed neither a clear winner nor any end in sight. The Confederates surprised the Union forces by winning the Battle of Bull Run in Virginia in the summer of 1861, but Union troops under General Ulysses S. Grant (1822–1885) took control of Tennessee in early 1862. A few months later, the Union lost the Battle of Shiloh in Kentucky but captured the strategically important city of New Orleans. In Virginia, General George McClellan (1826–1885) pushed Union troops toward Richmond, only to be held up by fierce battles with Confederates under the command of General Thomas "Stonewall" Jackson (1824–1863) and General Robert E. Lee (1807–1870), the top commander of the Confederate army.

With the war not going as well as expected, Lincoln realized that a drastic measure was called for, especially one that could deplete the labor force that supported the Southern economy and thus weaken the Confederate war effort. On September 22, 1863, close on the heels of a Union victory at the bloody Battle of Antietam in Maryland, Lincoln issued a Preliminary Emancipation Proclamation (the first draft of the Emancipation Proclamation). Often characterized as a blanket statement of freedom for all slaves, it was not exactly that. In fact, this document reflected Lincoln's mixed feelings about the slavery issue and about the purpose of this war. The proclamation declared that, effective January 1, 1863, slaves in the rebellious Confederate slaves would be

free. Not included were the approximately 450,000 slaves who lived in the loyal border states, the 275,000 in Union-held Tennessee, or those in the parts of Virginia and Louisiana that were under Union control.

The Emancipation Proclamation changes the war

Despite its limitations, the Emancipation Proclamation did succeed in transforming, according to *A Short History of Reconstruction*, "a war of armies into a war of societies." From this point on, the destruction of slavery—the institution that formed the backbone of Southern society—would be the central issue of the Civil War. This fact was not lost on the abolitionists and free blacks of the North, who greeted the news with excitement. As noted in *Climbing Up to Glory: A Short History of African Americans During the Civil War and Reconstruction*, Frederick Douglass wrote, "We shout for joy, that we live to record this righteous decree."

Artist Thomas Nast's vision of the difference emancipation would make in the lives of the freed slaves. To the left, scenes of life before the Civil War, showing the horrors of the auction block, punishment by flogging, and a branding; in the center and to the right, life after the war, showing a happy family life, a mother sending her children off to school, and a worker receiving wages. *The Library of Congress.*

In the South, the news spread quickly along the "grapevine telegraph," the secret communication network by which the slaves shared information and gossip, in spite of their masters' best efforts to keep them ignorant. Some slaves openly expressed their joy and some fled to Union lines, including a few who might have been expected to stay put. As reported in *Been in the Storm Too Long: The Aftermath of Slavery,* an elderly man responded to a suggestion that he was too old to flee slavery with this comment: "Ise eighty-eight year old. Too ole for come? Mas'r joking. Never too ole for leave de land o' bondage." Many other slaves, however, chose a more muted response. Long accustomed to protecting themselves by hiding their true opinions and feelings, they kept quiet and waited to see what would happen next.

Even in the North, there were many whites who did not share black people's happiness about the coming end of slavery and approval of the war that would bring it about. In the summer of 1863, protesters opposed to the war staged a bloody, destructive riot in New York City. They burned down not only the city's draft office (where soldiers were enlisted into the army) but other government buildings, homes of prominent Republicans, and symbols of the abolitionist movement such as the Colored Orphan Asylum. The rioters also murdered an unknown number of black people in the streets before Federal troops got control of the situation.

The riot seemed to signal mixed feelings on the part of U.S. citizens about the conflict in which so many young men were losing their lives. But President Lincoln did not waver. Instead of backing away from the direction in which he was leading the country, Lincoln became even more convinced that the Emancipation Proclamation had been necessary and that slavery must be abolished. He did not expect to be reelected in 1864, so he was surprised when the voters did choose him as their leader for the next four years—and by a landslide yet, over his former general, George McClellan. Voters continued to count on Lincoln's leadership.

African American soldiers fight for freedom

One of the most important consequences of the Emancipation Proclamation was that it cleared the way for

African Americans to enlist in the Union army. By the end of the war, about 186,000 black soldiers (130,000 of them former slaves) would have served, making up 10 percent of the army's total enrollment. Even though they were forced to serve in segregated units led by white officers and were paid less than white soldiers, there is no doubt that the African American troops played an important role in the eventual Union victory. Their admirable performance gave skeptical whites a broader view of black people's ability and courage. Further, the experience of fighting in the war helped many African Americans develop the public status and personal confidence they would later carry into roles as political leaders in the Reconstruction governments.

Prejudice gives way to necessity

Even before the war began, Frederick Douglass had called for the enlistment of free blacks, arguing that allowing them to fight would both strengthen the Union forces and highlight the moral urgency of abolishing slavery. But such a development was blocked by both law and prejudice. Even though African Americans had fought in every previous war in colonial history and in U.S. history, the popular belief was that blacks made poor soldiers and that white soldiers should not have to serve alongside them. In addition to the general idea that allowing black soldiers to fight was treating them too much as equals, there was also fear about a violent uprising or rebellion of blacks if they were provided with weapons.

President Lincoln himself had initially been opposed to the enlistment of black soldiers, but as the war dragged on, he changed his position. Even before the Emancipation Proclamation went into effect, realizing that nothing else would bring the influx of troops that was sorely needed to secure a Union victory, Lincoln signed the Militia Act. This guaranteed that slaves who enlisted in the Union army would earn their freedom.

Many African Americans saw joining the army as a chance to prove their loyalty to their country, even if many citizens of that country thought ill of them and some thought it would be best if they left and settled somewhere

Frederick Douglass: A Respected Spokesperson

Frederick Douglass was the most prominent black leader of the nineteenth century and an eloquent spokesperson for African Americans. Long active in the abolitionist movement (to end slavery), he was one of the Reconstruction era's strongest advocates for black civil rights. Perhaps what gave Douglass his special authority was his firsthand knowledge of several different levels of black experience. Born into slavery, he had escaped to the North and gradually risen to a high status, even serving as an advisor to the president of the United States.

Douglass was born in Easton, Maryland, around 1817 to a slave mother. It was not known who his father was, but he may have been Aaron Anthony, who owned Douglass's mother, Harriet Bailey. Douglass was owned by Anthony's daughter, Sophia, and her family. Before her husband put a stop to the practice, Sophia started to teach Douglass to read. He continued to educate himself, and by the time he was a teenager he was committed to the ideals of liberty and equality that he had read about.

Desperate to gain his freedom, Douglass plotted an escape in 1835, but the plan was discovered before it could be carried out. Three years later, while working in Baltimore, Douglass managed to escape to New York. He married and settled in New Bedford, Massachusetts, working as a day laborer and raising five children. In 1841, Douglass delivered a rousing speech to the Massachusetts Anti-Slavery Society, sharing details of his early life in slavery. Famous abolitionist William Lloyd Garrison (1805–1879) was in the audience. He befriended Douglass, whose public-speaking skills had impressed him, and soon Douglass was launched on a career as an abolitionist and orator.

In 1845, Douglass published his autobiography, in which he recounted vividly the brutal treatment he had endured as a slave and his escape to freedom. Having gained public attention through the book, Douglass feared that he might be recaptured by his former master, who technically still owned him. Thus he fled to England for two years, where he raised enough money through speaking engagements to purchase his freedom.

Returning to the United States, Douglass founded a newspaper called the *North Star* (named for the star that escaping slaves had followed to the North) and began a distinguished career as a journalist. He spoke out not only against slavery but in favor of education for blacks and of

else. Most African Americans felt that, for better or worse, the United States was their home, and they wanted to show that they could and would defend it. Both soldiers and black

Frederick Douglass.

recruit young African American men to become soldiers; in fact, two of his own sons fought with the Fifty-fourth Massachusetts regiment, one of the first and best known of the black military units. Once Reconstruction began, Douglass pushed for the expansion of civil and political rights—especially the right to vote, which he felt was most essential—for blacks. When Congress passed the Fifteenth Amendment, which guaranteed voting rights to all male citizens, Douglass supported it, even though feminist leaders had criticized the amendment for limiting suffrage to men.

During the last decades of his life, Douglass held a number of federal government jobs. He served as U.S. marshal and recorder of deeds in the District of Columbia, and held diplomatic posts in Santo Domingo (now the Dominican Republic) and Haiti. In 1881, the third and final version of his autobiography, *The Life and Times of Frederick Douglass,* was published. He continued speaking out on civil rights and equality, and caused something of a controversy when, after the death of his first wife, he married his white secretary. Douglass died of a heart attack in 1895, not long after attending a meeting on women's suffrage.

women's suffrage. Although he stressed the traditional values of self-reliance, hard work, and morality, Douglass differed from more conservative white abolitionists in urging blacks to take political action—including violence, if necessary—to gain equality, rather than waiting for kindhearted white people to grant it to them.

During the Civil War, Douglass met with President Abraham Lincoln several times to urge him to make the abolition of slavery the central issue of the conflict. He also advocated the enlistment of black troops in the Union army. Once this was approved, he began working hard to

leaders hoped that joining the fight to preserve the Union might be a first step in gaining even more rights for African Americans.

Black regiments perform well

The first black troops were called up and organized for duty in the fall of 1862, although most recruitment did not occur until the following spring. The first regiment, formed in November 1862, was the First South Carolina Volunteers. These soldiers were paid $10 per month instead of the $13 paid to white soldiers; they also had $3 deducted for their uniform, while white soldiers were paid $3 extra to cover the uniform cost. To protest this inequity, the men of the First South Carolina refused to accept any pay at all and fought for free. A double standard for black and white soldiers was also applied in regard to bounties (one-time bonuses paid upon enlistment) and pensions (money paid to former soldiers after their duty had ended), with black soldiers eligible for neither.

Nevertheless, many blacks were eager to join the army and generally optimistic about the results of their actions. As noted in *Been in the Storm So Long: The Aftermath of Slavery,* Thomas Long of the First South Carolina Volunteers said, "Now things can never go back, because we have showed our energy and courage and our natural manhood." Urging on the recruitment efforts, Douglass encouraged African Americans to fight for their own people's freedom, pointing out that "liberty won by white men would lose half its luster."

Black regiments formed as far west as Kansas, and in former Confederate strongholds like Mississippi, Virginia, and Louisiana. Six months after the Emancipation Proclamation went into effect, more than thirty regiments had formed; by December 1863, fifty thousand black soldiers had enrolled. One of the most famous regiments was the Fifty-fourth Massachusetts, whose story was dramatized in the 1989 movie *Glory.* Bound for Hilton Head Island, South Carolina, the regiment (which included two sons of Frederick Douglass) left Boston in May 1863, sent off with a parade lined with twenty thousand cheering spectators. Two months later, the regiment made an assault on Fort Wagner, located on Charleston Bay. Although they lost the battle and sustained heavy losses (including their white commander, Robert Gould Shaw [1837–1863]), the Fifty-fourth Massachusetts was honored for its valiant fighting.

Southern blacks react with pride

Although the Confederate response to the Union's black soldiers—they were known to immediately execute any they captured, rather than holding them as prisoners of war as they would white soldiers—may have dampened their spirits, they must have been lifted by the response of the black people they encountered as they made their way through the South. The surprise and amazement many felt when they saw the Union regiments made up of blue-uniformed African Americans quickly turned to pride. The troops were greeted by cheers and hugs as they marched through cities, towns, and rural areas.

Almost as many African Americans served the Union army in noncombat jobs (such as cook, carpenter, blacksmith, scout, and guide) as fought in battles. Of those who did serve as soldiers, about one-third were counted as dead or missing by the end of the war. Of this number, only 2,751 had died in combat; the rest succumbed to diseases like diarrhea and dysentery (an infection of the intestinal tract producing fever, pain, and severe diarrhea), which also killed many more white soldiers than the actual fighting. Most observers and commentators agreed that the African American troops had performed as well as the white ones, and seventeen of them (along with four sailors) were awarded the Congressional Medal of Honor.

Through their willingness to sacrifice their lives in defense of the Union, African Americans hoped that they had proved their loyalty to the nation. As the war drew to a close and the effects of the Emancipation Proclamation began to be felt, the dream of freedom seemed more and more real. In a few years, the war would end and freedom would come, but in the meantime several important developments would have to unravel along the way to those much-hoped-for outcomes.

For More Information

Books

Ames, Mary. *From a New England Woman's Diary in Dixie in 1865.* Norwood, MA: Plimpton Press, 1906. Reprint, New York: Negro Universities Press, 1969.

Blassingame, John W., ed. *Slave Testimony.* Baton Rouge: Louisiana State University Press, 1977.

Foner, Eric. *A Short History of Reconstruction.* New York: Harper & Row, 1990.

Golay, Michael. *Reconstruction and Reaction: The Emancipation of Slaves, 1861–1913.* New York: Facts on File, 1996.

Higginson, Thomas Wentworth. *Army Life in a Black Regiment.* Boston: Fields, Osgood & Co., 1870. Reprint, Mineola, NY: Dover Publications, 2002.

Jenkins, Wilbert L. *Climbing Up to Glory: A Short History of African Americans During the Civil War and Reconstruction.* Wilmington, DE: Scholarly Resources, 2002.

Litwack, Leon F. *Been in the Storm So Long: The Aftermath of Slavery.* New York: Vintage Books, 1979.

Litwack, Leon F. *Frederick Douglass.* New York: W. W. Norton, 1991.

McCutcheon, Marc. *Everyday Life in the 1800s.* Cincinnati: Writer's Digest Books, 1993.

McPherson, James M. *The Struggle for Equality: Abolitionists and the Negro in the Civil War and Reconstruction.* Princeton, NJ: Princeton University Press, 1965.

Stampp, Kenneth M. *The Era of Reconstruction: 1865–1877.* New York: Vintage Books, 1965.

Wagner, Margaret E., Gary W. Gallagher, and Paul Finkelman, eds. *Civil War Desk Reference.* New York: Simon & Schuster, 2002.

Web Sites

Louisiana State University. *The United States Civil War Center.* http://www.cwc.lsu.edu/ (accessed on August 31, 2004).

"Reconstruction." *African American History.* http://afroamhistory.about.com/od/reconstruction/ (accessed on August 31, 2004).

"Reference Resources: Civil War." *Kidinfo.* http://www.kidinfo.com/American_History/Civil_War.html (accessed on August 31, 2004).

"US Civil War." *Internet Modern History Sourcebook.* http://www.fordham.edu/halsall/mod/modsbook27.html (accessed on August 31, 2004).

The Civil War Draws to a Close

2

Passing through Mathews County, Virginia, one of eleven states that seceded (separated themselves) from the Union to become the Confederacy, a Union officer encountered a slave woman named Eliza Sparks. Stopping to admire her baby, the officer asked for the child's name. The woman answered that the baby's name was Charlie Sparks, just like his father's. As the officer rode off he called out, "Goodbye, Mrs. Sparks!" As recorded in *Been in the Storm Too Long: The Aftermath of Slavery,* the woman was pleasantly surprised to be shown such respect by a white person. "Now what do you think of dat?" she said. "Dey all call me Mrs. Sparks!" In the days before the Civil War (1861–65), the African American people who had lived in the Southern United States for over two hundred years as slaves were known—to whites, at least—only by their first names. Among the many rights denied them was the simple one of being addressed with respect, as an adult human being like any other.

The last two years of the American Civil War (1861–65) would be full of moments like that experienced by Eliza Sparks, moments when sometimes thrilling, sometimes

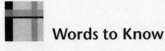

Words to Know

Civil War: The bloody conflict that divided the United States from 1861 to 1865. It pitted the Northern Union (federal government) against the Confederacy, the eleven Southern states that had seceded, or broken away, from the United States. Initially sparked by the secession of the Confederacy and the desire to keep the Union together, the war eventually became a struggle to free the four million blacks held as slaves in the South.

Confederacy: The eleven Southern states that seceded (separated themselves) from the Union, sparking the Civil War. These states, also known as the Confederate States of America, included Virginia, North Carolina, South Carolina, Georgia, Florida, Mississippi, Alabama, Arkansas, Louisiana, Tennessee, and Texas.

Contrabands: Slaves who became refugees when, as the Union army advanced through the South, they fled from their masters and sought refuge in the Union camps. The word contraband refers to property confiscated by an invading army during war.

Davis Bend, Mississippi: The site of a successful experiment in which blacks were given control by the Union army of their own land and labor. The setting was a large plantation confiscated from the family of Confederate president Jefferson Davis.

Forty Acres and a Mule: The slogan that became a popular representation of what African Americans hoped the federal government would give them after the Civil War, in compensation for their many years of unpaid labor.

Free blacks: African Americans who had never been slaves, or who had escaped from slavery into the North.

Gideon's Band: A group of Northern teachers and missionaries whose abolitionist ideals inspired them to travel to the Sea Islands of South Carolina as the Civil War was ending to help the freed slaves.

Plantation: A large farm or estate on which basic crops like cotton, tobacco, sugar, and rice were grown. Before the Civil War, the Southern economy was dependent on the agricultural production of the plantations, which in turn depended on the unpaid labor of slaves.

Proclamation of Amnesty and Reconstruction: Also known as the Ten Per Cent Plan, a plan created by President Abraham Lincoln that would allow most Southerners who took an oath of loyalty to the United States and agreed to accept the abolition of slavery to receive a full pardon and the restoration of all rights guaranteed to U.S. citizens.

Racism: The belief that there are characteristics or qualities specific to each race, which often results in discrimination (treating people differently based on race).

Reconstruction era: The period stretching roughly from the end of the Civil War in April 1865 to the inauguration of President Rutherford B. Hayes in 1877. During Reconstruction, representatives of the U.S. government—including the president and Congress—and the military would join with both white and black Southerners to try to reorganize the political and social structure of the devastated, defeated South.

Sea Islands: A chain of islands located off the coasts of South Carolina and Georgia. They were the site of an early experiment in distributing confiscated land to former slaves, and the destination of Gideon's Band, a group of teachers and missionaries who helped the freed slaves.

Secession: The separation of the eleven Southern states of the Confederacy from the rest of the Union, an act that sparked the Civil War.

Slavery: The practice of making human beings the property of others and forcing them to obey. Slaves captured in Africa were brought as unpaid laborers to the Southern United States, beginning in the seventeenth century. They endured harsh living and working conditions and, often, brutal punishment. By the time of the Civil War, there were about four million slaves in the United States. The 1863 Emancipation Proclamation declared most of them free. The end of the Civil War, followed by the passage of the Thirteenth Amendment to the Constitution, brought an end to slavery.

Special Field Order #15: A document issued by Union general William T. Sherman that allowed blacks to settle on 40-acre plots located along the South Carolina and Georgia coasts. Hopes for independence were dashed when this so-called "Sherman land" was returned to its Confederate owners soon after the end of the war.

Unionists: Southerners who opposed secession and continued to support the Union throughout the Civil War.

Wade-Davis Bill: Legislation that called for a majority of a Southern state's white males to sign an oath saying they had never aided the Confederacy before a new state constitution could be drawn up. Only those who signed the oath could vote on a new constitution, which had to outlaw slavery but did not have to ensure blacks the right to vote. President Abraham Lincoln opted not to sign the bill.

shocking evidence of change would boldly appear before both black and white Southerners. As the Union army made its slow and steady progress across the South—from its occupation of the important port city of New Orleans, Louisiana, in the spring of 1862, to its victory in Vicksburg, Mississippi, in the summer of 1863, to the march of General William T. Sherman (1820–1891) across Georgia to the sea in late 1864—the slave system was breaking up, and the old ways were being destroyed. How these familiar things would be replaced was, however, still an open and complex question.

The Emancipation Proclamation changes the war

The Civil War is often viewed as a fight about slavery, but that is not exactly how it began. It started as a conflict between a Confederacy determined to detach itself from the Union and preserve its own way of life, and a Union just as determined to hold all of its individual states together as one nation. But the war's purpose changed on January 1, 1863, when President Abraham Lincoln (1809–1865; served 1861–65) signed the Emancipation Proclamation, a document that declared that a large number of the African Americans held in the Southern states as slaves were forever free. From that point on, the war was about slavery, and President Lincoln was committed to ensuring the freedom of the four million enslaved blacks in the South.

News of the Emancipation Proclamation reached some slaves fairly quickly, especially in areas where Union troops were present to confirm their freedom. It took longer for the news to reach some of the more remote regions, and on plantations (large farms or estates on which slaves worked on basic crops like cotton, tobacco, sugar, and rice) in these areas life went on much as it had before. Though most former slaves would remember for the rest of their lives the day they heard that they were free, not all felt inclined to immediately leave the only homes they had ever known and set out on their own. For one thing, the Union victory—however likely it seemed—was not yet secured, and in many areas there were still Confederate forces around. For another, the prospect of freedom brought con-

fusion in addition to joy, for the slaves were now forced to think about where they would go and what they would do to support themselves.

In addition to such practical concerns, the years of slavery had woven a complex web of mutual dependency between the slaves and their owners. Slaves were dependent on their masters for everything material—food, clothing, and shelter—and in many cases they had lived a long time or even grown up with the white people they served. Although sometimes modified by feelings of affection and loyalty, the habit of obedience and submission to the traditional authority and power of these white people was strong. Meanwhile, the white slaveholders were dependent on their slaves both practically and emotionally. It was not just that they needed the slaves to work their fields, though that was certainly true. They often believed they had treated their slaves like members of the family and they were truly shocked to find that their slaves did not want to stay with them.

This Reconstruction era illustration shows African Americans receiving news of the Emancipation Proclamation, signed by President Abraham Lincoln (left) on January 1, 1863, with much rejoicing. *The Library of Congress.*

Contrabands in the Union camps

Many of those who did choose to leave their masters followed the Union troops as they made their way through the South. African Americans streamed by the thousands into the Union camps, creating a big problem for the commanders who found themselves responsible for caring for these refugees, who came to be known as contrabands (a word that refers to property confiscated by an invading army during war). Many were put to work for wages, as army laborers or even as workers in the cotton, rice, and tobacco fields abandoned by fleeing whites. Wages were low and conditions harsh, however, for the camps provided neither adequate shelter, food, or sanitation, and disease was widespread.

In addition, African Americans who had arrived among the Union forces with high expectations about how they would be treated often encountered the same kind of prejudice and even abuse they had experienced from Southern whites. Racist attitudes against blacks (as well as anyone not of northern European descent) existed all across the United States, and not just in the South. On the other hand, the experience of meeting for the first time the enslaved human beings for whom the war was being fought changed the outlook of at least a few Union soldiers. As noted in *Been in the Storm So Long: The Aftermath of Slavery,* one soldier described his encounter with the evidence of slavery's brutality, when he saw the scars left by the whippings that slaves routinely received for misbehavior: "Some of them were scarred from head to foot where they had been whipped. One man's back was nearly all one scar, as if the skin had been chopped up and left to heal in ridges.... That beat all the antislavery sermons ever yet preached."

Meanwhile, white Southerners feared the worst as the Union troops advanced and more and more blacks became aware of the change that was coming. Many whites expected their slaves to erupt in vengeful violence against their masters, but—despite a few occurrences of black violence against whites—this expected bloodbath never came. Reports were made, however, of slaves suddenly talking back to their masters or refusing to submit to the discipline and punishment they had previously endured. Gradually, African Americans were beginning to lower the masks they had used to disguise

their true feelings and opinions, masks that had given them one form of protection against the inhumanity of slavery. As noted by one slaveholder in *Been in the Storm So Long: The Aftermath of Slavery,* what was hidden behind these masks sometimes came as a surprise to those who had never questioned either slavery or their slaves' outward demeanor: "I believed that these people were content, happy, and attached to their masters. But events and reflection have caused me to change these opinions."

African Americans prepare cotton for a cotton gin. *The Library of Congress.*

Rehearsals for Reconstruction

As the Civil War wound down and a Union victory drew closer, political leaders, journalists, and ordinary citizens turned their attention to some important issues. They wondered how the Confederacy would be accepted back into the Union, and whether the Congress or the president would decide the terms of this process. They wondered what labor system would replace slavery in the Southern states, the economy of which was so dependent on the toil of those who were now free. Perhaps most troubling was the question of how African Americans would fit into politics and society in both the South and the North.

In late 1863, President Lincoln would provide a partial answer to these questions, but it was an answer that many believe he intended only as a short-term, temporary solution. His Proclamation of Amnesty and Reconstruction would offer a plan for admitting Southerners back into the Union and for reorganizing their state governments. Before it would come to be, however, several notable experiments in Reconstruction had already taken place, or were already in the process of taking place. These early efforts at rebuilding highlighted the many challenges ahead.

Changes in a border state

Maryland was one such Reconstruction testing ground. Maryland was one of the border states, one of the Southern states, along with Delaware, Kentucky, West Virginia, and Missouri, that had voted not to secede from the Union. Maryland was excluded from the terms of the Emancipation Proclamation. But unlike Delaware and Kentucky, where slavery was allowed to continue, Maryland was dominated during the war by an antislavery sentiment. Before the war, there had been eighty-seven thousand slaves in Maryland, almost all of them on large tobacco plantations located in the rural southern part of the state. This area's large landowners had long controlled state politics, but after the occupation of Maryland by the Union army early in the war, the small farmers, manufacturers, and laborers of the northern part of the state—and particularly those who lived in the large city of Baltimore—gained more power.

After a strong showing in Maryland's 1863 election, this group (called Unionists because of their support for the Union) set in motion a reconstruction of the state that included the abolition (outlawing) of slavery as well as the establishment of free, tax-supported public schools. From that point forward, legislative representation would be based on the white population alone. (Previously, population counts in slaveholding areas had included blacks, even though they could not vote. This method of counting gave these areas more legislative representatives and thus more power.) In addition, voters would have to take a strict oath of loyalty to the United States. In its lack of endorsement, or even much concern, for the rights of black people beyond freeing them from slavery, Maryland's reconstruction reflected the viewpoint of many other Southern governments in the earliest days of the Reconstruction era.

Further experiments in Tennessee and Louisiana

Early models for Reconstruction were also tried out in Tennessee and Louisiana. After capturing the city of Nashville in February 1862, the Union took control of Tennessee. President Lincoln rewarded Unionist senator Andrew Johnson (1808–1875) for his loyalty to the federal government by appointing him military governor (a temporary leader who serves during wartime) of the state. Johnson became known for the tough stand he took against the Confederates, declaring, as quoted in *A Short History of Reconstruction,* that "treason must be made odious [unpleasant; distasteful] and traitors punished." This unforgiving stance made Johnson seem like one of the Radical Republicans in Congress, who were calling for harsh measures against those who had turned against the Union. (Later, it would become clear that, as U.S. president, Johnson was not a Radical after all.) At the end of 1863, Johnson called for the abolition of slavery, although he confided that his motive was not so much sympathy for the slaves as disdain for the slaveholders: "Damn the Negroes, I am fighting those traitorous aristocrats, their masters." A year later, hoping to extend their influence in the South by rewarding a Unionist, the Republicans elected Johnson as Lincoln's second-term vice president.

Louisiana provided the only example of an early attempt at reconstruction that took place in the Deep South (which included such states as Alabama, Mississippi, and Florida). The Union capture of New Orleans in April 1862 was a major feat, for this was the largest city in the South. Its white population included a large number of foreigners and Northerners drawn to New Orleans by its thriving banking and commercial industries. The city was also home to the largest free black population in the Deep South, a communi-

New Orleans: A Unique Black Community

In addition to the nearly four million blacks who were living as slaves in the Southern United States, there were about 180,000 free blacks in the nation. Free blacks were those who had never been slaves, those who had escaped to freedom in the North, or those who had somehow accumulated enough money to purchase their own freedom. Eleven thousand of them were living in New Orleans, Louisiana, one of the most important cities in the South. The free black community in New Orleans was the largest in the Deep South before the war.

Many of the free blacks in New Orleans were the mulatto, or mixed-heritage, descendants of French settlers and slave women. Among these individuals, known as Creoles, were a sizable number who were well educated and wealthy. There were craftsmen such as bricklayers and carpenters, and there were professionals like doctors, architects, and undertakers. Some free blacks owned plantations, and some were even slaveholders. Sugar planter Antoine Dubuclet (1810–1887), for example, owned one hundred slaves.

Although the laws of the state and nation prohibited the free blacks of New Orleans, like other African Americans, from voting, they did enjoy unusual freedom. They could own property, they could sue (and be sued), and they could travel without restriction, something most slaves could not do without permission from their masters.

The Union army occupied New Orleans in the spring of 1862. Almost immediately, hundreds of free blacks volunteered to join the Northern cause and fight against the Confederacy. In August, the military commander in charge of New Orleans, Major General Benjamin Butler (1818–1893), authorized the formation of three black regiments: the First, Second, and Third Louisiana Native Guards. By November, the regiments had three thousand members, with officers drawn from the free black community (unlike the black regiments of the North, which were commanded by white officers).

ty dominated by biracial individuals (people of mixed racial heritage; then called mulatto) who had achieved remarkable levels of wealth, education, and status. Unlike in many other places, free blacks in New Orleans were allowed to travel freely and could testify in court against whites.

Most of the sugar planters in the southern part of the state were Unionists, but they were divided in their ideas about slavery. Some planters wanted to keep slavery or at

Soldiers of the 107th Colored Infantry, Fort Corcoran, Washington, D.C. *AP/Wide World Photos. Reproduced by permission.*

to the segregation (separation) of the races in public places. They formed aid societies (such as the Bureau of Industry) to provide the former slaves with food and fuel and to help them find employment.

Even though they made an effort to assist the freed people, the Creoles of New Orleans did not see themselves as having much in common with those who had been slaves. Some did not even want their children to attend school alongside the offspring of the former slaves. As quoted in *A Short History of Reconstruction,* an observer noted that they "tended to separate their struggle from that of the Negroes. Some believed they would achieve their cause more quickly if they abandoned the black to his fate. In their eyes, they were nearer to the white man; they were more advanced than the slave in all respects."

In the eyes of many white Southerners, however, there was no difference between these and other categories of African Americans when it came to the denial of equality. The struggle ahead would be shared by all of them.

With the end of the Civil War and the coming of freedom, free blacks from New Orleans were at the forefront of those speaking out for the expansion of black civil and political rights, especially black suffrage (the right to vote). They also called for government funding of public schools for children of all races, and an end

least compensate slaveholders for their lost labor; others favored emancipation and other reforms that would make Louisiana more like a Northern state. Lincoln put General Nathaniel B. Banks (1816–1894) in charge of Louisiana, instructing him to oversee the creation of a new state constitution that abolished slavery. Serious disagreements about the rights of African Americans soon developed between the different groups, however. A prominent leader of the free blacks

Free black leader P. B. S. Pinchback. *The Library of Congress.*

named P. B. S. Pinchback (1837–1921), who would later briefly serve as lieutenant governor of Louisiana, called for political rights to be extended only to that community, which set itself apart from (and even above) the slave population.

Several free black leaders from Louisiana even paid a visit to the president to argue the case for extending political rights—especially the right to vote—to blacks, and their intelligence and eloquence appear to have influenced the qualified endorsement for voting rights that Lincoln later made. In the end, though, the pleas of Pinchback and other black leaders were ignored. Louisiana's new constitution did make New Orleans the new center of power in the state. (In the same manner as Maryland's constitution, it also established a minimum wage and free public education.) Louisiana's slaves were declared free, but they were not granted the further rights for which Pinchback and his friends had argued.

The Sea Islands experiment

Perhaps the most pressing and thorny issue facing white and black Southerners alike was that of labor. How would the economy of the South survive without the unpaid toil that had been provided by the slaves for so long? What would happen to the many acres of land that had been abandoned or confiscated during the war? How would blacks support themselves? Would they become independent farmers, or work for others for wages? Would their employers treat them fairly? The complexities of these questions were revealed in the labor experiments that took place in several areas of the South, including the Sea Islands (a chain of islands located off the coast of South Carolina), the plantations of southern Louisiana, and at Davis Bend, Mississippi.

An African American village in Georgia, after the Civil War. © *Bettmann/Corbis.*

The Sea Islands came under Union control relatively early in the war, with the Navy occupation of the city of Port Royal in November 1861. Virtually all white residents of the Sea Islands had fled, leaving ten thousand slaves behind. The newly freed black people reacted to the departure of the whites, and the arrival of the Union troops, by looting houses and shops and burning cotton gins, the processing machines used in the production of the much despised "slave crop," cotton. Having thus expressed their feelings about their former lives as slaves, the blacks went about planting their own corn and potato crops on the abandoned land, which they felt entitled to occupy by virtue of their long years of unpaid labor. The former slaves' efforts at independent survival were not allowed to continue for long, however, as a new population of whites soon arrived on the Sea Islands, and these newcomers had different ideas about how the former slaves should employ themselves.

The new arrivals included military officers, government agents, and investors hoping to cash in on the cotton and rice still growing in the fields of the Sea Islands. Another important new presence was a group called Gideon's Band, made up of idealistic Northern teachers and missionaries, all of them fired with abolitionist fever, who wanted to teach and otherwise help the freed slaves. In their sensitivity to the wishes of the Sea Island blacks, however, the Gideonites were destined to clash with those who had come to the area with a plan to use the former slaves as laborers.

In 1863 and 1864, the confiscated land of the Sea Islands was auctioned off, and almost none of it went to the African Americans who had previously toiled on it. Eleven plantations were purchased by a group of Boston investors headed by Edward S. Philbrick (1827–1889). Although he was a strong supporter of abolition, Philbrick also believed that the labor of the freed slaves could help him to make a lot of money. Apparently unimpressed by the more than two hundred years that the Sea Island blacks had spent working for free, Philbrick did not want to give them any free land. Instead, he proposed to pay them wages to work in the same cotton fields previously owned by their former masters.

In the end, even though he had made some money, Philbrick decided to return to Boston. The big profits he had anticipated never materialized. The black people of the Sea Islands were not enthusiastic about raising cotton, which they associated with slavery; nor did they respond well to the gang-labor system that was used. Unlike in other areas of the South, where slaves had worked in gangs supervised by an overseer, the Sea Islands blacks had been assigned daily tasks they had to complete. This had given them more control over the pace and length of their work day. Generally, though, the failed labor experiment in the Sea Islands demonstrated a fundamental difference in viewpoint. Whereas the Northerners envisioned the freed slaves working for wages on plantations, the blacks wanted to farm their own land.

Regulations for control of blacks

A labor system that was more typical of experiments tried across the South occurred in southeastern Louisiana, where former slaves were offered plantation work that came with strict rules. Responding to plantation owners' desire to control blacks—and to keep Southern society as much as it had been before the war as possible—General Banks issued labor regulations in Louisiana that created a situation closely resembling slavery. Blacks who were unemployed could be charged with vagrancy (being without a home or job), and to avoid that charge they had to sign yearly labor contracts. They would receive either 5 percent of the crop proceeds or $3 per month plus food, shelter, and medical care.

Perhaps most restrictive, though, was the rule that they would not be allowed to leave the plantation without the owner's consent; one of the worst aspects of slavery had been the inability to move around when and where one wished. Blacks resisted signing the contracts, and the white plantation owners did not like the contracts either because they prohibited the kind of physical punishment they felt was necessary to make blacks work. Even though this attempt to answer the looming questions about labor did not work, the army extended it to the rest of the Mississippi Valley—with similar results—after the fall of Vicksburg in the summer of 1863. A similar system would even become law under the Black Codes established in the Southern states soon after the end of the war (see Chapter 5).

A Mississippi community run by blacks

Davis Bend, Mississippi, was the site of what was referred to in *A Short History of Reconstruction* as "the largest laboratory of black economic independence." In the years leading up to the war, this plantation owned by Jefferson Davis (1808–1889), the president of the Confederacy, and his brother Joseph Davis (1784–1870) had been the setting for an attempt to establish a model slave community. The idea was that if slaves were provided with good food and housing and allowed to set up their own government to resolve conflicts, they would be happy with their lot and would give their masters less trouble. Indeed, one result had been that the Davises gained a reputation among the region's black population as particularly kind and fair masters. In any case, the owners had fled Davis Bend during the war, and when Gen-

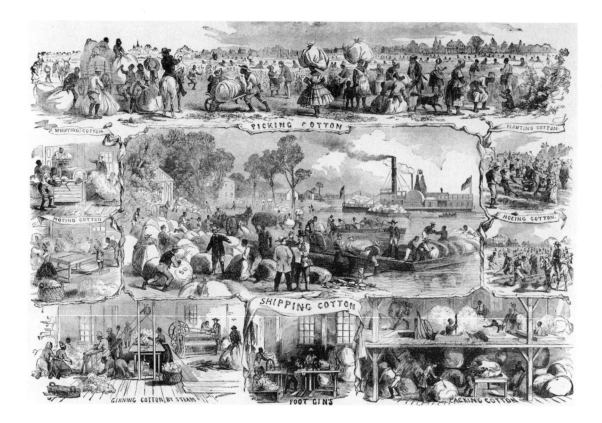

Production of cotton captured by the Federal Army during the Civil War, on the Sea Islands, at Port Royal, South Carolina. African Americans are shown gathering, processing, packing, and shipping cotton. © Corbis.

eral Sherman arrived in the area with his troops, the former slaves were running the plantation.

Sherman decided to follow the example set by the Davises. He declared that the plantation would be run by freed slaves, who would establish their own government with elected judges and sheriffs. By 1865, the five thousand blacks who had settled on the plantation lands had raised almost two thousand bales of cotton, bringing in a profit of $160,000. But in 1867, the land was returned to Joseph Davis. In the end, the model that gave blacks control over their own work and community was not followed. Rather, the Louisiana version, featuring labor contracts and military officers in charge, prevailed.

Lincoln's Ten Per Cent Plan

Even as these experiments were taking place, government leaders were wondering what the president would propose as the best way to rebuild the Southern states. It was almost a year after the signing of the Emancipation Proclamation that Lincoln came up with such a plan, issuing his Proclamation of Amnesty and Reconstruction on December 8, 1863. Under this plan, any Southerner (excluding slaves) who took an oath of loyalty to the United States and agreed to accept the abolition of slavery would receive a full pardon and the restoration of all rights guaranteed to U.S. citizens. Not included in the offer were high-ranking Confederate civil and military officers, although even they could apply for individual pardons. (It was believed that had Lincoln lived, he would have been very generous in granting such pardons.)

Lincoln's proposal is often referred to as the Ten Per Cent Plan, because it stated that when the number of loyal citizens in a state reached 10 percent of the number who had voted in 1860, this minority could establish a new state government. Although the new constitution had to abolish slavery, the states could otherwise deal with blacks (in other words, extend other rights) as they saw fit. Abolitionists immediately criticized the plan because it failed to guarantee black suffrage (the right to vote) and equality before the law.

It seems that Lincoln wanted to appeal to those Southerners who, before the war, had voted against seceding from the Union. He did not want to offend them now by offering African Americans too many rights, and he probably saw the plan as a way to shorten the war and gain support for emancipation rather than as a long-term arrangement. As reported in *The Era of Reconstruction: 1865–1877,* Lincoln explained his position by noting that this kind of government was only "what it should be as the egg is to the fowl.... We shall sooner have the fowl by hatching the egg than by smashing it." Nevertheless, this plan for state governments to be ruled by a minority proved more divisive than helpful.

The Wade-Davis Bill

Some of that division existed within Lincoln's own Republican party. Different ideas about the postwar status of the freed blacks would eventually lead to the emergence of a powerful group called the Radical Republicans, who would push through a truly revolutionary program of Reconstruction. During the last year of the war, however, the Republicans' main concerns did not include winning suffrage for blacks. Rather, they wanted to make sure that the newly freed blacks received equal protection under the law, and that sincere Unionists (not those who had just taken a loyalty oath in order to gain power) were in control of the Southern state governments.

In pursuit of these goals, U.S. senator Benjamin F. Wade (1800–1878) of Ohio and U.S. representative Henry Winter Davis (1817–1865) of Maryland introduced to Congress a bill that was meant to delay the start of Reconstruction. The Wade-Davis Bill specified that a majority of a state's white males must pledge their loyalty—signing a strict promise, called an Ironclad Oath, that they had never aided the Confederacy—to the U.S. Constitution before a new state constitution could be drawn up. Only those same white males could vote on the new constitution, which had to outlaw slavery but did not have to ensure blacks the right to vote.

Still reluctant to offend Southerners, Lincoln ensured the death of the Wade-Davis Bill by pocket-vetoing it (neither signing nor vetoing it, until at last its eligible time frame for signing expired), which earned him stinging criticism from the bill's sponsors. Lincoln's response was that he did not want to commit to any one plan, and that the individual states could choose to go along with the Wade-Davis plan if they wished. Historians have characterized Lincoln's actions of this period as reflecting his view that the war must first be won and emancipation ensured before proposing radical changes to Southern society.

An important amendment, and a new agency

In January 1865, the Thirteenth Amendment to the Constitution was ratified (approved by both houses of Congress and signed), thus officially abolishing slavery in the United States of America. Still, some abolitionists noted that the freedom thus gained by African Americans would ring hollow until they also earned political rights. Meanwhile, free blacks in Louisiana continued to push for black suffrage, and they were winning sympathizers.

THE FREEDMAN'S BUREAU!

AN AGENCY TO KEEP THE **NEGRO** IN IDLENESS AT THE **EXPENSE** OF THE WHITE MAN.

TWICE VETOED BY THE **PRESIDENT,** AND MADE A LAW BY **CONGRESS.**

SUPPORT CONGRESS & YOU SUPPORT THE NEGRO.   SUSTAIN THE PRESIDENT & YOU PROTECT THE WHITE MAN

For 1864 and 1865, the FREEDMAN'S BUREAU cost the Tax-payers of the Nation, at le⸱   TWENTY-FIVE MILLIONS OF DOLLARS.   For 1866, THE SHARE of the Tax-payers o⸱ Pennsylvania will be about ON⸱ ⸱ON OF DOLLARS. **GEAR⸱** is FOR the Freedman's Bureau. **CLYMER** is OPPOSED to it.

The question of whether, or how much, the federal government should get involved in assisting the freed slaves as they attempted to take their places in U.S. society was at least partially answered by the creation of the Freedmen's Bureau in March 1865. Originally established to last for just one year, this new government agency was authorized to distribute clothing, food, and fuel and generally oversee the interests of the freed people. Importantly, the bureau was also authorized to divide land that had been abandoned or taken over by the federal government (usually for nonpayment of taxes) into 40-acre lots. These lots were to be available for freed slaves or loyal whites to rent and would eventually be sold.

A racist political advertisement proclaiming the positions on the Freedmen's Bureau of the Pennsylvania gubernatorial candidates in 1866. Republican John White Geary defeated Democrat Hiester Clymer. *© Corbis.*

Special Field Order #15

Even before the creation of the Freedmen's Bureau, an action taken by General Sherman soon after his arrival on the Georgia seacoast added a new complication to the land

issue. After a 285-mile march from the west that left a trail of destruction in its wake, Sherman's troops reached Savannah in November of 1864. Thousands of slaves followed, despite Sherman's attempts to discourage them from leaving their own areas. Desperate for ideas on what to do with so many homeless people, Sherman and Secretary of War Edward M. Stanton (1814–1868) met with the city's black leaders, who expressed the desire of the black population and refugees to obtain and farm their own plots of land.

As a result of this meeting, Sherman issued Special Field Order #15, which set aside the Sea Islands and a segment of the coastal rice-growing region south of Charleston, South Carolina (extending inland thirty miles), for black settlement. Each family would receive 40 acres as well as a mule loaned by the army. By June, 40,000 blacks had settled on 400,000 acres of what came to be known as "Sherman land." This bold move by Sherman suggested to the freed slaves and others that truly radical changes were underway. The idea that their generations, worth of unpaid labor would now be compensated for with free land made perfect sense to blacks and represented one of their most cherished dreams. Like other Americans, they associated ownership of land with success, contentment, and freedom itself. They wanted to work for themselves and support their families and never again have to answer to any master or overseer. This dream, however, was not recognized by most Southern whites. The promise represented by Sherman's order—which would be encoded in the popular slogan "Forty Acres and a Mule"—would eventually be taken back, and Sherman himself would later say that he had never intended it to be permanent.

Blacks celebrate the war's end

As Sherman's army moved north into South Carolina, it was more and more evident that the war was almost over. On February 18, 1865, Union forces entered Charleston, greeted by cheers from jubilant blacks. Among the troops were the members of the Fifty-fourth Massachusetts Regiment, an army unit made up of black volunteers who had helped to prove that African Americans were willing and able to defend their nation. Five weeks later, the black population of Charleston celebrated the Union victory with a parade in front of ten thousand cheering spectators that featured four thousand marchers, including soldiers as well as schoolchildren and members of fire companies and the skilled trades.

Similar scenes of jubilation marked the arrival of the forces headed by General Ulysses S. Grant (1822–1885) in Richmond, Virginia, the Confederate capital, on April 3. The Union occupation of Richmond was a momentous occasion for the city's blacks, for it convinced them that they were really free. President Lincoln himself traveled down from Washington, D.C., to walk the streets of the enemy stronghold, surrounded by a group of sailors as bodyguards. To his embarrassment, Lincoln was received as a savior by the freed slaves, some of whom threw themselves at his feet.

Wondering where to go from here

On April 9, Confederate general Robert E. Lee (1807–1870) surrendered to Grant at Appomattox Courthouse, Virginia, officially ending the war. Although the fighting was over, great challenges lay ahead for white and black Southerners and for the political and military leaders who would begin the work of reconstructing their society. At this point, Lincoln had no specific plan for Reconstruction that promised success. The early experiments in Reconstruction had not produced any workable guidelines, nor had they been widely accepted.

On April 11, in what is generally regarded as his last speech as president, Lincoln made a qualified endorsement of black suffrage, suggesting that perhaps blacks with proven intelligence or who had served their country through military service could be allowed to vote. This suggests that Lincoln might eventually have become a committed supporter of expanded rights for blacks, but no one will ever know. Four days later, Lincoln was dead, shot by John Wilkes Booth (1838–1865), an actor with strong Confederate sympathies who blamed the president for the South's downfall.

Across the nation, African Americans responded with deep sadness to the death of the man they closely associated with their freedom. Many blacks were among the twenty-five thousand people who viewed Lincoln's body in Washington, D.C., and many joined the spectators who lined the streets of that city as his casket passed by. In the South, blacks showed their grief over Lincoln's death by wearing black clothing and armbands; they honored the president with church services that often ended with whole congregations in tears.

The shocking loss of Lincoln brought African Americans not only sadness but apprehension. Without the wise and just leadership of the fallen president, they wondered, would they be permitted to become full citizens of the United States? Slavery was gone for good, but freedom was not yet completely won. As noted in *A Short History of Reconstruction* by the great, black abolitionist and leader Frederick Douglass (c. 1817–1895), "The work does not end with the abolition of slavery, but only begins."

For More Information

Books

Berlin, Ira A., et al., eds. *Freedmen: A Documentary History of Emancipation, 1861–1867.* New York: Cambridge University Press, 1982.

Blassingame, John W., ed. *Slave Testimony.* Baton Rouge: Louisiana State University Press, 1977.

Foner, Eric. *A Short History of Reconstruction.* New York: Harper & Row, 1990.

Golay, Michael. *Reconstruction and Reaction: The Emancipation of Slaves, 1861–1913.* New York: Facts on File, 1996.

Jenkins, Wilbert L. *Climbing Up to Glory: A Short History of African Americans During the Civil War and Reconstruction.* Wilmington, DE: Scholarly Resources, 2002.

Litwack, Leon F. *Been in the Storm So Long: The Aftermath of Slavery.* New York: Vintage Books, 1979.

Oubre, Claude F. *Forty Acres and a Mule: The Freedmen's Bureau and Black Land Ownership.* Baton Rouge: Louisiana State University Press, 1978.

Rose, Willie Lee. *Rehearsal for Reconstruction: The Port Royal Experiment.* Athens: University of Georgia Press, 1999.

Stampp, Kenneth M. *The Era of Reconstruction: 1865–1877.* New York: Vintage Books, 1965.

Web Sites

Louisiana State University. *The United States Civil War Center.* http://www.cwc.lsu.edu/ (accessed on August 31, 2004).

"Reconstruction." *African American History.* http://afroamhistory.about.com/od/reconstruction/ (accessed on August 31, 2004).

"Reference Resources: Civil War." *Kidinfo.* http://www.kidinfo.com/American_History/Civil_War.html (accessed on August 31, 2004).

"US Civil War." *Internet Modern History Sourcebook.* http://www.fordham.edu/halsall/mod/modsbook27.html (accessed on August 31, 2004).

Slavery's End Brings Both Joy and Confusion

3

January 1, 1863, was a day of joy for African Americans. On that day, President Abraham Lincoln (1809–1865; served 1861–65) signed the Emancipation Proclamation. The proclamation declared that most of the four million black people who had, beginning in the seventeenth century, been enslaved in the Southern United States were forever free. The Civil War (1861–65) had raged for two years by then, pitting the Northern defenders of the Union against the Southern members of the Confederacy (the name for the states that had separated themselves from the United States to form their own country) in a bloody conflict.

At first, the war had seemed to be more about the rights of individual states than about freeing the slaves, but President Lincoln's Emancipation Proclamation had changed the focus of the struggle. From that day on, the Civil War was about freedom. When the war ended in April 1865, the period referred to as the Reconstruction era began. It would last roughly until the inauguration of President Rutherford B. Hayes (1822–1893; served 1877–81) in 1877, but its consequences would be felt throughout the following century.

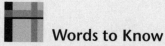

Words to Know

Black suffrage: The right of African Americans to cast votes in elections. The Fifteenth Amendment to the Constitution, passed in 1870, guaranteed that voting rights could not be denied on the basis of race or "previous condition of servitude."

Civil War: The bloody conflict that divided the United States from 1861 to 1865. It pitted the Northern Union (federal government) against the Confederacy, the eleven Southern states that had seceded, or broken away, from the United States. Initially sparked by the secession of the Confederacy and the desire to keep the Union together, the war eventually became a struggle to free the four million blacks held as slaves in the South.

Confederacy: The eleven Southern states that seceded (separated themselves) from the Union, sparking the Civil War.

These states, also known as the Confederate States of America, included Virginia, North Carolina, South Carolina, Georgia, Florida, Mississippi, Alabama, Arkansas, Louisiana, Tennessee, and Texas.

Forty Acres and a Mule: The slogan that became a popular representation of what African Americans hoped the federal government would give them after the Civil War, in compensation for their many years of unpaid labor.

Freedmen's Bureau: A federal agency that existed from 1865 to 1869 that assisted the former slaves in their transition to freedom. The program helped African Americans by distributing clothing, food, and fuel; handling legal cases; dispensing medical care; and setting up black schools.

During this period of both achievements and setbacks, representatives of the U.S. government—including the president and Congress—and the military would join with both white and black Southerners to try to reorganize the political and social structure of the devastated, defeated South.

Slaves rejoice

The news of freedom arrived at different speeds to the slaves working on farms and plantations (large estates on which basic crops like cotton, tobacco, and rice were grown) throughout the South. In some places, the advance of the Union army had already broken down the slave system, by

Mutual benefit societies: Organizations created by African Americans following the end of slavery. These societies lent strength and support to the black communities that began to thrive during the Reconstruction era and were often organized around professions or reform movements.

Racism: The belief that there are characteristics or qualities specific to each race, which often results in discrimination (treating people differently based on race).

Reconstruction era: The period stretching roughly from the end of the Civil War in April 1865 to the inauguration of President Rutherford B. Hayes in 1877. During Reconstruction, representatives of the U.S. government—including the president and Congress—and the military would join with both white and black Southerners to try to reorganize the political and social structure of the devastated, defeated South.

Segregation: The separation of people or groups which, in the Southern United States, was based on race.

Special Field Order #15: A document issued by Union general William T. Sherman that allowed blacks to settle on 40-acre plots located along the South Carolina and Georgia coasts. Hopes for independence were dashed when this so-called "Sherman land" was returned to its Confederate owners soon after the end of the war.

Vagrancy: Being without a home or a job. Beginning in the Reconstruction era, vagrancy laws made joblessness a crime, thus forcing unemployed blacks to accept work on white Southerners' plantations.

which unpaid, often mistreated black workers had toiled in the fields to raise millions of dollars worth of crops. In more remote areas, slaves did not know they were free until after the war ended. Some of them were informed by their masters, and others by Union soldiers or by agents of the Freedmen's Bureau, the agency that had been established several months earlier to help the freed slaves begin their new lives.

Wherever they were and however they heard, the former slaves remembered to their dying days the moment when they understood that they were free. As recounted in *A Short History of Reconstruction,* former slave Houston Holloway recalled that he "felt like a bird out of a cage. Amen. Amen. Amen. I could hardly ask to feel any better than I did

A Letter from a Former Slave

The following letter, dictated by a former slave on August 7, 1865, originally appeared in the *Cincinnati Commercial* and, a couple weeks later, the *New York Tribune*. It was also reprinted in *Been in the Storm So Long: The Aftermath of Slavery*.

To My Old Master, Colonel P. H. Anderson

Big Spring, Tennessee

Sir: I got your letter and was glad to find you had not forgotten Jourdon, and that you wanted me to come back and live with you again, promising to do better for me than anybody else can. I have often felt uneasy about you. I thought the Yankees would have hung you long before this for harboring Rebs they found at your house. I suppose they never heard about your going to Col. Martin's to kill the Union soldier that was left by his company near their stable. Although you shot at me twice before I left you, I did not want to hear of your being hurt, and am glad you are still living. It would do me good to go back to the dear old home again and see Miss Mary and Miss Martha and Allen, Esther, Green, and Lee. Give my love to them all, and tell them I hope we will meet in the better world, if not in this. I would have gone back to see you all when I was working in the Nashville hospital, but one of the neighbors told me Henry intended to shoot me if he ever got a chance.

I want to know particularly what the good chance is you propose to give me. I am doing tolerably well here; I get $25 a month, with victuals [food] and clothing; have a comfortable home for Mandy (the folks here call her Mrs. Anderson) and the children, Milly, Jane, and Grundy, go to school and are learning well; the teacher says Grundy has a head for a preacher. They go to Sunday-School, and Mandy and me attend church regularly. We are kindly treated; sometimes we hear others saying, "Them colored people were slaves" down in Tennessee. The children feel hurt when they hear such remarks, but I tell them it was no disgrace in Tennessee to belong to Col. Anderson. Many darkies would have been proud... to call you master. Now, if you will write and say what wages you will give me, I will be better able to decide whether it would be to my advantage to move back again.

that day.... The week passed off in a blaze of glory." More simply but just as profoundly, as noted in *Been in the Storm So Long: The Aftermath of Slavery*, another former slave, Richard Caruthers said, "That the day I shouted."

The end of the war and the emancipation of blacks meant something altogether different for the white Southerners who had depended on their slaves' unpaid labor for their livelihood. Defeated by a hated enemy and faced with the huge challenge of rebuilding their shattered lives, these whites expressed a multitude of negative emotions. They were angry and embittered, worried about the future, and

As to my freedom, which you say I can have, there is nothing to be gained on that score, as I got my free papers in 1864 from the Provost-Marshal-General of the Department at Nashville. Mandy says she would be afraid to go back without some proof that you are sincerely disposed to treat us justly and kindly—and we have concluded to test your sincerity by asking you to send us our wages for the time we served you. This will make us forget and forgive old scores, and rely on your justice and friendship in the future. I served you faithfully for thirty-two years and Mandy twenty years. At $25 a month for me, and $2 a week for Mandy, our earnings would amount to $11,680. Add to this the interest for the time our wages have been kept back and deduct what you paid for our clothing and three doctor's visits to me, and pulling a tooth for Mandy, and the balance will show what we are in justice entitled to.... If you fail to pay us for our faithful labors in the past we can have little faith in your promises in the future. We trust the good Maker has opened your eyes to the wrongs which you and your fathers have done to me and my fathers, in making us toil for you for generations without recompense. Here I draw my wages every Saturday night, but in Tennessee there was never any pay day for the Negroes any more than for the horses and cows. Surely there will be a day of reckoning for those who defraud the laborer of his hire.

In answering this letter please state if there would be any safety for my Milly and Jane, who are now grown up and both good-looking girls. You know how it was with poor Matilda and Catherine. I would rather stay here and starve and die if it comes to that than have my girls brought to shame by the violence and wickedness of their young masters. You will also please state if there has been any schools opened for the colored children in your neighborhood, the great desire of my life now is to give my children an education, and have them form virtuous habits.

P.S. Say howdy to George Carter, and thank him for taking the pistol from you when you were shooting at me.

From your old servant,

Jourdon Anderson

most of all bewildered about their new relationship with the black people around them. Revealing her belief that blacks could not possibly be independent beings, in charge of their own lives, a former slaveholder quoted in *Been in the Storm So Long: The Aftermath of Slavery* asked, "If they don't belong to me, whose are they?"

This comment highlights the racist attitude common among Southern whites (and also among most Northerners of the period) that held that blacks were inferior to people of northern European descent, were incapable of caring for themselves, and were not suited for anything but serving white people. Southerners had, of course, used this racist belief to justify slavery itself, and in the years to come they would use it to keep African Americans from taking their place in society. .

The changes freedom brought

Meanwhile, blacks were learning what freedom meant, and figuring out what to do with it. Probably the most important change was that they no longer had to put up with the brutalities they had endured as slaves, especially the harsh physical punishment they received for misbehavior and the unbearable pain and grief caused when members of families were torn apart as slaveholders sold individuals to other masters. The end of slavery brought a welcome opportunity to strengthen and reestablish family bonds and to begin the building of a strong black community supported by churches, schools, and mutual benefit societies (organizations whose members worked together to help each other).

Moving around, or staying put

Freedom also meant that former slaves were now free to move around as they wished, whereas before the Civil War they had to have a pass from their masters to leave their own plantations. Many freed people immediately exercised this cherished right, leaving their former homes to look elsewhere for work—far away, perhaps in a large city, or as near as the next plantation. They left to find lost family members or just to be on the move and thus experience freedom. One white family who had always treated their black cook kindly and who now offered to pay her well to continue working for them were told by her, as noted in *Reconstruction and Reaction: The Emancipation of Slaves, 1861–1913*, "If I stay here I'll never know I'm free."

Between 1865 and 1870, the black populations of the ten largest Southern cities doubled, whereas the white populations increased by only 10 percent. In the immediate aftermath of the war, many African Americans believed that the city offered them the most advantages—that there, protected by the more abundant Union soldiers and agents of the

Freedmen's Bureau, they would be able to make the most of their freedom. There too, they would find the basis of what would eventually grow into thriving black communities.

Both black leaders and the Freedmen's Bureau, however, urged blacks to stay in the countryside and continue working on the farms and plantations. They cited such grim realities of city life as scarce jobs, inadequate housing, widespread poverty and disease, and strict vagrancy laws (which punished those who were unemployed and homeless). For the first time, blacks were crowded together into separate neighborhoods or areas of the cities, a trend that would continue into the twentieth century.

Some freed slaves chose to stay where they were or to return after a brief taste of the free life somewhere else. Sometimes they stayed out of loyalty to their former masters but more commonly as a practical choice. With few possessions, little money, and no experience on how to survive on their

An illustration from *Harper's Weekly* shows a representative of the Freedmen's Bureau preventing violence between whites and blacks.

own, many slaves felt they had no choice but to continue in lives very similar to their old ones, except that they must now be paid wages or otherwise compensated for their labor. There were other changes too, especially in the way black people conducted themselves around white people. Some of these changes were viewed with curiosity or amusement by whites, but more often they were shocked and outraged by this evidence of a new way of life to which they must adjust.

New ways of behaving

Blacks expressed their freedom in large and small ways, each of which challenged or overturned the authority that whites had always had over them. They began holding their own meetings and church services; purchasing previously forbidden things like dogs, guns, and liquor; and dressing as they pleased. Women especially enjoyed this new pleasure, often donning brightly colored clothes, hats with veils, and parasols (decorative small umbrellas used as protection from the sun). Blacks might refuse to yield a sidewalk to a white person, decline to tip a hat to a white person they did not like, or even talk back to someone who addressed them in a demeaning way.

White Southerners were highly sensitive to these signs of what they considered disrespect, disobedience, or "sauciness." Sometimes they only made fun of black people for trying to imitate white people, but sometimes whites used violence to force blacks to behave as they thought black people should. It seemed that once that there was no market price on them, African American lives were cheap. Many were beaten and even killed for offending whites in various ways, including the most trivial. For example, among the one thousand murders of blacks by whites reported by the Freedmen's Bureau in Texas between 1865 and 1868 was one that resulted from a black man's failure to remove his hat in the presence of a white person.

Before the Civil War, blacks and whites had lived in close contact with each other. After the war, it became important to whites to keep up a strict segregation (separation) in all aspects of life, especially in public places. Justifying to some Northern visitors his prejudice against blacks, one white Southerner, noted in *Been in the Storm So Long: The Af-*

termath of Slavery, claimed, "I haven't any prejudices against 'em because they're free, but you see I can't consider that they're on an equality with a white man. I may like him, but I can't let him come to my table and sit down like either of you gentlemen. I feel better than he is."

Whites also worried that the freeing of the slaves would lead to miscegenation (sexual relations between blacks and whites), thus violating white racial "purity." Blacks found this concern particularly ironic, since every plantation slave quarters had its share of biracial children born from the rape of slave women by their white masters or overseers. Blind to this history of sexual violence by whites against blacks, whites viewed all black men—especially the much hated black Union soldiers who were now in their midst—as potential rapists.

Family reunions

One of the freed people's most urgent matters of concern was locating family members from whom they had been separated during slavery. This was a monumental task, because slaves generally did not have last names. Furthermore, they may have been sold more than once after leaving their families, making it difficult to track them across the many miles they may have traveled. Blacks made valiant, heart-wrenching efforts to locate their lost husbands, wives, children, parents, siblings, and other relatives. They often placed newspaper advertisements like this one that appeared in the Nashville Colored Tennessean: "During the year 1849, Thomas Sample carried away from this city, as his slaves, our daughter, Polly, and son…. We will give $100 each for them to any person who will assist them… to get to Nashville or get word to us of their whereabouts."

Family ties had always been important to African Americans, as had the idea of marriage. During slavery, most couples who wished to marry took part in a simple ceremony that involved stepping or jumping over a broomstick. Once they were free, many of these couples hurried to legalize their marriages, both for the dignity this process would bring to their union and for the legal protections it would offer their families. There was also a rush to acquire the last names that slaves—who were often given even their first names by their masters—had been denied. Many chose the names of famous people, especially those associated with freedom and democracy, such as Lincoln, Jefferson, and Madison. Others adopted names of former masters (often the earliest one remembered in a family's history), and some just chose names they liked. In any case, the ability to freely choose one's own name was much cherished.

Another big change in black family life after emancipation involved the withdrawal of black women from working in the fields or as house servants. Once again, whites ridiculed black women for "playing the lady" or imitating white behavior, but this was a meaningful step for many black families. Now that they had control over when and where their family members worked, they could choose to keep the mother of the family at home, tending to her own household instead of caring for other people's fields, homes, and children. This would prove to be only a temporary luxury, though, since economic conditions would soon call for every member of the family who was able to contribute to its income.

The church: A cornerstone of black life

In addition to the family, the church was a cornerstone of black life during the Reconstruction era. During slavery, blacks had generally not been allowed to establish their own churches. Instead, they had participated in the congregations of white-run churches, always relegated to the back rows of seats and never given any role in church administration. Nevertheless, the slaves had created their own vibrant form of Christianity, with Jesus Christ viewed as a personal savior who gave strength and comfort during hard times and would eventually deliver black people out of slavery. When freedom arrived, many blacks felt that it had come about through the kind of divine intervention for which they had always hoped and prayed.

Following the Civil War, the white churches did not offer an equal role for their black members, but in any case many blacks were eager to start their own churches. They did so very successfully, pooling their money to buy land and construct buildings and meanwhile holding services wherever they could find the space. In addition to providing religious services, churches played a central role in black life. They pro-

vided the settings for schools, social events, and political meetings; promoted moral values; mediated family conflicts; and disciplined members for misbehavior such as adultery.

Ministers were among the community's most respected leaders, admired for their public-speaking skills, organizational abilities, and wisdom in resolving problems. Many of them became active in the black political life of the Reconstruction era (during which over one hundred ministers were elected to legislative seats). Entering political life seemed to them a natural outgrowth of their concern for and knowledge of the people they served.

Also contributing to the growth of strong black communities were the mutual benefit societies, organizations established to help blacks help each other. They were often organized around professions or trades, such as fire fighting, carpentry, or stone masonry; life necessities, like burial; or topics or activities of interest, such as debating, drama, tem-

An African American congregation at a black church in Washington, D.C., in 1876. *The Granger Collection, New York. Reproduced by permission.*

The Black Church: A Source of Strength

Spirituality has always been an important value to African Americans. After being brought to the United States as slaves, many blacks adopted the Christianity practiced by their owners. However, both during and after the days of slavery, they worshiped in their own ways and places. For example, most of them had a very direct, immediate view of Jesus Christ, considering him a personal savior who would one day lead blacks out of slavery.

Many slaveholders were concerned about the spiritual welfare of their slaves and allowed them to attend church (although private religious practice was strictly forbidden). Before the Civil War, both slaves and free blacks attended the same churches as Southern whites, including those of the Baptist, Methodist, Presbyterian, Episcopalian, and other Protestant sects. Some were also Catholics. Although they had to follow the same rules of behavior as white members, blacks were always seated separately at services and had no role or say in church matters.

The spiritual instruction that slaves received also tended to reinforce their separate, unequal status. White preachers would urge them to obey their masters if they wanted to go to heaven. For their part, many slaves considered these white ministers hypocrites who preached to others to hold Christian values while approving of—and often participating in—the evil institution of slavery. African Americans also tended to find the services in white churches dull and uninspiring. Thus some of them held their own religious services in secluded areas, often at great risk of harsh punishment.

When slavery ended, African Americans were quick to establish their own churches, where they could take up leadership roles, express themselves just as they wished, and access the social services offered by black church groups. In addition, even after the war, the white churches maintained their segregated ways and offered no particular welcome or reassurance to black members. In some cases, however, white Southerners helped blacks establish churches by donating land, money, or temporary facilities or even performing some of the work to raise the church buildings.

The vast majority of African Americans, whether churchgoing or not, emerged from slavery into extreme poverty. Until they had enough money to meet construction costs, the new black churches initially met in temporary places like warehouses and private homes (and in one case, a railroad boxcar). Sometimes churches of different denominations—some of the most popular included the African Methodist Episcopal (AME) Church and the AME Zion

Church—would share meeting space or pool resources. Despite the impoverishment of the black community, the churches raised astonishing amounts of cash.

In addition to raising money for the building of black schools (and sometimes providing the facilities), the churches provided a number of much-needed social welfare services. These included lending aid to the homeless, the poor, the sick, the elderly, prison inmates, orphans, and black war veterans. They also organized societies to help with burial expenses.

The churches soon became important and busy centers of black religious, social, and eventually political life. They commonly offered three services on Sunday, in addition to Wednesday night prayer meetings, but some also provided regular weekday services. Churches catering to the majority of the African American population tended to feature very expressive, noisy services that stressed God's immediate presence. Churches frequented by members of the small black middle and upper classes tended to resemble white churches in their more orderly, quiet nature and standard hymns.

The churches provided a place for blacks to affirm their social status, reinforce their feeling of belonging to a community, and lend their lives a deeper sense of meaning. The churches upheld a strict code of behavior by which card-playing, drinking, and gambling were forbidden and adultery discouraged. Ministers helped resolve family disputes, and members knew that they could be expelled or banished because of misbehavior.

The black ministers were especially admired for their preaching, which was often dramatic and filled with vivid imagery, and for the guidance and advice they provided. Thus it is not surprising that clergymen dominated the black political leadership that emerged during the Reconstruction era. For example, of the 255 African Americans in South Carolina's legislature between 1868 and 1876, 43 were ministers. By contrast, black women, who made up the bulk of church membership and played an important part in fundraising and organization efforts, were not afforded an equal role in church leadership.

Because they were centers of African American life, the black churches and preachers were particularly targeted by such white terrorist groups as the Ku Klux Klan, who used violence and intimidation to keep blacks from exercising their rights. Nevertheless, the churches continued to provide a strong base of support for African American communities during the difficult years that followed.

perance (the movement to stop the use of alcohol), or equal rights. These organizations offered social contact and support as well as, in many cases, sickness and death benefits for members. They tended to be dominated by the self-improvement philosophy that blacks were widely being encouraged to adopt in their churches and schools and by the Freedmen's Bureau. In some of the larger cities such as Nashville, New Orleans, and Atlanta, the mutual benefit societies also offered various forms of relief for the poor, including orphanages, soup kitchens, and "poor relief" (similar to modern welfare or public assistance) funds.

Education: The key to advancement

Before the Civil War, all the slave states except Tennessee had prohibited the education of slaves. Although some slaves still managed to learn to read and write, either through the indulgence of their masters or by their own initiative, about 90 percent of adult blacks in the South were illiterate (unable to read or write) in 1860. Blacks emerged from slavery with a deep desire to acquire education, which was central to their idea of what freedom meant. They recognized that they would be able to take better advantage of the opportunities and choices that lay before them if they could read and write. Students of all ages filled the newly established classrooms in large numbers.

Most of the funding for the schools built for Southern blacks during Reconstruction came from charitable organizations in the North and from the Freedmen's Bureau (replaced after 1868 by state government contributions). But blacks took an active role in getting many schools started, often setting them up temporarily in churches, homes, and even pool halls until school buildings could be constructed. It became a common sight around the South to see black people of all ages and occupations peering into books, whether in a classroom or on a lunch break from work.

In the years to come, African Americans would proudly remember that, as poor as their communities were, blacks had raised one million dollars for schools by 1870. The money was used to construct school buildings and to pay teachers, many of whom were boarded in black homes. Following in the footsteps of the first white teachers, most of

them women, who had come from the North to help the freed slaves, the first black teachers were often thrust into their roles—owing to the desperate need for teachers—before they had attained much education themselves. Like the ministers of the black churches, these teachers were much respected and were called upon to take leadership roles in the community, sometimes even moving from there into political office. Seventy black teachers served in state legislatures during Reconstruction.

African Americans of all ages attended school during Reconstruction.
© Bettmann/Corbis.

Rebuilding the South

Among all the questions still unanswered as the Civil War came to a close lay a central truth: the Confederacy had been defeated. The eleven states that had separated themselves from and fought the Union for four years were now under martial law (military officers were in charge of keeping order) and were occupied by Federal troops. Many of these soldiers were black—since most white troops had been in the army longer and were thus discharged earlier—a fact that annoyed many Southerners. To the bitterness of defeat and the humiliation of occupation was added the reality of a changed physical and social environment.

Northern journalists who visited the South in the days following the end of the Civil War reported scenes of total desolation. They saw barns, homes, and fences destroyed; bridges and railroads torn up; livestock dead; and fields grown wild. They saw the remains of walls and chimneys standing where the Union army had marched through, burning everything in its path. The loss of farm animals, buildings, and machinery had a devastating impact on Southern agriculture. The loss of life—including more than one-fifth of the South's white male adult population as well as thirty-two thousand black Southerners who had served in the Union army—was also devastating. In addition, those who had converted their money to Confederate currency, which was now useless, were bankrupt.

Bleak prospects for the future

The Southern United States did not consist entirely of rich farming land and huge plantations on which slaves had toiled. In fact, there were many other areas of the South, such as the upcountry or mountainous areas of western Virginia and North Carolina and eastern Tennessee, that were populated by small farmers who had owned few or no slaves. Yet the politics, economy, and culture of the South had always been dominated by the small minority of slaveholding plantation owners. This group was reeling now from the effects of the war, not only economically (owing to the loss of property, including the approximately two billion dollars they had invested in slaves) but physically and psychologically. As they returned to their homes, the former Confederates expected to be treated harshly by the victorious Union. They thought they might lose their property or civil rights, and that they might even be prosecuted for treason. Their world had changed forever, and the future must have seemed very bleak to these white Southerners.

Perhaps the most complex and thorny issue of the Reconstruction era was that of labor. No one was sure exactly how the new economy of the South would be organized now that farmers and plantation owners would have to pay the workers who raised their crops. Nor was it known exactly how, now that they could make their own decisions, black people would choose to support themselves, how much real freedom they would be given in making decisions about labor, and how much they would depend on the government for help. As in other aspects of postwar life, labor was complicated by the vastly different ideas about it held by white and black Southerners.

Questions of labor and land

Faced with the prospect of a free labor system in which physical punishment of workers was outlawed, many former slaveholders disbelieved it was possible. In their racist view, African Americans were lazy and would not work unless they were forced, by the whip or by some other strong form of persuasion. They did not believe that blacks had the ambition, economic know-how, or intelligence needed to succeed on their own. The former slaves, however, looked back on their several centuries of hard, forced labor and the many luxuries their white owners had purchased through that labor and concluded that they were, in fact, very hard workers. In black eyes, it was the plantation owners who were lazy and who had, in fact, stolen the fruits of black toil.

That is not to say that blacks did not want to make some major changes in the labor system, even beyond prohibiting physical punishment. They wanted to work shorter hours than they had during slavery, when they would often be in the fields from before sunup until nine or ten o'clock at night. They wanted to control the conditions under which they worked (which usually meant eliminating the overseer and giving individuals or groups of individuals responsibility for their own tasks) and to achieve as much independence as possible. Most important of all, blacks yearned to own and farm their own land.

Immediately following the end of the war, blacks cherished a persistent belief that the government would be giving them the abandoned or confiscated land owned by those who had rebelled against the United States. This idea made perfect sense to blacks, who felt that they should now be rewarded for their years of unpaid labor and the contribution they had made to the growth and prosperity of the nation. Union general William T. Sherman (1820–1891) had seemed to confirm this belief when, soon after his triumphant arrival on the Georgia coast, he issued Special Field Order #15. This document made a large area of land along the coasts of Georgia and South Carolina available to black farmers, four hundred thousand of whom subsequently settled on 40-acre plots of "Sherman land." It also led to the popularity of the slogan "Forty Acres and a Mule" to represent black hopes.

As it turned out, though, the order was deemed a temporary measure. Under a liberal pardon from President Andrew Johnson (1808–1875; served 1865–69), who had assumed office after the assassination of Abraham Lincoln on April 15, 1865, former Confederates would be allowed to return to and reclaim the lands they had left during the war. Although some blacks would resist the efforts to force them off the land they had occupied with such high hopes, most would have to leave. Without enough money to buy their own land, blacks would have to become wage laborers or (more favorably in their own eyes) sharecroppers, who leased and farmed a piece of land and then gave the owner a share (usually half) of the crops they raised.

Just as blacks were finding ways to explore and develop their new economic freedom, Southern whites were looking for ways to create a new system that resembled the old one as much as possible. That would mean giving blacks as few rights, as few choices, and as little independence as possible. Most important, it would mean denying blacks access to land, because land meant money and power. Thus white Southerners banded together, agreeing to refuse to rent or sell land to the freed people. They also tried to gain authority over blacks by getting them to sign labor contracts that strictly controlled not only how they worked but how they lived, restricting them, for example, to their plantations unless they had permission from their employers. Under the state governments that would soon be set up under President Johnson's Reconstruction program, these measures would be encoded into laws called Black Codes (see Chapter 5).

The Freedmen's Bureau

The government agency assigned to help with all of the post–slavery era changes, the Freedmen's Bureau, had a very big job. Intended to operate only temporarily, the Bureau was supposed to assist not only in the creation of a workable free labor system but in establishing schools; dispensing aid for the poor, old, sick, and insane; resolving disputes both among blacks and between blacks and whites; and making sure that blacks received equal justice under the law. As noted in *Been in the Storm So Long: The Aftermath of Slavery,* a North Carolina Bureau officer declared rather grandly, "We desire to instruct the colored people of the South, to lift them up from subservience and helplessness into a dignified independence and citizenship."

This would have been a tall order under the best of circumstances, but it took place in an atmosphere of mutual distrust and hostility between blacks and whites, and with only nine hundred agents to cover the entire South. For example, one agent named John DeYoung was responsible for 3,000 square miles (with a population of about eighty thousand) in South Carolina.

Discussing the Freedmen's Bureau's mission with its commissioner, General Oliver Otis Howard (1830–1909), General Sherman commented, as quoted in *A Short History of Reconstruction,* "It is not in your power to fulfil one tenth of the expectations of those who framed the Bureau. I hear you have Hercules' task." Even though white Southerners detested the Freedmen's Bureau as a symbol of their defeat and losses, the agency often worked in whites' favor by trying to persuade blacks to work on the plantations. Blacks, meanwhile, invested much trust in the Bureau and remained its loyal supporters to the end.

Building schools, and fighting violence

Black people especially admired General Howard, who was considered a true advocate for black people's rights and interests. Howard put a strong focus on education, which he saw as an essential element in improving the lives and prospects of African Americans. Much energy went into coordinating the activities of the Northern charitable organizations that were responsible for setting up most schools. By 1869, almost three thousand schools (not including the private ones) had been established, serving over 150,000 students. Considered the crowning achievement of the Freedmen's Bureau, this feat laid a basis for a public school system in the South.

The first teachers were some five thousand white volunteers—most of them women—from the northeastern United States. Before the war, many had been involved in the abolitionist movement (the movement to abolish slavery). They were now eager to help the former slaves learn to read and write. Further, they wanted the freed people to learn how to be good citizens, and they emphasized self-reliance, discipline, frugality, temperance, religiousness, cleanliness, and punctuality. These were the values stressed throughout mainstream U.S. society during the mid-nineteenth century, and it was thought that black people must adopt them if they were to join that society.

Another important task of the Freedmen's Bureau was dealing with the violence that was occurring across the South as whites reacted in anger and brutality against their changed relationships to blacks. During the waning months of the war, considerable numbers of Union soldiers (many of them black) had been present in the South to help prevent or address such violence, especially in cities and towns. But after May 1865, few troops were still around, as most had been sent to other places (particularly the parts of the West where U.S. forces were battling with Native Americans).

The Freedmen's Bureau was, ideally, supposed to work with local courts to ensure that blacks could attain justice against those who attacked, cheated, or otherwise mistreated them. In reality, though, the white Southern courts were not willing to offer blacks equal rights. Blacks were not allowed to serve on juries and could testify only against other blacks. In any case, their testimony would not have been believed or given much weight by most whites. As recounted in *Been in the Storm So Long: The Aftermath of Slavery,* a Freedmen's Bureau agent in Georgia noted with frustration that "no jury would convict a white man for killing a freedman, or fail to hang a Negro who had killed a white man in self defense."

The struggle for civil rights begins

For the first time since their arrival in the United States, blacks were now free to gather together and discuss what their role in the nation should be. During the spring and summer of 1865, black people organized a large number of meetings, parades, and petitions supporting civil rights and suffrage (the right to vote). In a number of states, they held conventions with locally elected delegates—many of them ministers, teachers, and former Union soldiers—who discussed the important topics of the day.

The most critical of these issues were equality before the law and suffrage, promises that blacks felt had been guaranteed by the words of the Declaration of Independence. Tens of thousands of young men both black and white had died in the Civil War to defend these rights. Participants in the conventions declared that African Americans were loyal to the United States, had made sacrifices in the country's defense, and were now ready to play an equal part in its society.

Before his assassination, President Lincoln had suggested that he might be in favor of a limited form of black suffrage. Revered by blacks as the man who had led them out of slavery, Lincoln had been a thoughtful and adept politician who often demonstrated an ability to compromise and to change his mind. His untimely death had made the future even more uncertain. The ability of the man who succeeded him, Andrew Johnson, to guide the nation at such a difficult time was unknown. In the past, Johnson had expressed contempt for the slaveholding plantation owners. But as his term began, no one knew whether his antislavery stance extended to more rights for former slaves.

Blacks did have a strong base of support in the U.S. Congress, where the Radical Republicans had already begun to push for black suffrage and civil rights. But Congress was not scheduled to meet until December 1865. During the seven months between the war's conclusion and the end of the year, African Americans as well as their friends in Congress and elsewhere would be dismayed by the turn of events. President Johnson's ideas about the rebuilding of the South would hold disappointments for those who hoped that a better society could be created in the states of the former Confederacy.

For More Information

Books

Berlin, Ira A., et al., eds. *Freedmen: A Documentary History of Emancipation, 1861–1867*. New York: Cambridge University Press, 1982.

Blassingame, John W., ed. *Slave Testimony.* Baton Rouge: Louisiana State University Press, 1977.

Foner, Eric. *A Short History of Reconstruction.* New York: Harper & Row, 1990.

Golay, Michael. *Reconstruction and Reaction: The Emancipation of Slaves, 1861–1913.* New York: Facts on File, 1996.

Jenkins, Wilbert L. *Climbing Up to Glory: A Short History of African Americans During the Civil War and Reconstruction.* Wilmington, DE: Scholarly Resources, 2002.

Litwack, Leon F. *Been in the Storm So Long: The Aftermath of Slavery.* New York: Vintage Books, 1979.

Oubre, Claude F. *Forty Acres and a Mule: The Freedmen's Bureau and Black Land Ownership.* Baton Rouge: Louisiana State University Press, 1978.

Smith, John David. *Black Voices from Reconstruction, 1865–1877.* Gainesville: University of Florida Press, 1997.

Stampp, Kenneth M. *The Era of Reconstruction: 1865–1877.* New York: Vintage Books, 1965.

Wagner, Margaret E., Gary W. Gallagher, and Paul Finkelman, eds. *Civil War Desk Reference.* New York: Simon & Schuster, 2002.

Web Sites

Louisiana State University. *The United States Civil War Center.* http://www.cwc.lsu.edu/ (accessed on August 31, 2004).

"Reconstruction." *African American History.* http://afroamhistory.about.com/od/reconstruction/ (accessed on August 31, 2004).

"Reference Resources: Civil War." *Kidinfo.* http://www.kidinfo.com/American_History/Civil_War.html (accessed on August 31, 2004).

"US Civil War." *Internet Modern History Sourcebook.* http://www.fordham.edu/halsall/mod/modsbook27.html (accessed on August 31, 2004).

The President's Plan for Reconstruction

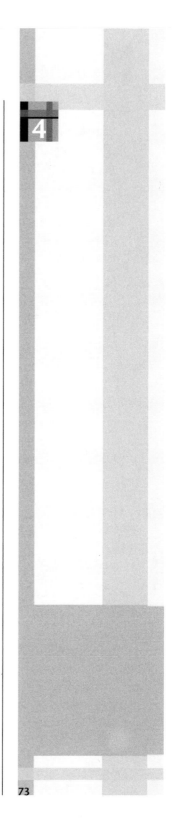

4

For more than four million African Americans living in the Southern United States, the end of the Civil War (1861–65) brought the freedom they had hoped for during all the long years of slavery. Ever since the arrival of the first white colonists in the New World, blacks captured in Africa and transported across the sea on slave ships had toiled without pay in fields and as house servants in the South. They had endured harsh conditions with remarkable strength and adaptability. Freedom brought great joy and expanded opportunities, but it also created new challenges. Probably the most threatening was the resentment of white Southerners, who found this changed society—and especially their new relationship with blacks—hard to accept.

A changed society

Northern journalists who traveled south in the days following the war's April 1865 conclusion found a devastated landscape littered with the debris of the bloody conflict: torn-up railroads, bridges, and fences; fields overgrown with

Words to Know

Amnesty: An official pardon for those convicted of political offenses.

Black Codes: Laws put in place by the Southern governments formed under the Reconstruction plan of President Andrew Johnson, which returned power to the former leaders of the Confederacy. They limited the economic options and civil rights of the former slaves through strict regulations on both their working conditions and their behavior.

Freedmen's Bureau: A federal agency that existed from 1865 to 1869 that assisted the former slaves in their transition to freedom. The program helped African Americans by distributing clothing, food, and fuel; handling legal cases; dispensing medical care; and setting up black schools.

Proclamation of Amnesty: A document issued by President Andrew Johnson soon after he took office, that established that most Southerners would be allowed to take an oath of allegiance that would offer them a complete pardon and amnesty and would restore to them any property other than slaves that the federal government had seized during the war.

weeds; ruined walls and chimneys left in the wake of an invading army that had burned everything in its path. They found black people both jubilant and in need of help as they tried to establish independent lives. White Southerners, meanwhile, were reeling not only from their personal losses but from the collapse of their society and economy. Their resentment over that collapse was heightened by the presence of the blue-coated soldiers (many of them black) who had so recently been their enemies; the South was now occupied by the Union army.

Meanwhile, all around were the former slaves whose unpaid labor had allowed the owners of the plantations (large estates where basic crops like cotton, tobacco, and rice were grown) to live in wealth and leisure. Whites now had to pay their employees to perform both the hard, tedious labor and the menial tasks previously reserved for their slaves, and in some cases—for Confederate money was now worthless and many whites were bankrupt—they even had to do this work themselves. As noted in *Been in the Storm So Long: The*

Racism: The belief that there are characteristics or qualities specific to each race, which often results in discrimination (treating people differently based on race).

Radical Republicans: A group of senators and representatives with a history of activism in the abolitionist movement who turned their energies, during the Reconstruction era, toward trying to create a truly democratic society in the South.

Reconstruction era: The period stretching roughly from the end of the Civil War in April 1865 to the inauguration of President Rutherford B. Hayes in 1877. During Reconstruction, representatives of the U.S. government—including the president and Congress—and the military would join with both white and black Southerners to try to reorganize the political and social structure of the devastated, defeated South.

Thirteenth Amendment: The amendment in the U.S. Constitution, passed in 1865, that officially abolished slavery in the United States.

Unionists: Southerners who opposed secession and continued to support the Union throughout the Civil War.

Aftermath of Slavery, one young lady complained, "It does seem a waste of time for people who are capable of doing something better to spend their time sweeping and dusting while scores of lazy negroes that are fit for nothing else are laying around idle."

Such racist views, which held that blacks were inferior in every way to whites, that they lacked energy and intelligence, and that they were made for nothing better than to serve white people, were widespread in the South, as indeed they were in all parts of the United States in the nineteenth century. This attitude would severely hamper the efforts of African Americans and others to win for blacks the civil rights that whites took for granted. During the era of Reconstruction—the period stretching roughly from the end of the Civil War in April 1865 to the inauguration of President Rutherford B. Hayes (1822–1893; served 1877–81) in 1877—both black and white Americans would participate in the effort to rebuild the South. It was a time of struggle, marked by hope and achievement but also marred by brutality and injustice. In the months immediately following the war's end, though, it seemed that injustice would rule the day.

The president's plan

As the war was drawing to a close and a Union victory seemed inevitable, President Abraham Lincoln (1809–1865; served 1861–65) had devised a plan for readmitting the Southern states into the Union and reorganizing their state governments. Referred to as the Ten Per Cent Plan, Lincoln's program allowed the states to form governments as soon as only 10 percent of eligible voters (white males who had been able to vote in 1860) signed a loyalty oath, vowing their faithfulness to the Union. It is likely that Lincoln had intended this only as a temporary measure, but he died before his intentions—and his full vision of the new Southern society—could be known. Assassinated on April 15, 1865, Lincoln left a nation not only grieving for its fallen leader but uncertain about how to mend the wounds the war had left, how to bind the divided nation into one again.

The man called upon to take Lincoln's place was Andrew Johnson (1808–1875; served 1865–69), a former U.S. senator from Tennessee who had been rewarded for his loyalty to the Union (both before and during the war) with the position of vice president. Thrust into the task of guiding the nation through what was probably the darkest hour in its history so far, Johnson was an unknown quantity. No one was sure exactly where or how he would lead the country.

The Radical Republicans are optimistic

Nevertheless, the Radical Republicans in Congress felt optimistic. This group of senators and representatives, dominated by such men as U.S. representative Thaddeus Stevens (1792–1868) of Pennsylvania and U.S. senator Charles Sumner (1811–1874) of Massachusetts, had been pushing for a transformed Southern society. They hoped to break the power of the large landowners (and former slaveholders) and to ensure that African Americans had the same civil and voting rights as whites. The Radicals had been unhappy with Lincoln's plan for Reconstruction. They felt it did not impose harsh enough penalties on those who had rebelled, and they believed that governments established by only 10 percent of the population were not very democratic. Based on Johnson's previous statements, the Radicals expected him to propose a plan more in keeping with their own ideas.

Before the start of the Civil War, Johnson had been a determined supporter of the Union (or Federal government). When Southern leaders proposed that eleven states secede (separate) from the Union and form their own government (subsequently named the Confederate States of America), Johnson had voted against such a move. During the first year of the war, he had remained loyal to the Union. When Tennessee had been occupied by the Union army in 1862, Lincoln had named Johnson the state's military governor.

Two years later, Johnson had joined Lincoln on the Republican ticket as candidate for vice president. During the campaign, he had used harsh language to denounce the rebellious Confederates. As quoted in *The Era of Reconstruction: 1865–1877,* Johnson declared, "I say the traitor has ceased to be a citizen, and in joining the rebellion has become a public enemy." Referring to the punishment to come when the war was finally over, Johnson said the "traitors must be punished and impoverished."

It was this kind of language that convinced both the Radicals and the more moderate Republicans in Congress that Johnson shared their views. Immediately after becoming president, Johnson continued to talk in the same way, calling for the arrest of Confederate leaders like President Jefferson Davis (1808–1889) and threatening to charge the rebels with treason and break up the great Southern estates into small farms. However, even though he was committed to the abolition of slavery, Johnson did not propose that the Federal government get involved in ensuring civil rights for blacks. These matters, he suggested, should be left up to the individual states once the South was reorganized.

Johnson surprises everyone

Ten days into Johnson's administration, U.S. senator Zachariah Chandler (1813–1879) of Michigan, a Radical and a member of the Committee on the Conduct of the War, re-

Andrew Johnson: Advocate for White Workers

Throughout his political life, Andrew Johnson considered himself a champion of ordinary working people. During the Reconstruction era, however, he proved that he did not feel the same concern for ordinary African Americans.

Johnson was born on December 25, 1808, in Raleigh, North Carolina. His family struggled financially and Johnson received no formal schooling. While apprenticing with a tailor (working with and learning a trade), he learned the basics of reading and writing. After two years, Johnson and his brother ran away to Tennessee; the rest of the family eventually joined them. Settling in the eastern Tennessee town of Greeneville, Johnson worked in a tailor's shop. He married a quiltmaker named Eliza McCardle (1810–1876), who helped Johnson continue his education. The couple would raise five children.

After becoming interested in debating, Johnson was elected to a local government position in 1828. Two years later, he became mayor of Greeneville; five years later, he was elected to the Tennessee state legislature. Although he did not win reelection in 1835, he was elected again in 1839. He continued to support the interests of the non-slave-owning white workers of eastern Tennessee against those of the wealthier slave owners who lived in the middle and western parts of the state. Johnson was not, however, opposed to slavery and even owned slaves himself.

In 1840, Johnson joined the Democratic Party and ran successfully for state senator. In that office, he gained a reputation for strong opinions and for a reluctance to compromise. From 1843 to 1853, Johnson served as a U.S. congressman. In his deep reverence for the federal Union and for the U.S. Constitution, he modeled himself after his hero, former president Andrew Jackson (1767–1845; served 1829–37). This created friction with many other Southern Democrats, who were already drifting away from the Union.

As a member of Congress, Johnson proposed a Homestead Act that would offer as many as 160 acres of federal land to anyone who was willing and able to farm it. The bill repeatedly failed to be approved by the Senate and was not passed until 1862. Meanwhile, in 1853, Johnson was elected governor of Tennessee, after which he signed into law the first public school system in the state. Four years later, he became a U.S. senator. Once again he pushed for the passage of the Homestead Act, which was actually opposed by Southern members of his own party (who feared it might include limits on slavery) and supported by Northern Republicans.

Even though he was not against slavery, Johnson was a strong nationalist who did not support the growing anti-Union sentiment in the South. Tennessee was not one of the original seven states to secede from the United States, but Ten-

Andrew Johnson. *The Library of Congress.*

nesseans did vote to join the Confederacy after the successful Confederate attack on Fort Sumter, South Carolina, in April 1861. Having opposed secession, Johnson left Tennessee and spent most of the first years of the war in Washington, D.C., while continuing to visit his family in Union-held Nashville. Johnson was the only Southern senator who did not resign his seat.

By March 1862, the Union army had taken control of most of Tennessee, and President Abraham Lincoln rewarded Johnson for his loyalty to the Union by making him the state's military governor. Thus Johnson oversaw the restoration of order and establishment of a new state government. In the summer of 1864, anticipating an end to the war and hoping to gain favor with Northerners who sympa-

thized with the South, Lincoln convinced the Republican Party to nominate Johnson as his running mate in the upcoming presidential election. In November, Lincoln and Johnson defeated former Union general George B. McClellan.

Less than two months into the new term, Lincoln was assassinated and Johnson was propelled unexpectedly into the office of the president. Johnson's plan for the Reconstruction of the South proved so lenient that the region's old leaders were able to regain power. Constantly at odds with the Radical Republicans who dominated Congress—a situation made worse by his difficult personality—Johnson was eventually impeached (tried for misbehavior) and nearly missed being removed from office.

For the 1868 election, the Republicans passed over Johnson and nominated instead popular Civil War general Ulysses S. Grant (1822–1885; served 1869–77). After leaving Washington, Johnson returned to a hero's welcome in Greeneville. He made several unsuccessful bids for the U.S. House of Representatives and Senate before being elected senator in 1874, becoming the first (and so far only) ex-president to serve in that office. Johnson served just less than five months; he suffered two strokes and died on July 31, 1875. In accordance with his instructions, he was buried with his body wrapped in a U.S. flag and his head resting on a copy of the U.S. Constitution.

ported with relief that Johnson was, as noted in *The Era of Reconstruction: 1865–1877,* "as radical as I am." Believing that the Senate and House of Representatives must have a say in the reorganization of the South, Chandler and his colleagues assumed that Johnson would delay the formation of any Reconstruction program until December, when the next session of Congress was scheduled to begin. Thus, they were shocked when Johnson quickly put his own plan into motion, making it clear that he saw Reconstruction as the responsibility of the president, not of Congress.

On May 29, Johnson issued two proclamations. The first, often referred to as the Proclamation of Amnesty, established that most Southerners would be allowed to take an oath of allegiance (loyalty) that would offer them a complete pardon and amnesty (protection from prosecution) and would restore to them any property—except for slaves, of course—seized by the federal government during the war. White Southerners were relieved to hear that most of them would not face treason charges or lose any of their civil rights or property. Exempted were fourteen classes of citizens, including not only Confederate civil and military leaders but anyone who had supported the Confederacy and whose property was valued at $20,000 or more. As noted in *A Short History of Reconstruction,* this was meant to punish the members of what Johnson had called "the pampered, bloated, corrupted aristocracy" of wealthy Southern plantation owners. These people could, however, apply for pardons from the president.

The second proclamation laid out the steps for the states to form new governments. The president would appoint provisional (temporary) governors, who would call for state conventions and supervise the election of convention delegates. All those who had been eligible to vote in 1860 and had taken the loyalty oath would be allowed to vote and run for office. Once the conventions had established voting and office-holding regulations, elections for state governors, legislators, and members of the federal Congress could take place. Each state was also required to proclaim that secession had been an illegal act, cancel any debts left over from the Confederacy, and ratify the Thirteenth Amendment to the Constitution (the document that officially outlawed slavery).

By the end of the year, when Congress met, Johnson would declare Reconstruction complete. Despite the relatively harsh requirements he had laid out, the new state governments organized under his program would take a much different shape than anyone—including Johnson himself—originally expected, with the South's old, wealthy planter class firmly in charge again. Understanding why this happened requires a look into Johnson's background and how his fundamental beliefs differed from those of the Radical Republicans.

A Southern Unionist

Both Johnson and the Radicals shared a hatred for the Southern aristocracy, which they saw as a spoiled, lazy minority that had grown wealthy through the labor of others. But this is where their views parted. Unlike Johnson, the Radicals envisioned a transformed South where blacks would have civil rights and where U.S. business interests would be aided by federal protections. Johnson's idea of change in the South really extended only to the rise of the small farmer, who the president felt had been held down by the wealthy plantation owners. Like Southerners before the Civil War, Johnson still believed in a decentralized form of government; that is, one that gave the individual states a great deal of freedom to govern themselves independently. He envisioned the new South as a kind of a rural paradise in which—importantly—white people were in charge.

Like Abraham Lincoln, Andrew Johnson had risen from poverty to the most important office in the nation. Born in North Carolina, he moved as a young man to east Tennessee to make his own living in a tailor's shop. He had no formal education, and his wife taught him to read and write. Johnson entered politics as a town alderman (a member of a city council) and later became a mayor, then a state legislator, then a five-term member of the U.S. Congress. He served for two terms as Tennessee's governor before becoming a U.S. senator, a position in which he worked for tax-supported free public schools and the Homestead Act (which made 160-acre plots of federally owned land available for anyone who wanted to settle on them).

Johnson had always been a strong defender of ordinary working people, but he did not feel the same way about African Americans. He had not always been opposed to slavery and even owned slaves himself before the Civil War.

Eventually he did come out against slavery, but his stance was based more on a fear of miscegenation (sexual relationships between blacks and whites, which some thought would mar the "purity" of the white race) and on the advantage slavery gave to wealthy people than on the injustice of slavery. In fact, as reported in *The Era of Reconstruction: 1865–1877,* Johnson once said that he wished that "every head of a family in the United States had one slave to take the drudgery and menial service off his family." Johnson believed in democracy, but felt that it applied only to whites. The main goal of his Reconstruction program was to make the white small farmers of the South its new leaders.

It was not only Johnson's ideas that brought him into clashes with the Radicals, and eventually with all the Republicans in Congress. His personality did not help his case. Unlike Lincoln, Johnson was not able to make the most of his impoverished background and use it as a bond with the masses of ordinary U.S. citizens. Instead, he felt bitter and resentful toward wealthy people, who, he believed, had treated him with scorn. He lacked self-confidence and often failed to act decisively at important times. In addition, he was known as an intolerant, inflexible person who was unwilling to compromise. All these qualities served him poorly in his attempt to put through his own plan for Reconstruction.

Conflicting ideas about the future

Other issues central to the way white Southerners reacted to Johnson's plan involved land and labor. The war ended with the occupation of the eleven Confederate states by the Union army. This gave Union military officers responsibility for deciding what to do about the tens of thousands of former slaves who must now seek paid work to support themselves. It was widely believed by these officers and by agents of the Freedmen's Bureau, the federal agency established in March 1865 to aid the former slaves in their transition to freedom, that the best course for blacks was to remain on their plantations as field workers or domestic servants. They were discouraged from moving to the large Southern cities (such as Atlanta, Georgia, and Charleston, South Carolina), owing to fears about the problems that overcrowding and unemployment might breed. (Nevertheless, many blacks—especially in the weeks and months immediately following their emancipation—did flock to the cities, in search of work, protection, or the support of a growing African American community.)

The Northern whites concerned with the matter of land and labor assumed that the South would make a smooth transition from slavery to a free market system (where people work for wages and then buy what they need to survive). What they failed to anticipate were both the attitude of white Southerners and the hopes and dreams that African Americans had nurtured through generations of slavery. While white plantation owners wanted low-paid, well-disciplined workers to raise their crops, blacks yearned to farm land that belonged to them. These two conflicting ideas of the future would create a big problem in the South in the years to come.

Blacks long to own land

The Freedmen's Bureau had originally been authorized to distribute about 850,000 acres of Southern land that had either been abandoned or confiscated by the Union army during the war. The Freedmen's Bureau official in charge of this issue was General Rufus Saxton (1824–1908), who was revered by African Americans for his firm commitment to the idea of landownership as the best way for blacks to take up their lives as freed people. Indeed, blacks closely associated landownership with freedom itself and, like most Americans, with success. They also felt that their more than two centuries of unpaid labor entitled them to be compensated with free land.

During the summer of 1865, Saxton began settling blacks on land in South Carolina, Georgia, and Florida. In the Sea Islands (located off South Carolina) and along the coast of South Carolina and Georgia, thousands of blacks had been farming confiscated land since early 1864, authorized by Union general William T. Sherman (1820–1891) when, after his victorious arrival on the coast, he issued Special Field Order #15. In addition, the original plan for the Freedmen's Bureau had authorized the agency to distribute confiscated land to the former slaves.

As the summer progressed, however, Confederates who had fled their plantations began returning, surprised

Company A of the First
South Carolina Volunteers,
the first black military
organization, takes an oath
of allegiance before General
Rufus Saxton. © *Corbis.*

and outraged to discover former slaves farming their land
and even living in their homes. The question of how this situation would be resolved was answered at the end of May,
when President Johnson issued his Proclamation of Amnesty,
restoring all confiscated property to former supporters of the
Confederacy as long as they signed a loyalty oath. By September, Johnson had specifically ordered that most confiscated land be restored to its former owners.

In October, General Oliver Howard (1830–1909), the
much-respected director of the Freedmen's Bureau, traveled
to Edisto Island (part of the Sea Island chain) to inform the
black settlers there of the government's decision and to do
what he could to ease the shock and pain of this news. At a
meeting attended by about two thousand former slaves, voices from the crowd expressed the disappointment and frustration felt by all. Howard asked that a committee be formed to
create a plan to facilitate a smooth transition of ownership.
The committee's response, as quoted in *Reconstruction and Re-*

action: The Emancipation of Slaves, 1861–1913, is a moving testament to the strength of their feelings:

> You ask us to forgive the owners of our island. *You* only lost your right arm in the war and might forgive them. The man who tied me to a tree and gave me 39 lashes and who stripped and flogged my mother and my sister and who will not let me stay in his empty hut except I will do his planting and be satisfied with his price and who combines with others to keep away land from me well knowing I would not have anything to do with him if I had land of my own— that man, I cannot well forgive. Does it look as if he has forgiven me, seeing how he tries to keep me in a condition of helplessness?

Despite the protests not only of blacks but of sympathetic whites like Howard, Saxton, and the group known as Gideon's Band (white Northerners who had come to the Sea Islands before the war's end to educate and otherwise help the freed slaves there), the army soon began removing most blacks from the land they had occupied in Virginia, Louisiana, Georgia, and South Carolina. The few who resisted—using weapons to drive off the former owners—were also eventually forced to leave. In early 1866, responding to complaints from Southern whites that Saxton was working against their interests, Johnson removed him from his post. This added to the general sense of betrayal blacks felt as their dreams of owning land seemed to fade away.

General Rufus Saxton. *The Library of Congress.*

The unexpected results of Johnson's plan

As President Johnson embarked on his plan for Reconstruction, he envisioned that the leaders who had dominated Southern politics before the war—that is, the wealthy class of plantation owners, who actually represented a very small minority of the total Southern white population—

Oliver Otis Howard: Admired by African Americans

A Civil War general assigned to the difficult task of taking charge of the newly formed Freedmen's Bureau, Oliver Otis Howard soon gained the esteem of the former slaves for his dedication to the cause of justice and advancement for blacks. In fact, as noted in *Been in the Storm So Long: The Aftermath of Slavery*, Howard "may have been second only to Abraham Lincoln in the esteem of the ex-slaves."

Born in 1830 in Leeds, Maine, Howard was the son of a prosperous farmer who died when the boy was nine years old. After earning a degree from Bowdoin College in 1850, Howard immediately entered the U.S. Military Academy at West Point, New York, graduating near the top of his class in 1854. He subsequently served in a variety of military posts (including math instructor at West Point). Soon after the start of the Civil War, Howard was made colonel of the Third Maine Regiment, and three months later he was promoted to the rank of brigadier general of volunteers. He was made a brigadier general of the regular army in 1864.

During the war, Howard took part in many famous battles, including the first Bull Run, Fair Oaks (where he lost an arm), Antietam, and Gettysburg. He accompanied General William T. Sherman on his "March to the Sea," and was horrified by the looting and successive violence he witnessed. On May 12, 1865, President Andrew Johnson appointed Howard commissioner of the Bureau of Refugees, Freedmen, and Abandoned Lands (better known as the Freedmen's Bureau), a position for which President Lincoln had previously selected him.

The Bureau was charged with assisting the former slaves in their transition to freedom by dispensing food, clothing, fuel, medical care and other forms of aid; eventually it would also play a role in organizing schools and dispensing justice for blacks who had been mistreated or cheated. Howard took on an extremely challenging task, as his agency faced not only a shortage of agents to carry out its work but the animosity of white Southerners, who resented the Bureau's advocacy of blacks. One of his most heart-wrenching moments came when, in October 1865, he had to inform a large gathering of South Carolina blacks that they would have to va-

would now be replaced with Unionists (those who had remained faithful to the federal government throughout the Civil War). Johnson assumed that the majority of Southerners shared his contempt for what he called the slaveocracy, those who had accumulated wealth and lived in leisure while their slaves did all the labor.

General Oliver Otis Howard. © *Corbis.*

cate the land they thought the government had given them.

Though plagued by charges of corruption and incompetence by some its agents, the Bureau achieved a great deal in its short life, including distributing fifteen million food rations to poverty-stricken Southerners, both black and white; dispensing medical care to a million people; and spending $5 million on helping to set up black schools. Howard's real concern for the problems facing African Americans made him a hero to the people he was dedicated to helping.

Howard was one of the founders of a leading black educational institution, Howard University in Washington, D.C. He served as the university's president from 1869 until 1874. Throughout the 1870s, he was involved in the U.S. government's military efforts to ease white settlement of the West by bringing the Native Americans who lived in the region under control. Howard helped to negotiate a treaty with the Apache Indians and commanded military expeditions against the Nez Perce, the Bannocks, and the Paiutes. He later wrote a number of books based on his experiences among Native Americans.

During the 1880s, Howard served in a number of army positions, including superintendent of West Point. At the time of his retirement in 1894, he was commander of the Division of the East. Howard spent the remainder of his life at his home in Burlington, Vermont, busy with writing, religious and educational activities, and speaking engagements. He died on October 26, 1909.

As it turned out, he was wrong. Although ordinary white Southerners had felt some envy and resentment for the planter class, in many ways they also respected and admired these traditional leaders of a society and culture cherished by whites at all economic levels. Most people in the South, after all, had supported secession, and most—as now became obvious—were still willing to accept the old leaders. Thus the people who had dominated Southern politics before the war, and even those who had been active in the Confederacy, quickly realized that Johnson's lenient plan would allow them to take their own places at the head of their society.

Former confederates receive pardons

Few of the arrests of Confederate "traitors" that Johnson had threatened were made, and even the former president of the Confederacy, Jefferson Davis, spent only two years in prison. The fact that little desire for any real change existed was borne out by the results of the state government elections held in the South in the fall of 1865. Although many Unionists were elected in the states of the Upper South (such as Maryland and Missouri), almost all of those elected in the Deep South (which included such states as Mississippi, Georgia, and South Carolina) were plantation owners and former Confederate military leaders and office holders. Some had even bragged, during the campaign, of their activities during the war. One of them was Alexander H. Stephens (1812–1883), who had been vice president of the Confederacy under Davis and who now had been elected a senator in Georgia.

The fact was that many of the officials elected under Johnson's plan for state reorganization were not eligible to take the required amnesty oath. This left Johnson in an embarrassing bind, for he did not want to declare invalid the results of the program he himself had designed. Johnson's solution was to begin issuing presidential pardons in large numbers and with very little difficulty for the applicants. By 1867, in fact, he would issue 13,500 pardons. Thus Johnson seemed to completely turn his back on his earlier ideas.

Historians have proposed a number of reasons for this turnaround. Perhaps Johnson felt that this was the only way to ensure white supremacy in the South or to make sure that he would win reelection when the time came. Perhaps he lacked the strong will it would take to push through economic and social changes that were sure to meet resistance from white Southerners. It has also been suggested that Johnson derived some pleasure from his power to grant pardons to the Southern aristocrats he so resented, and that they took advantage of this weakness. In any case, by the end of the year Johnson was in a position of either admitting that his program had backfired or coming out against the Radicals in Congress, as well as, eventually, the moderate Republicans who had been more inclined to support him.

Schurz reports on conditions in the South

Even before reaching that point, Johnson hoped to prove that true reform was underway. He had sent out some military and government officials to report on conditions in the South. One of these was General Ulysses S. Grant, who returned from a one-week tour and reported that all was well. A much less favorable report was filed by a former Union general, politician, and journalist named Carl Schurz (1829–1906), whose advice Johnson chose to ignore. Schurz claimed that even though Southerners admitted defeat and were cooperating with efforts to reorganize their governments, they were still bitter and reluctant to acknowledge that they had done anything wrong in either seceding or fighting the Union. They were eager to end the federal occupation of their society, hostile to the Northerners among them, and extremely unwilling to accept the fact that blacks were now free and must now be considered ordinary U.S. citizens.

In his report, Schurz chronicled numerous acts of violence by whites against blacks, including shootings, hangings, and arson attacks on schools and churches. He found that Southerners were just as opposed to educating blacks as they had been during slavery, still just as convinced that the Southern society created by whites would be threatened by blacks who could read and write. As recounted in *Reconstruction and Reaction: The Emancipation of Slaves, 1861–1913*, former slave Douglass White, who had served in the Union army, described what had often happened when he and his neighbors had sent their children off to school in Louisiana: "Big white boys and half-grown men used to pelt them with stones and run them down with open knives, both to and from school. Sometimes they came home bruised, stabbed, beaten half to death, and sometimes quite dead." Sensing the vulnerability of blacks to attacks and exploitation by whites, Schurz urged the president to provide federal protection for African Americans. "Nothing renders society more restless," he warned, "than a social revolution but half accomplished."

Carl Schurz: An Immigrant Devoted to Democracy

An active politician who served as a general in the Civil War (1861–65), Carl Schurz was also the author of a chilling report that convinced many Northerners to support the Radical Republicans' plan for the Reconstruction of the South.

Born to poor parents in Germany in 1829, Schurz was a good student with a special interest in music. He was just about to enter college when his father went bankrupt and was sent to debtor's prison. After helping to arrange for his father's release, Schurz finally entered the University of Bonn. He intended to become a history professor, but in 1848 he became a student leader in the democracy movement that was sweeping across Europe. Caught up in the political disorder that soon engulfed his country, Schurz was labeled a rebel, imprisoned, and sentenced to death.

Making a dramatic escape through the prison sewer system, Schurz fled to Paris, then London, but he returned to Germany to make a daring and successful rescue of a friend who was still imprisoned. Again he went to Paris, but he was forced to leave when authorities there viewed him as a troublemaker. He moved to London, where he married a German woman. The couple left for the United States in 1852.

After arriving in New York, Schurz quickly became involved in politics. He and his growing family settled in Philadelphia, Pennsylvania, where Schurz became a U.S. citizen and studied English intensely while working as an editor of a German-language newspaper. Schurz then moved his family to Wisconsin, where there were many German immigrants and where his ability to speak both German and English made him an asset to local politicians. He became active in the Republican Party while also earning a law degree and practicing law.

Schurz often spoke out on the issues of the day, especially the abolition of slavery. In 1860, he served as a Wisconsin delegate at the Republican political convention, and he subsequently campaigned for nominee Abraham Lincoln. When Lincoln became president, he made Schurz the U.S. minister to France, but the Civil War drew Schurz back to the United States. In 1862, he was commissioned a brigadier general of volunteers, serving under General John C. Frémont (1813–1890). Schurz led troops in the second battle of Bull Run and at Chancellorsville, Chattanooga, and Gettysburg.

After the war, Schurz returned to his work as a newspaper editor. He made a

Even though the president refused to acknowledge it, Schurz's report was submitted to Congress, and Northerners were shocked by its contents. Adding to their dismay and dis-

Carl Schurz. *The Library of Congress.*

newspaper in St. Louis, Missouri. In 1869, he was elected to the U.S. Senate, where he spoke out against several of the policies of President Ulysses S. Grant. Schurz campaigned for Rutherford B. Hayes in the 1876 presidential election, and when Hayes was elected he made Schurz secretary of the interior. Thus, Schurz had held the two highest positions possible for a naturalized citizen—U.S. senator and cabinet secretary.

As head of the Department of the Interior, Schurz oversaw the relocation of Native Americans onto reservations, a process that would continue throughout the last quarter of the nineteenth century. As he became more familiar with American Indians, Schurz grew more sympathetic to their plight. He believed that they should be treated with dignity but that they should become integrated with white society (rather than being allowed to live as they always had, which was their wish).

Schurz resigned this post in 1881 but stayed active in politics as well as through writing and editing. He served for six years as editor of the well-known *Harper's Weekly* magazine, and continued to speak and write (including his autobiography) until his death in 1906.

tour of the South and recorded his observations in a report that, while ignored by President Andrew Johnson, was submitted to the U.S. Congress. Northerners were shocked by Schurz's descriptions not only of the physical devastation of the South but of the brutal ways in which blacks there were being treated. His account—and his plea for federal assistance for the South and especially for the former slaves—helped to drum up support for the Reconstruction plan devised by the Radical Republicans in Congress.

Later, Schurz became editor of the *Denver Post*, then of a German-language

gust was news of the infamous Black Codes, a set of policies adopted by the Southern states under the Johnson program. In setting the terms of his Reconstruction plan, Johnson had left the treatment of blacks, their role in society, and any decisions to grant them civil and political rights up to the individual states.

Southern states enact the Black Codes

Left to their own devices, the former states of the Confederacy chose to restrict voting rights to whites only. As reported in *Reconstruction and Reaction: The Emancipation of Slaves, 1861–1913*, they agreed with Mississippi governor Benjamin Humphreys (1808–1882), who declared that "ours is and it shall ever be, a government of white men." Neither did the states make any provision for the establishment or support of black schools. They saw blacks as bound for no greater goal than being agricultural workers or servants without education, skills, or property. Motivated both by their desire to maintain a pool of cheap labor and by a real belief in the limitations of blacks, they considered no other role acceptable. Through the Black Codes, they tried to ensure that no other role would be possible.

The Black Codes rose out of a white conviction that African Americans were lazy by nature and would not work unless they were forced to, and that they should be kept under strict control and denied most civil rights. The laws represented an attempt by the state to limit black people's options and thus ensure a stable work force for the plantations, backed up by rigid enforcement of labor agreements or contracts that restricted not only work conditions but behavior. Often these contracts called for the kind of gang labor (driven by overseers) that the blacks had learned during slavery to hate, as well as complete obedience to the plantation owner (which might mean not leaving or having visitors without permission). This tactic did not always work, as blacks sometimes signed contracts but then refused to comply with all of the rules. The labor shortage that immediately followed the war gave blacks some bargaining power, especially in Florida and Texas. Bad harvests in the autumns of 1865 and 1866, however, chipped away some of that leverage.

The Codes did grant blacks the right to marry and to own and sell property; at the same time, however, they called for segregation of public places, prohibited interracial marriage, and prevented blacks from serving on juries or testifying

against whites. Blacks were forced, in effect, into signing labor contracts, because unemployed blacks could be arrested as vagrants, the definition of which also included those who were seen as idle, disorderly, or even careless with money. In South Carolina, blacks had to obtain special licenses and pay high fees if they wanted to perform work other than agricultural labor. In Mississippi, which had some of the most severe Black Codes of all the states, blacks must have written evidence each January that they had signed labor contracts. If at any point during the year they broke their contracts, all of the wages they earned up to that point could be forfeited. In Louisiana and Texas, the laws applied to all members of the family who were able to work (a way to keep women and children working in the fields); in Florida, they made "disrespect" a crime, and in North Carolina, even the "intent" to steal was against the law.

As reported in *Reconstruction and Reaction: The Emancipation of Slaves, 1861–1913,* the Black Codes were designed to show that, in the words of Georgia politician Emerson

As a result of the Black Codes, African American men were rounded up and accused of being vagrants, homeless and jobless wanderers. *The Granger Collection, New York. Reproduced by permission.*

Etheridge (1819–1902), "the Negroes are no more free than they were forty years ago, and if anybody goes about the country telling them they are free, shoot him." It was evident that white Southerners were, in fact, trying to recreate the conditions of slavery, and that they were more than willing to use violence to achieve that goal. Northerners were outraged, and even some Southerners agreed that the laws had gone too far; a few of the states even modified early versions of their codes to remove any references to race, though of course the codes were not meant to restrict anyone but blacks.

Opposition to Johnson's program grows

Leaders of the African American community called on Congress for help. A group of them even met with President Johnson in early 1866 to express their dissatisfaction with his program, which had allowed former Confederates to shape the new Southern governments according to their own ideas. Pressed to explain why he would not support black suffrage, Johnson asserted that he would not risk further tension or possibly a race war between blacks and whites. As reported in *Reconstruction and Reaction: The Emancipation of Slaves, 1861–1913,* black leader Frederick Douglass (c. 1817–1895), who had spearheaded the fight for freedom and was now working for the expansion of black civil rights, told the president, "You enfranchise [give the vote to] your enemies and disenfranchise your friends."

But by now it seemed that it was too late for Johnson to turn back. He defended the Black Codes as restrictions necessary to the well-being of the former slaves, thus putting himself firmly on the side of the plantation owners for whom he had once expressed such contempt. Meanwhile, though, the discontent stirred by the president's program was growing.

At first, supporters of Johnson's plan had included Northern businessmen, who hoped for a quick return to agricultural production in the South. After all, cotton had been the nation's leading export, and many Northerners, including merchants, lawyers, bankers, insurance brokers, and shipowners, benefited from the cotton trade. In addition, the New England textile industry needed a steady influx of cotton to keep its looms humming. But the news of the Black Codes and of ever-increasing attacks on blacks by resentful, angry whites helped the Radical Republicans make their case not only against Johnson's program but in favor of black suffrage.

When the Thirty-ninth Congress met in December 1865, Johnson proclaimed in the face of evidence to the contrary that Reconstruction had already been accomplished and that the Southern state governments were headed by leaders loyal to the Union. The stage was now set for a showdown with the Radicals. In the months to come, Johnson would face an overwhelming tide of opposition as the moderate Republicans in Congress rallied to the Radical cause. Many would claim that Johnson had himself brought about the downfall of his short-lived Reconstruction program.

For More Information

Books

Ayers, Edward L. *The Promise of the New South: Life After Reconstruction.* New York: Oxford University Press, 1992.

Benedict, Michael Les. *A Compromise of Principle: Congressional Republicans and Reconstruction, 1863–1869.* New York: Norton, 1974.

Foner, Eric. *A Short History of Reconstruction.* New York: Harper & Row, 1990.

Golay, Michael. *Reconstruction and Reaction: The Emancipation of Slaves, 1861–1913.* New York: Facts on File, 1996.

Jenkins, Wilbert L. *Climbing Up to Glory: A Short History of African Americans During the Civil War and Reconstruction.* Wilmington, DE: Scholarly Resources, 2002.

Litwack, Leon F. *Been in the Storm So Long: The Aftermath of Slavery.* New York: Vintage Books, 1979.

McPherson, James M. *The Struggle for Equality: Abolitionists and the Negro in the Civil War and Reconstruction.* Princeton, NJ: Princeton University Press, 1965.

Murphy, Richard W. *The Nation Reunited: War's Aftermath.* Alexandria, VA: Time-Life Books, 1987.

Smith, John David. *Black Voices from Reconstruction, 1865–1877.* Gainesville: University of Florida Press, 1997.

Stampp, Kenneth M. *The Era of Reconstruction: 1865–1877.* New York: Vintage Books, 1965.

Wagner, Margaret E., Gary W. Gallagher, and Paul Finkelman, eds. *Civil War Desk Reference.* New York: Simon & Schuster, 2002.

Wharton, Vernon L. *The Negro in Mississippi, 1865–1900*. New York: Harper & Row, 1965.

Web Sites

Louisiana State University. *The United States Civil War Center.* http://www.cwc.lsu.edu/ (accessed on August 31, 2004).

"Reconstruction." *African American History.* http://afroamhistory.about.com/od/reconstruction/ (accessed on August 31, 2004).

"Reference Resources: Civil War." *Kidinfo.* http://www.kidinfo.com/American_History/Civil_War.html (accessed on August 31, 2004).

"US Civil War." *Internet Modern History Sourcebook.* http://www.fordham.edu/halsall/mod/modsbook27.html (accessed on August 31, 2004).

The Radical Republicans
Clash with the President

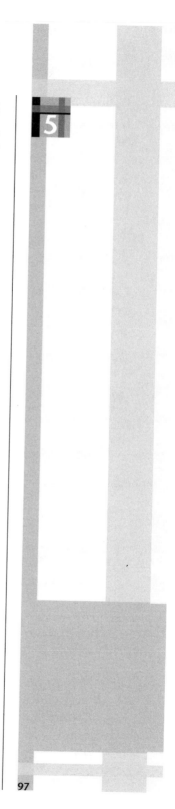

5

For some African Americans, the end of slavery came with the January 1863 signing of the Emancipation Proclamation, the document that proclaimed most of them free. For others, it came in April 1865 with the end of the Civil War (1861–65). This bloody, four-year conflict had divided the nation, pitting the Northern Union (federal government) against the Confederacy, the eleven Southern states that had seceded (broken away) from the United States. In any case, all of the four million former slaves rejoiced in their freedom.

The end of slavery did not, however, bring with it an easy solution to the problems facing black people. As noted in *The Era of Reconstruction: 1865–1877,* according to respected African American leader Frederick Douglass (c. 1817–1895), a former slave who fought first for the abolition of slavery and later for black civil rights, the freed people "were sent away empty-handed, without money, without friends, and without a foot of land to stand upon. Old and young, sick and well, they were turned loose to the open sky, naked to their enemies."

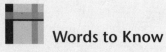

Words to Know

Black suffrage: The right of African Americans to cast votes in elections. The Fifteenth Amendment to the Constitution, passed in 1870, guaranteed that voting rights could not be denied on the basis of race or "previous condition of servitude."

Civil Rights Act of 1867: Legislation that guaranteed that all persons born in the United States (except for Native Americans) were to be considered U.S. citizens with full protection of "person and property" under the law. Fears that the bill would be ruled unconstitutional resulted in the framing of the Fourteenth Amendment, which enshrined the same guarantees in the U.S. Constitution.

Democratic Party: The political party that had been dominant in the South before the Civil War and which regained control at the end of Reconstruction. Generally, Democrats were conservatives who opposed the kinds of changes advocated by the Republicans, especially those that, they felt, gave the federal government too much power.

Fourteenth Amendment: A constitutional amendment, passed in 1868, that made it illegal for any state to deny equality before the law to any male citizen. Although it did not guarantee that blacks could vote, it gave an advantage to states that did allow black suffrage.

Freedmen's Bureau: A federal agency that existed from 1865 to 1869 that assisted the former slaves in their transition to freedom. The program helped African Americans by distributing clothing, food, and fuel; handling legal cases; dispensing medical care; and setting up black schools.

Race riots: Outbreaks of violence that highlighted racial tensions in both the North and South. Major riots occurred in New York, Memphis, and New Orleans.

Racism: The belief that there are characteristics or qualities specific to each race, which often results in discrimination (treating people differently based on race).

Radical Republicans: A group of senators and representatives with a history of ac-

The enemies Douglass referred to were all around them, in the form of white Southerners embittered by defeat and unwilling to accept the realities of their postwar lives, especially their changed relationship with the black people who had been their unpaid laborers and servants. During the period known as the Reconstruction era, which lasted from the end of the Civil War in April 1865 to the inauguration of

tivism in the abolitionist movement who turned their energies, during the Reconstruction era, toward trying to create a truly democratic society in the South.

Ratification: The process of both houses of the U.S. Congress or a state legislature approving and signing a bill.

Reconstruction Acts of 1867: The legislation devised by the Radical Republicans in Congress as a plan for remaking Southern society. The first act divided the ten Southern states—Tennessee had already been readmitted to the Union—into five military districts ruled by military commanders until the new state governments wrote and approved constitutions. The states had to ratify the Fourteenth Amendment as well as guarantee suffrage for all male citizens. Three subsequent Reconstruction Acts refined some of the issues brought up by the first.

Reconstruction era: The period stretching roughly from the end of the Civil War in April 1865 to the inauguration of President Rutherford B. Hayes in 1877. During Reconstruction, representatives of the U.S. government—including the president and Congress—and the military would join with both white and black Southerners to try to reorganize the political and social structure of the devastated, defeated South.

Republican Party: The political party that dominated both the U.S. Congress and the new Southern governments during the Reconstruction era. Before the war, most Republicans had tended to live in the North and had favored protections for business interests, public support for internal improvements (like roads and services), and social reforms. As the Reconstruction era progressed, the Republican Party grew more conservative, and its influence in the South decreased as that of the white Southern Democrats increased.

Veto: Refuse to approve.

Women's suffrage: A movement to win for women the right to vote.

President Rutherford B. Hayes (1822–1893; served 1877–81) in 1877, African Americans and whites from both North and South attempted to form a new society in the states of the former Confederacy. Their efforts were hampered not only by racial hostility and the conflicting interests of the various groups but by the economic devastation that had followed in the wake of the war. Reconstruction brought both achievements and disappointments, and it set in motion consequences that continue to be felt in the twenty-first century.

Johnson's bold Reconstruction stance

After the assassination of President Abraham Lincoln (1809– 1865; served 1861–65) in April 1865, Vice President Andrew Johnson (1808–1875), a former U.S. senator from Tennessee, was thrust unexpectedly into the highest office in the nation. Instead of waiting for Congress to convene—an event scheduled for December 1865—Johnson abruptly put into effect his own plan for readmitting the Southern states into the Union and reorganizing their state governments.

Expected to deal harshly with those who had rebelled against the Union, Johnson surprised everyone by treating them leniently. Owing to Johnson's liberal signing of presidential pardons, many Confederate military and civil leaders were able to regain power in the South. The governments they formed then went about trying to recreate the conditions of slavery, using laws called Black Codes to limit the economic options and civil rights of the former slaves.

Formerly a champion of ordinary, working people, Johnson seemed to have aligned himself with the South's most powerful class, the wealthy owners of the sprawling plantations (the large estates where basic crops like cotton, tobacco, and rice were grown). In the North and in Washington, D.C., opposition to Johnson's policies was growing. People were shocked to hear about the Black Codes and about the violence that blacks were increasingly subjected to as white Southerners vented their anger and frustration and tried to keep the former slaves in their place. The popular outcry helped the cause of the Radical Republicans, a group of senators and representatives who had long been active in the abolitionist movement (the movement dedicated to ending slavery) and now hoped to remake the South as a true democracy for both whites and African Americans.

A Republican majority in Congress

When the Thirty-ninth Congress met in December 1865, the Republican Party held a strong majority in both

the Senate and the House of Representatives. Members of this political party, most of whom lived in the Northern United States, tended to favor protections for business interests, public support for internal improvements (like roads and services), and social reforms. Making up a very small minority of the Thirty-ninth Congress was the Democratic Party, which had been dominant in the South before the war. Democrats were opposed to the kinds of changes proposed by the Republicans, especially those that, they felt, took away individual freedom and local government control by making the federal government too strong.

Among the Republicans in Congress, several subgroups existed. The largest of these was made up of moderates, whose approval would have to be won for any policy or law to be passed. The small group of conservatives did not have much of a voice, but the equally small group of Radicals, most of them veterans of the tough antislavery fight, were extremely vocal. Prominent Radicals in the Senate in-

An 1865 political cartoon evaluating the efforts of President Abraham Lincoln and Vice President Andrew Johnson to repair the Union. © *Bettmann/Corbis.*

Thaddeus Stevens: The Great Leveler

Thaddeus Stevens was a champion of ordinary people, especially slaves. Outspoken and sometimes harsh, Stevens is remembered for his commitment to democratic values and his leading role in the congressional Reconstruction plan.

Stevens was born in 1792 in Danville, Vermont, the second of four sons. His mother, a nurse, ran the family farm after Stevens's father left the family. Accompanying his mother on her nursing rounds, Stevens saw how the poor suffered, and his experiences probably influenced his dislike of class divisions and inequality.

In 1807, Stevens's mother sold the farm and moved her family to nearby Peacham, so her boys could attend school. Stevens graduated from Dartmouth College in 1814, then moved to Gettysburg, Pennsylvania, where he taught school while preparing for a law career. He also became interested in politics and joined the Anti-Masons Party, which shared his distrust of secret organizations like the Masons.

Elected to Pennsylvania's state legislature, Stevens gained a reputation as a strong-minded, uncompromising, outspoken idealist. He served for six terms, during which time he began his lifelong crusade against slavery and in favor of civil and political rights for blacks. He continued to practice law, often defending runaway slaves and others who could not pay him.

Stevens won a seat in the U.S. House of Representatives in 1849. In his first speech before the House, he declared his opposition to slavery and his refusal to compromise with the powerful Southerners in Congress. As a congressman, Stevens opposed all bills that were favorable to the South, as well as the despised Fugitive Slave Law, which encouraged the capture of slaves who had escaped to the North so that they may be returned to their Southern masters. His belief in the equality of all people and his wish for a classless society gained him the nickname "the Great Leveler."

After serving two terms, Stevens left Congress and returned to his law practice and also became involved in an iron manufacturing business. As the slavery debate heated up, however, Stevens was drawn back to politics. At the age of sixty-seven, he was again elected to the House of Representatives, arriving in time to take part in the debates that led up to the Civil War. Once again he was known for his quick wit and honesty, as well as his sarcasm and occasional lack of politeness.

One of the few to realize that the Civil War would probably be longer and bloodier than expected, Stevens worked hard to raise the money the military would need to pay salaries, buy weapons, and provide pensions. By 1863, the now-powerful Stevens had turned his attention to the question of how the South would be readmitted and reconstructed once the war was over. Not surprisingly, Stevens took an extreme stance, advocating black suffrage, strict readmission requirements,

Thaddeus Stevens. *The Library of Congress.*

and harsh penalties for those who had supported the Confederacy.

Stephens considered the Reconstruction plan that President Abraham Lincoln initially proposed, known as the Ten Per Cent Plan, too lenient toward the South. Following Lincoln's assassination, Stevens was shocked when the new president, Andrew Johnson, put his own plan—even milder than Lincoln's—into motion without any input from Congress. In December 1865, Stevens took a leading role in the refusal by Congress to seat Southerners elected under Johnson's program.

Like other members of the group of Radical Republicans who now dominated national politics, Stevens believed that Reconstruction offered an ideal opportunity to create a perfect form of democracy in the South. In early 1866, intense debates about Reconstruction occurred in Congress. Believing that former slaves deserved to be compensated for their many decades of unpaid labor, that owning land would give them an economic boost, and that those who had been disloyal to the Union should be punished, Stevens recommended an extreme plan. He proposed that the federal government confiscate all the Southern plantations of more than 200 acres of land and divide them into 40-acre plots to be distributed to the freed people. Any remaining land would be sold and the proceeds used to repay wartime debts.

Most members of Congress rejected this plan. But other measures supported by Stevens, such as the Reconstruction Acts, the Civil Rights Bill, and the Fourteenth Amendment, were approved and became law. President Johnson, however, fiercely opposed this legislation and frequently clashed with Congress. In February 1868, the arguments reached a climax: Stevens formally recommended impeachment (a process that could have resulted in his removal from office) of the president.

Following hearings, Johnson was acquitted by only one vote, allowing him to remain president. The disappointed Stevens's health was failing, and he died six months later. By his special request, he was buried in a racially integrated cemetery; the inscription on his tombstone read in part: "Equality of Man before the Creator."

cluded Charles Sumner (1811–1874) and Henry Wilson (1812–1875) of Massachusetts and Benjamin Wade (1800–1878) of Ohio. Prominent Radicals in the House of Representatives included Thaddeus Stevens (1792–1868) of Pennsylvania, George W. Julian (1817–1899) of Indiana, and James M. Ashley (1824–1896) of Ohio. Most of the Radicals were from New England or the upper Midwest, areas dominated by small farms and towns and by the concepts of free labor and liberal (open-minded) social reform.

Idealistic people like Stevens and Sumner recognized this as an important moment in history, a golden opportunity to push through the kinds of changes they desired. An iron manufacturer with a blunt manner and a reputation for fighting hard for his beliefs, Stevens was a passionate advocate of equality for African Americans. Considered somewhat self-righteous but principled and responsible, Sumner too had fought long and hard, not only against slavery but in favor of women's rights and prison reform. He was much admired by both black abolitionists and ordinary African Americans as a defender of their rights. Now Stevens and Sumner would spearhead the battle to win black suffrage (the right to vote), which many considered the most essential right because it gave citizens the power to make changes in their society.

In addition to the issue of black civil and political rights, the Radical Republicans also had a vision of economic reform for the South, which they hoped to model after the North as much as possible. They looked down on the plantation system, which had created wealth and leisure for whites by exploiting the labor of enslaved blacks. As noted in *The Era of Reconstruction: 1865–1877*, in the Radical Republicans' view, "new railroads, new factories and foundries, all the busy, profitable industry of the North, were linked with the grand march of humanity toward a more productive and fuller life, while the world of the Southern plantation embodied the ways of sloth, backwardness, and darkness itself." Achieving the new Southern society they envisioned would, however, prove more difficult than they had guessed.

An intense debate begins

The moderate Republicans in Congress were not initially prepared to go as far as the Radicals in reconstructing the shattered South. Nevertheless, when the roll was called on the first day of the Thirty-ninth Congress, the Radicals were in agreement: The names of the Southern senators and representatives elected under Johnson's program were not to be recognized—they would not be permitted to take their seats. Thus Johnson was put on notice that the plan he had implemented in the nearly eight months of his presidency had not been found acceptable by the legislators chosen by U.S. citizens to represent their interests. From this point on, Johnson would face an uphill battle.

Nevertheless, the moderate Republicans still dominated Congress. These moderates included U.S. senators Lyman Trumbull (1813–1896) of Illinois, John Sherman (1823–1900) of Ohio, and William Pitt Fessenden (1806–1869) of Maine and U.S. representatives James G. Blaine (1830–1893) of Maine and John A. Bingham (1815–1900) of Ohio. Although unwilling to seat the new Southern legislators, they continued to hope for a compromise with the president. As 1866 began, an intense debate commenced as the senators and representatives discussed the role that black people would play in the life of the nation. Although the Republican majority did not yet accept black suffrage, they did support civil rights for blacks (such as the right to a trial by jury and to equal protection of the laws).

Johnson, however, allied himself with those white Southerners whose racist attitudes prevented them from seeing blacks as anything but inferior and unworthy of full U.S. citizenship. As noted in *The Era of Reconstruction: 1865–1877*, Johnson used his Annual Message to Congress to express his views on the subject, claiming that "wherever [blacks] have been left to their own devices they have shown a constant tendency to lapse into barbarism." Further, he warned of the danger of "Africanizing" the South, or creating a society in which blacks were given more consideration than whites. In refuting the idea that the U.S. government was made only for white men, Thaddeus Stevens declared that "to say so... violates the fundamental principles of our gospel of liberty. This is man's government, the government of all men alike."

Johnson's supporters in Congress—made up primarily of the Democrats, who had opposed him when they thought he agreed with the views of his predecessor, Abraham Lincoln, but began to support him when he expressed

Charles Sumner: A Fierce Fighter for Black Rights

A U.S. senator for twenty-three years, Charles Sumner began his career as a passionate abolitionist. Once African Americans gained their freedom, Sumner led the fight to expand their political and civil rights. During the Reconstruction era, he was one of the most prominent of the Radical Republicans, who created a Reconstruction program that resulted in the nation's first multiracial state governments.

Born in Boston, Massachusetts, in 1811, Sumner was the son of a prominent lawyer and politician. A shy and studious boy, he graduated from Harvard College at the age of nineteen. He went on to attend Harvard Law School and earned his degree in 1834, but he soon discovered that he did not care for practicing law. Sumner spent three years traveling through Europe, where he met some of the leading writers and political figures of the period. When he returned to Boston, he was in demand at parties and gatherings.

Nevertheless, Sumner found both his law practice and his social life unfulfilling. But a new interest in reform movements created a spark. He began to speak out for prison reform and against war, offending some listeners with his rather aggressive, self-righteous speaking style but impressing others. Sumner also became involved with the antislavery movement, and he was one of the few who spoke out against the nation's war with Mexico (1846–48).

Two years later, Sumner's involvement in a new political organization called the Free Soil Party (whose members opposed the extension of slavery into the new territories of the United States) led to his election to the U.S. Senate. There his combative speeches against slavery made him unpopular with Southerners, who considered him a radical abolitionist. Many Northerners, however, agreed with Sumner's views and appreciated his passionate efforts to end slavery. Sumner became a member of the Republican Party soon after its formation in the middle of the 1850s.

In May 1856, Sumner gave a three-hour speech against the Kansas-Nebraska Bill, which threatened to nullify (negate) the earlier Missouri Compromise by allowing the settlers in these two states to make their own decisions on whether to allow slavery. His "Crime Against Kansas" speech was full of colorful insults against various people who had publicly defended slavery. The next day, an angry congressman named Preston Brooks (1819–1857)— whose cousin had been one of those insulted by Sumner—attacked him on the Senate floor with a walking stick.

Seriously injured, Sumner spent the next three years as an invalid. Although he won reelection in 1857, he did not return to the Senate until June 1860. He marked his return with another fiery speech against slavery, which was thought to give a boost to the successful bid by Abraham Lincoln for the presidency. As the tension over the slavery issue mounted and the Southern states moved toward seces-

Charles Sumner. *The Library of Congress.*

sion, Sumner refused to go along with those who wanted to reach a compromise with the South. He called for an immediate and unqualified end to slavery.

During the Civil War, Sumner pressed Lincoln to completely abolish slavery, but Lincoln insisted—during the first years of the war, at least—that the purpose of the war was to reunite the country, not emancipate the slaves. Sumner also pushed for blacks to be allowed to enlist in the Union army and for harsh punishments for Confederates once the Union won the war. In February 1862, he charged that the Southerners had committed "state suicide" by seceding, which meant that they had given up all their rights and that the military could now confiscate all their property, including their slaves.

While Sumner's advocacy of black rights made him a hero among African Americans, his outspoken manner alienated some of his colleagues, including some who basically agreed with his views. More focused on principles than on practical matters, Sumner did not play a major role in actually implementing the important legislation of the Reconstruction era.

When tensions between President Andrew Johnson and the Radical Republicans in Congress resulted in an impeachment trial, Sumner's was one of the loudest voices calling for the president's removal from office. He was bitterly disappointed when Johnson was acquitted by one vote. After the election of President Ulysses S. Grant (1822–1885; served 1869–1877), Sumner used his longtime position as chairman of the powerful Senate Foreign Relations Committee to block bills and appointments the president favored. Sumner was eventually ousted from his committee chair position.

As the Reconstruction era drew to a close and more conservative views began to prevail, Sumner's influence diminished. In the 1872 presidential election, Sumner supported the Democratic candidate, Horace Greeley (1811–1872), but Grant was reelected. As 1874 began, Sumner faced an uphill battle for reelection and also suffered from heart disease. In March—after urging his colleagues, from his sickbed, to support a new Civil Rights Act to protect black rights—Sumner died.

ideas similar to their own—accused the Radicals of hypocrisy. They charged that these upper-class Northerners were using the equality issue to mask their true aims, which were to punish white Southerners and to promote Northern business interests. In addition, the Democrats claimed, they only wanted blacks to vote in order to keep their own party in power.

There may have been some truth in some of these charges (the Radicals did hope, for example, that when blacks were able to vote they would use their ballots to keep Republicans in office), but the idealism of men like Stevens and Sumner had certainly been proved by their long years of activism. Indeed, the deep hatred of these and other leaders for slavery had eventually helped to shift the focus on the Civil War from state's rights and keeping the Union intact to winning freedom for blacks. Most historians now agree that their interest in gaining equality for African Americans was sincere.

The Freedmen's Bureau bill

One of the first actions Congress had taken after refusing to recognize the Southern legislators was to create a Joint Committee on Reconstruction to investigate and report on conditions in the South. Already reports were arriving that documented the mistreatment of blacks in the South. Perhaps the most revealing report was compiled by ex-Union general Carl Schurz ([1829–1906]; see Chapter 4 for more details). As the new year began, it was clear that the agents of the Freedmen's Bureau, the federal agency established in March 1865 to assist the former slaves in their transition to freedom, needed more power to punish those who denied blacks their rights or physically assaulted them. To that end, Senator Trumbull introduced a bill to extend the life of the Freedmen's Bureau (which had been authorized to operate for only one year) and broaden the power of its agents to protect blacks.

Much hated by white Southerners because of its advocacy of black rights, the Freedmen's Bureau had been criticized even by some Northern leaders. Some of the agents, it was charged, had misled African Americans into thinking they would receive free land; others had been incompetent and corrupt, and some had even collaborated with plantation owners by pressuring blacks to sign unfair labor contracts. Generally, though, it was agreed—especially among black people themselves—that the Freedmen's Bureau had done a great deal of good. By 1869, when it finally did close, the Bureau's agents had distributed $15 million worth of food rations to destitute Southerners, both black and white; dispensed medical care to a million people; and spent $5 million on setting up black schools.

It came as a surprise to almost everyone when President Johnson vetoed (refused to approve) the Freedmen's Bureau bill. He claimed that it was not necessary and too expensive to extend the Bureau's life and even asserted, as noted in *A Short History of Reconstruction,* that giving blacks assistance was unfair to "our own people" (meaning whites). Even Johnson's supporters had urged him to sign the bill, as it would help to keep the moderate Republicans on his side. Congress immediately overrode the bill, and it became law.

Johnson's lack of sympathy for the challenges faced by African Americans was evident. He gave further evidence of insensitivity—as well as arrogance and tactlessness—when, during an unplanned speech at the White House, he referred to his congressional opponents as traitors, claiming they were as bad as those who had rebelled against the Union during the Civil War.

The Civil Rights Bill

The next important piece of legislation introduced during this period was the Civil Rights Bill, which guaranteed that all persons born in the United States (except for Native Americans) were to be considered U.S. citizens with the right to make contracts, bring lawsuits in court, and receive full protection of "person and property" under the law. This bill was intended to give fuller meaning to the Thirteenth Amendment which, when added to the Constitution the previous year, had officially outlawed slavery but had not specified exactly what black people's new freedom entailed.

The Civil Rights Bill was in direct opposition to the Black Codes, which had made a legal distinction between the rights that blacks and whites enjoyed. It was truly a revolutionary document, in that it overturned not only the Black

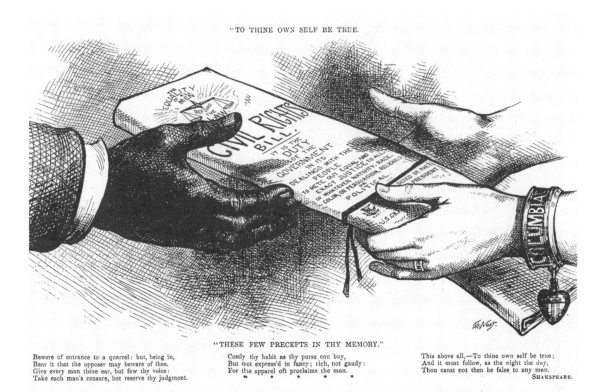

"THESE FEW PRECEPTS IN THY MEMORY."

Beware of entrance to a quarrel: but, being in,
Bear it that the opposer may beware of thee.
Give every man thine ear, but few thy voice:
Take each man's censure, but reserve thy judgment.

Costly thy habit as thy purse can buy,
But not express'd in fancy; rich, not gaudy:
For the apparel oft proclaims the man.
* * * * *

This above all,—To thine own self be true;
And it must follow, as the night the day,
Thou canst not then be false to any man.

SHAKSPEARE.

"To Thine Own Self Be True," the title of a political cartoon showing a black hand receiving the Civil Rights Bill enacted on April 9, 1866, from white hands. Harper's Weekly.

Codes of the South but many discriminatory laws that existed in the Northern states. It also proved that the Republicans in Congress were united in their belief that civil rights for the former slaves must be part of any Reconstruction program.

Again, Johnson caused ripples of surprise and outrage when he vetoed the bill, on the grounds that it gave too much power to the federal government and also discriminated against white people. Once more, Congress overrode Johnson's veto and enacted the Civil Rights Bill on April 9, 1866, the first time in U.S. history that this override had happened with such a major piece of legislation.

Republicans prepare to shape Reconstruction

Near the end of April, the Joint Committee on Reconstruction submitted its report on conditions in the South. The testimony that witnesses provided caused alarm and shock. Many instances of violence and injustice against blacks were reported by military officers, Freedmen's Bureau agents, former slaves, and others, as was the continuing, bitter resentment that white Southerners held toward the U.S. government. The committee concluded that until the Southern states could guarantee civil rights for all citizens, and until the former leaders of the Confederacy had been excluded from holding public office, their legislators must not be allowed to participate in the federal government.

Johnson's refusal to support the legislation that had united the Republican majority in Congress proved fatal to his program, for it had driven the moderates into the Radical camp. Johnson now lacked the support he needed to get his own policies approved and enacted. The Republicans, meanwhile, would now be able to create the kind of Reconstruction plan they had long and idealistically envisioned.

By passing the Civil Rights Bill, the Republicans had shown their commitment to civil rights for blacks. Yet there were fears that the bill might someday be found unconstitutional (not in keeping with the ideas outlined in the Constitution, the central document of the U.S. government, and therefore not valid). Therefore, to safeguard the rights described in the Civil Rights Bill, the Republicans wanted to put a guarantee of those rights directly into the Constitution through an amendment. Thus they created the Fourteenth Amendment, which was approved by Congress in June 1866.

Elizabeth Cady Stanton (left) and Susan B. Anthony (right), founders of the National Woman Suffrage Association.
© Bettmann/Corbis.

The Fourteenth Amendment

The Fourteenth Amendment made it illegal for any state to deny equality before the law to any male citizen. Al-

The Fight for Women's Rights

Once slavery was abolished, many longtime antislavery crusaders turned their energies to the struggle for black suffrage. At the same time, the leaders of the fledgling women's movement were just as passionate about gaining the same right for women.

During the course of the nineteenth century, reform movements of various kinds gained momentum as public awareness of social problems increased. Across the nation—especially in the northeastern region—activists called not only for an end to slavery but for an improvement in conditions in prisons and mental institutions and for equality between men and women. At this time, women not only could not vote but were not allowed to own property, and they did not have equal access to education and employment. Many schools and universities were closed to female students, and very few career choices were available to them. Single women could work in factories, but they earned only half of what men did for the same job.

Around the middle of the century, Elizabeth Cady Stanton emerged as a leader of the struggle for women's rights. She was inspired to begin her fight after attending the World Antislavery Conference in London with her husband; Stanton and other women were not allowed to participate. She and fellow reformer Lucretia Mott (1793–1880) soon organized a political meeting in Seneca Falls, New York. Held in July 1848 and attended by 240 people (40 of whom were men), it was the first such gathering to focus on women's rights. Attendees produced a "Declaration of Sentiments" that detailed the injustices against women, especially the denial of the right to vote and own property and the lack of equal opportunity in education and employment.

In 1865, the document that would eventually become the Fourteenth Amendment to the U.S. Constitution was introduced to Congress. The amendment would give all male citizens voting rights, but women would be excluded. Most alarming to the feminist leaders was that for the first time, the words "male citizen" would be written into the Constitution. Even though they sympathized with the

though it did not guarantee that blacks could vote, it gave an advantage to states that did allow black suffrage, by reducing the number of a state's congressional representatives—which is determined by population—in proportion to the number of male citizens denied the right to vote. Before the war, three-quarters of the slaves had been included in population counts, but now they would all be counted. To avoid giving

Early women's rights leader Elizabeth Cady Stanton. © *Bettmann/Corbis.*

pertaining to owning property and entering careers), but it was not until the passage of the Nineteenth Amendment in 1920 that women received the right to vote. During the social unrest of the 1960s, the women's movement gained momentum as more and more women, as well as sympathetic men, demanded an end to discrimination in education, employment, law, and other areas. The Equal Pay Act, passed in 1963, required employers to pay the same wages for the same work. The Civil Rights Act (1964) also provided protection against job discrimination on the basis of both race and sex.

As the twentieth century drew to a close, feminist groups like the National Organization for Women (NOW) and the National Women's Political Caucus continued to apply pressure for societal and political change. By the beginning of the twenty-first century, women had made many advances, but some forms of discrimination continued (for example, some women were still paid less for the same work).

plight of blacks and their desire for suffrage, Stanton and other prominent women objected to the Fourteenth Amendment. Nevertheless, it was passed in July 1868. From this point on, the women's movement would separate itself from the abolitionists who had previously been its allies.

Over the next fifty years, women gradually gained more rights (especially

the Southern states an unfair advantage, though, they would lose representatives if they did not allow blacks to vote.

In addition, the Fourteenth Amendment decreed that anyone who had once sworn allegiance to the U.S. Constitution but later given aid to the Confederacy could not hold national or state office. This meant that the South's prewar leaders—many of whom had served as Confederate military

Social activist Victoria Woodhull reads her argument in favor of a woman's right to vote before a committee of the U.S. House of Representatives. *The Library of Congress.*

or civil officers—would not be allowed to govern the new Southern states, and the true Unionists (who had remained loyal to the federal government throughout the Civil War) would be in charge.

Among those who believed that the Fourteenth Amendment did not go far enough were women like Elizabeth Cady Stanton (1815–1902) and Susan B. Anthony (1820–1906), feminist leaders (those who support expanded rights for women) who thought women should also have the right to vote. They felt betrayed because, for the first time, the word "male" had been introduced into the Constitution in regard to suffrage, thus making their goal even harder to attain. The women's suffrage movement had previously been closely linked to abolitionism, but now the feminists severed that tie and took up their struggle alone.

Still, the Fourteenth Amendment was a document of major significance because it guaranteed that equality before the law would be protected by the federal government. The individual states were now required to uphold for all citizens those fundamental rights guaranteed by the Constitution's first eight amendments, including the rights to engage in free speech, to bear arms, and to be tried by an impartial jury.

President Johnson immediately denounced the amendment and advised the Southern states not to ratify it. (Ratification is the process of approval through which an amendment must pass to become part of the U.S. Constitution.) Ten of the eleven states of the former Confederacy took Johnson's advice; only Tennessee ratified the Fourteenth Amendment and thus was readmitted to the Union. At this point, Congress had not yet answered the question of how the remaining states could be readmitted.

Race riots in Memphis and New Orleans

Meanwhile, events occurring in two major cities of the South in the spring and summer of 1866 were causing great concern and horror in the North. The first occurred in May, when Memphis, Tennessee, became the scene of a bloody race riot. Following a collision of two taxis, one driven by a white and one by a black, police arrested the black driver. A group of black Civil War veterans came to the driver's aid, and a fight broke out between them, the police, and a white crowd. The violence lasted for three days, during which time the Memphis police and other whites attacked blacks and invaded black neighborhoods, burning hundreds of homes, schools, and churches and raping several black women. In all, forty-six blacks and two whites were killed.

Less than two months later, bloody clashes broke out in New Orleans, Louisiana, at a gathering of several hundred supporters of black suffrage. Union general Philip Sheridan (1831–1888), who would later serve as military governor of Louisiana, reported an "absolute massacre," with thirty-four blacks and three white radicals killed and more than a hundred people injured. Both of these violent outbreaks helped to further discredit the president's Reconstruction plan, as they seemed to many to prove what happened when former Confederates were treated too leniently.

The riot in New Orleans; white men murdering fleeing black men behind the Mechanic's Institute, where black and white legislators had gathered to discuss a new state constitution. © Corbis.

A disastrous speaking tour

As the summer progressed, Johnson and his supporters began to worry about the congressional elections that were coming up in the fall. Realizing that he needed to somehow turn the tide of opposition that seemed to be rolling over him, and believing that the common folk of the nation would rally behind him if they heard his message directly, Johnson embarked on a speaking tour. Referred to as a "swing around the circle," the tour took Johnson north through New York and then west to Ohio and Missouri before returning to the East Coast. Despite his intentions, Johnson's personal weaknesses made the tour a disaster.

Instead of dazzling crowds with his inspiring message, Johnson sparred with hecklers (people in a crowd who annoy and taunt a speaker) and indulged in long, rambling speeches full of self-pity and vindictiveness (feelings of revenge) toward those he regarded as his enemies. In Cleveland, Ohio, someone in the crowd yelled, "Hang Jeff Davis!"

Johnson yelled back, "Why not hang Thad Stevens and Wendell Phillips?" (Phillips [1811–1884], an abolitionist, was another Radical Republican.) In St. Louis, Missouri, Johnson claimed that he had been "slandered" (made the subject of lies) and "maligned" (spoken evil of) by his opponents.

Having previously misjudged the attitudes of ordinary Southerners toward their old leaders, Johnson had now misjudged those of ordinary Northerners. It seemed that they wanted those who had rebelled against the Union to be treated more harshly, and were even worried that Johnson's stance might disrupt the peace that been won at such a high cost. Even Johnson's supporters admitted that the tour had been a mistake, and he was roundly criticized for lowering himself to take part in exchanges with hecklers.

Republicans sweep the 1866 elections

During the campaign of 1866, most support for Johnson came from the Democratic Party, whose members tried to play on white fears about expanding rights for blacks. They claimed, for example, that the Republicans wanted to give black workers an advantage over white workers. Meanwhile, the Republicans also campaigned hard and used dramatic language and images to discredit Johnson. As recounted in *The Era of Reconstruction: 1865–1877,* Indiana governor Oliver P. Morton (1823–1877) called the Democratic Party a "common sewer and loathsome receptacle, into which is emptied every element of treason North and South, every element of inhumanity and barbarism which has dishonored the age."

When the election results came in, the widespread lack of support for Johnson was evident. The Republicans had won by a huge margin. They were now solidly in control of every Northern state legislature and government; in addition, they had more than the two-thirds majority needed to pass bills in both houses of the U.S. Congress. As the second session of the Thirty-ninth Congress met in December 1866, the Radicals were at their most powerful.

As the new year began, black suffrage seemed close to becoming a reality. In January, Congress approved a bill giving blacks in the District of Columbia the right to vote. Soon black suffrage was also expanded to the western territories (recently settled areas that were on their way to becoming states). Congress was still struggling, however, with a plan for the Reconstruction of the South. Some felt that this hesitancy was not such a bad thing, though, as a careful approach seemed preferable to Johnson's hastily implemented program.

Giving blacks the vote

In any case, the main issue that was holding up the process was black suffrage. Most believed that whatever Reconstruction act Congress passed must require the states to guarantee black voting rights, not only because it was the right thing to do but because the Republicans would need the political force of those black votes to move their programs forward. The act would probably require a limited period of military rule, and it would also need to prevent former Confederates from participating in government, at least temporarily. At the same time, blacks were going to need not only access to economic opportunity but training in how to manage their own affairs and how to be good citizens.

As noted in *The Era of Reconstruction: 1865–1877,* slavery had been "a poor training school for the responsibilities of citizenship." The very survival of black people under slavery had required them to be docile and obedient. Freedom, however, would require them to be independent and self-reliant and to overcome the sense of inferiority and, in some cases, fear of white people that they had absorbed over the years.

Some suggested that blacks were not ready for the responsibilities of citizenship, especially voting. Others, though, claimed that blacks could only learn about freedom by living it. As noted in *Been in the Storm So Long: The Aftermath of Slavery,* at a black political convention held in North Carolina soon after the end of the war, an African American leader named James Hood said, "The best way is to give the colored man rights at once, and then they will practice them and the sooner know how to use them."

The Republican plan for Reconstruction

Debate and discussion about the shape that Reconstruction should take finally resulted in the Reconstruction

Act of 1867, which was passed over Johnson's veto in March. The act divided the ten Southern states (Tennessee had already been readmitted to the Union) into five military districts ruled by military commanders, who were authorized to use the Army to protect lives and property. To be readmitted to the Union, the new state governments would have to write constitutions that guaranteed suffrage for all male citizens, and the constitutions would have to be approved by a majority of registered voters. In addition, each state must ratify the Fourteenth Amendment.

Three subsequent Reconstruction acts refined some of the issues brought up by the first. The second act empowered the military commanders to register voters, set up elections, and adopt state constitutions even if Southerners did nothing. The third act declared that the temporary military governments took precedence over the civil governments elected under Johnson's program. The fourth act made it harder for citizens to prevent the ratification of state constitutions.

The dream of black landownership

Although the Republican plan promised a more just society for all citizens than the one the president had created, African Americans were disappointed by its lack of any provision for the redistribution of land. Blacks associated the ownership of land with freedom itself and, like most Americans, they yearned for the economic independence it could afford. When slavery ended, they hoped that the government would compensate them for their long years of unpaid labor with free land.

Indeed, many Republicans agreed that the Southern plantation system should be broken up and the big estates divided into small farms. In an 1864 report on conditions in the South, Secretary of War Edwin Stanton (1814–1869) had predicted—as quoted in *The Era of Reconstruction: 1865–1877*—that "no such thing as a free, democratic society can exist in any country where all lands are owned by one class of men and cultivated by another."

Even before the end of the Civil War, a glimmer of hope that black dreams of landownership would come true had been provided by Union general William T. Sherman (1820–1891). Reaching Savannah, Georgia, after his victorious, destructive march across the South, Sherman had issued Special Field Order #15. This document allowed blacks to settle on 40-acre plots of land along the South Carolina and Georgia coasts; soon after the war, however, the land was returned to its Confederate owners (see Chapter 4 for more details). In addition, the original plan for the Freedmen's Bureau had authorized the agency to distribute land to the freed people.

During the discussions that had taken place before the passage of the Reconstruction Act, Senator Stevens had recommended that forty-four million acres of Southern land—which represented land owned by less than 5 percent of white Southern families—should be confiscated and redistributed to former slaves. In the end, though, there was too little public support for such a measure.

Despite its limitations, the Reconstruction Act of 1867 ushered in an exciting period in U.S. history. By giving African Americans the right to vote, it held out the promise that they would become equal participants in the life of the nation and that racist attitudes would be overcome. In *A Short History of Reconstruction,* this was "a radical departure, a stunning and unprecedented experiment in interracial democracy." The experiment would prove tragically short lived. For now, however, a brief period of hope and of genuine accomplishments had begun.

For More Information

Books

Ayers, Edward L. *The Promise of the New South: Life After Reconstruction.* New York: Oxford University Press, 1992.

Benedict, Michael Les. *A Compromise of Principle: Congressional Republicans and Reconstruction, 1863–1869.* New York: Norton, 1974.

Foner, Eric. *A Short History of Reconstruction.* New York: Harper & Row, 1990.

Franklin, John Hope. *Reconstruction After the Civil War.* Chicago: University of Chicago Press, 1961.

Golay, Michael. *Reconstruction and Reaction: The Emancipation of Slaves, 1861–1913.* New York: Facts on File, 1996.

Jenkins, Wilbert L. *Climbing Up to Glory: A Short History of African Americans During the Civil War and Reconstruction.* Wilmington, DE: Scholarly Resources, 2002.

Litwack, Leon F. *Been in the Storm So Long: The Aftermath of Slavery.* New York: Vintage Books, 1979.

McPherson, James M. *The Struggle for Equality: Abolitionists and the Negro in the Civil War and Reconstruction.* Princeton, NJ: Princeton University Press, 1965.

Murphy, Richard W. *The Nation Reunited: War's Aftermath.* Alexandria, VA: Time-Life Books, 1987.

Smith, John David. *Black Voices from Reconstruction, 1865–1877.* Gainesville: University of Florida Press, 1997.

Stampp, Kenneth M. *The Era of Reconstruction: 1865–1877.* New York: Vintage Books, 1965.

Wagner, Margaret E., Gary W. Gallagher, and Paul Finkelman, eds. *Civil War Desk Reference.* New York: Simon & Schuster, 2002.

Web Sites

Louisiana State University. *The United States Civil War Center.* http://www.cwc.lsu.edu/ (accessed on August 31, 2004).

"Reconstruction." *African American History.* http://afroamhistory.about.com/od/reconstruction/ (accessed on August 31, 2004).

"Reference Resources: Civil War." *Kidinfo.* http://www.kidinfo.com/American_History/Civil_War.html (accessed on August 31, 2004).

"US Civil War." *Internet Modern History Sourcebook.* http://www.fordham.edu/halsall/mod/modsbook27.html (accessed on August 31, 2004).

The Radical Republicans Move Forward with Reconstruction

6

At a Freedmen's Convention (a large political meeting made up largely of former slaves) held in Arkansas soon after the end of the Civil War (1861–65), an African American leader named William H. Grey (1829–1888) spoke about his people's newfound independence. As quoted in *Been in the Storm So Long: The Aftermath of Slavery,* Grey declared, "We have thrown off the mask, hereafter to do our own talking, and to use all legitimate means to get and to enjoy our political privileges. We don't want anybody to swear for us or to vote for us; we want to exercise these privileges for ourselves."

The spirit present in Grey's words coexisted with both the jubilation that African Americans of this period felt and their worries about the challenges that they faced. This mix of forces had been unleashed by the war's outcome: a victory for the Union (the federal government) over the Confederacy, the eleven Southern states that had seceded or separated themselves from the United States in order to protect the traditions of the South. These traditions centered around the enslavement of four million black people, who had been brought since the seventeenth century from Africa and

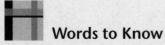

Words to Know

Carpetbaggers: The intentionally offensive nickname for Northerners who went to the South after the Civil War to participate in Reconstruction. Although many white Southerners felt they had come to take advantage of the devastated, demoralized South (and later, racist accounts of Reconstruction reinforced this view), most were actually educated, middle-class men with good intentions. Among their number were Union army veterans, teachers, and investors.

Civil Rights Act of 1867: Legislation guaranteeing that all persons born in the United States (except for Native Americans) were to be considered U.S. citizens with full protection of "person and property" under the law.

Democratic Party: The political party that had been dominant in the South before the Civil War and which regained control at the end of Reconstruction. Generally, Democrats were conservatives who opposed the kinds of changes advocated by the Republicans, especially those that, they felt, gave the federal government too much power.

Fourteenth Amendment: A constitutional amendment, passed in 1867, that made it illegal for any state to deny equality before the law to any male citizen. Although it did not guarantee that blacks could vote, it gave an advantage to states that did allow black suffrage.

Free blacks: African Americans who had never been slaves, or who had escaped from slavery into the North.

Freedmen's Conventions: Meetings held by African Americans following the end of the Civil War, at which they discussed the issues facing them and drew up statements to present to white leaders.

Impeachment: The process of charging an elected official with misconduct. On February 24, 1868, the House of Representatives passed a resolution to impeach President Andrew Johnson; he was specifically charged with violating the Tenure of Office Act and with bringing the office of the president into "contempt, ridicule, and disgrace." The trial results were one vote short of the two-thirds majority required to remove the president from office.

Integration: The intermixing of people or groups previously segregated (separated).

Mulattoes: People of biracial, or mixed black and white, heritage.

Radical Republicans: A group of senators and representatives with a history of activism in the abolitionist movement who turned their energies, during the Reconstruction era, toward trying to create a truly democratic society in the South.

Ratification: The process of both houses of the U.S. Congress or a state legislature approving and signing a bill.

Reconstruction Acts of 1867: The legislation devised by the Radical Republicans in Congress as a plan for remaking Southern society. The first act divided the ten Southern states—Tennessee had already been readmitted to the Union—into five military districts ruled by military commanders until the new state governments wrote and approved constitutions. The states had to ratify the Fourteenth Amendment as well as guarantee suffrage for all male citizens. Three subsequent Reconstruction Acts refined some of the issues brought up by the first.

Reconstruction era: The period stretching roughly from the end of the Civil War in April 1865 to the inauguration of President Rutherford B. Hayes in 1877. During Reconstruction, representatives of the U.S. government—including the president and Congress—and the military would join with both white and black Southerners to try to reorganize the political and social structure of the devastated, defeated South.

Republican Party: The political party that dominated both the U.S. Congress and the new Southern governments during the Reconstruction era. Before the war, most Republicans had tended to live in the North and had favored protections for business interests, public support for internal improvements (like roads and services), and social reforms. As the Reconstruction era progressed, the Republican Party grew more conservative, and its influence in the South decreased as that of the white Southern Democrats increased.

Scalawags: The intentionally offensive nickname for the white Southerners who joined the Republican Party and took part in the Reconstruction governments. Some scalawags saw this submission as the best route to gaining white control of the South again, whereas others were sincerely interested in creating a new, more just society.

Segregation: The separation of people or groups which, in the Southern United States, was based on race.

Union League: An organization, closely allied with the Republican Party, that African Americans across the South joined soon after the end of the Civil War. The group helped build schools and churches, care for the sick, assist workers in demanding fair wages and better working conditions, register black voters.

Veto: Refuse to approve.

forced to work in the fields and homes of white Southerners. During the Reconstruction era (which lasted roughly from the Civil War in April 1865 to the inauguration of President Rutherford B. Hayes [1822–1893; served 1877–1881] in 1877), both blacks and whites attempted to forge a new Southern society in which slavery no longer existed. However, anger, fear, and confusion about the future remained.

Two different plans for Reconstruction

During the months following the April 1865 conclusion of the Civil War, the U.S. Congress was the stage for another kind of battle. A group of senators and representatives known as the Radical Republicans opposed the Reconstruction program put forth by President Andrew Johnson (1808–1875; served 1865–69). Having gained that office unexpectedly when Abraham Lincoln (1809–1865; served 1861–65) was assassinated—only days after the war's end—by an enraged Southerner, Johnson had surprised everyone with a plan that allowed white Southerners to virtually recreate the days of slavery. The Republicans had managed to win public support for their own vision of a reconstructed South, which they saw as a place where free labor and industry would thrive and where, most importantly, access to equal civil and political rights would allow African Americans to become full, responsible U.S. citizens.

In March 1867, Congress passed the Reconstruction Acts over the president's veto (refusal to approve). This legislation divided the South into five districts, each of which would be under the control of a military commander until its citizens—including blacks but excluding those who had helped the Confederacy—organized a new government. The first step was to elect delegates to conventions at which the states' constitutions would be written. These constitutions were required to include suffrage (the right to vote) for all male citizens. In addition, each state had to ratify the Fourteenth Amendment, which said that the civil rights guaranteed to whites by the U.S. Constitution (such as the rights to free speech, to bear arms, and to practice one's own religion) could not be denied on the basis of race. Once a state's constitution had been approved by a majority of eligible voters, elections for local, state, and federal offices could be held.

The joy that blacks had felt with the dawn of freedom had diminished somewhat in the months following the war's end, for it seemed that their lives had actually changed very little. Although they were no longer slaves, their opportunities for advancement were still extremely limited. They continued to face many obstacles in their struggle to find work, to achieve the education they knew was essential to success, to attain the civil rights promised to other U.S. citizens, and even to keep their families safe from violence. The most troubling obstacle was the resentment and hatred of many white Southerners. They resisted the changes in their society through both brutal physical attacks on blacks and laws called the Black Codes, which attempted to keep African Americans under the economic and social control of whites (see Chapter 4).

The Freedmen's Conventions

The passage of the Reconstruction Acts gave African Americans new hope that equality might be within their reach. Even before this event, however, blacks had already launched what would become a period of intense political activity. During the year that followed the war's end, this took the form of electing delegates to the Freedmen's Conventions. President Johnson's Reconstruction plan, announced during the summer of 1865, called for the states to hold conventions at which delegates would organize new governments. But neither the president nor those who stepped up as leaders of the Southern states intended to include black people in these new governments. Thus African Americans held their own meetings, with the goal of discussing the issues facing them and eventually submitting statements on their views to the white leaders.

The Freedmen's Conventions took place in large cities, small towns, and tiny rural communities all over the South. Delegates often took great risks to participate, for those whites who believed blacks should have no say in Reconstruction (and some who feared the former slaves would organize a violent rebellion) did everything they could to prevent them from reaching the meetings. Many were threatened with violence or with the loss of jobs or credit in stores if they attended.

A cross section of black people

Nevertheless, a broad cross section of blacks made it to the Freedmen's Conventions. There were many uniformed veterans of the Union army, who had fought against the Confederacy to win their people's freedom. There were ministers, teachers, and tradesmen (such as carpenters and blacksmiths) as well as plantation workers. The earliest conventions were dominated by free blacks (those who had never been slaves or had escaped to the North and then returned after the war), but as time went on an increasing number of former slaves took part. African Americans took considerable pride in the sight of black people meeting in such numbers, for such a serious purpose. Commenting on a convention held in New Orleans, Louisiana, in early 1865, a black newspaper editor, as quoted in *Been in the Storm So Long: The Aftermath of Slavery,* called it "a great spectacle, and one which will be remembered for generations to come."

Among the most prominent black leaders at the conventions, some were Northern blacks who had come South to work as agents of the Freedmen's Bureau (the government agency established in March 1865 to help the former slaves make their transition to freedom), including Tunis G. Campbell (1812–1891) and Martin R. Delany (1812–1885). South Carolina native Francis L. Cardozo (1837–1903) had escaped slavery to become a minister in Connecticut. Leaders from among the ranks of the former slaves include such notable figures as Robert Smalls (1839–1915), whose bravery during the Civil War had made him famous, and Prince Rivers (c. 1824–?), a former coachman who had served as a sergeant in the Union army.

Some of the delegates were equipped with education and superior speaking skills. Others were poorly dressed and unable to read or write. A considerable number bore the visible scars of punishment they had received when they were slaves. Their differences were many, and included not only those of appearance (especially darker or lighter skin color) but of class, education, income, and occupation. The free black segment tended to be dominated by biracial people known then as mulattoes (people of mixed black and white heritage)—especially from the thriving community in New Orleans—many of whom did hold themselves above the former slaves. Generally, though, the convention attendees were united by the knowledge that they faced a common foe, an enemy who made no distinction between the different types of black people and treated them all just as poorly. They knew that they must come together to overcome the obstacles against them, and they meant to do without the help of whites—however well intentioned—as much as possible.

A reassuring tone

A writer in the black newspaper the *New Orleans Tribune* asked, "Who can better know our interest than we do? Who is better competent to discern what is good for us than we are?" Indeed, the conventions featured intense discussion and debate about the issues of most importance to African Americans. Many individuals offered testimony on conditions across the South, providing accounts and evidence of beatings, arson attacks, being cheated of wages, and other forms of mistreatment from white Southerners.

Despite the hatred for black people and their newfound freedom that whites had so openly expressed, the delegates of the Freedmen's Conventions thought it best to adopt a mild, friendly tone in the addresses and documents they would present to the wider state conventions. They did not want to scare whites, and hoped to win their trust by reassuring them that the former slaves intended to keep the peace and harbored no ill feelings toward those who had once enslaved them. They tried to point out that the past, present, and future lives of white and black Southerners were closely intertwined. They also stressed the idea that blacks felt just as loyal to the country of their birth as white Americans. "This is your country, but it is ours too;" declared the Freedmen's Convention of Georgia in 1866, as noted in *Been in the Storm So Long: The Aftermath of Slavery,* "you were born here, so were we; your fathers fought for it, but our fathers fed them."

By stressing the similarities between blacks and whites and appealing to a sense of common humanity, the delegates hoped to stem the tide of violence and mistreatment that had been steadily growing since the end of the war. Although they pointed out that almost all of them had remained peaceful and loyal to their former owners even during the war, when they might have been expected to rise up against them, they did not look back upon slavery with any fondness. It had been an experience marked by brutality and cruelty, and they had no wish to return to it.

Making black demands known

For now, the only leverage blacks could apply in making their demands was the threat of the continued presence of federal troops and agents—especially of the Freedmen's Bureau, which whites particularly hated—in the South. (Later, of course, after they were given the right to vote, they would be able to use their sheer numbers as leverage.) These demands included, first and foremost, the right to vote, to serve on juries, and to obtain education. Although economic issues—particularly that of landownership, and whether the federal government would compensate (repay) the former slaves with free land—were of great concern to blacks, they generally avoided making demands in this area because they did not want to alarm whites. Their statements were sprinkled with the references to such popular nineteenth-century values as hard work, honesty, thrift, neatness, morality, and Christianity. They asked for civil and political rights but not for "social" equality with whites, emphasizing that they did not wish to socialize with whites if whites did not desire such contact.

Not surprisingly, the Freedmen's Conventions came out in support of the important legislation passed by Congress in early 1866, including a bill to extend the life of the Freedmen's Bureau, the Civil Rights Bill, and the Fourteenth Amendment (see Chapter 5 for more details). They fully supported the decision of Congress not to recognize the representatives and senators elected under President Johnson's Reconstruction plan, which had favored the former supporters of the Confederacy and thus upheld the values of white supremacy. Historians now agree that it was the refusal of Johnson and of white Southerners to envision a society in which blacks were treated fairly that, in the end, itself brought about black suffrage.

The Reconstruction Acts spur political activity

Although not yet a part of the Constitution (as it would be with the passage of the Fifteenth Amendment in

1870), African Americans' right to vote was guaranteed by the Reconstruction Acts of 1867, which required the Southern states to approve the Fourteenth Amendment. Under the amendment, the number of congressional representatives of any state that prevented any of its male citizens from voting would be reduced. Suffrage meant more to blacks than any other right, for it gave them the power to take a prominent role in remaking their society. African Americans were now grappling with the complex questions of identity left in slavery's wake: Should they leave behind or celebrate their African heritage? Were they really inferior, as whites had always told them? Did they see beauty in themselves? Being allowed to vote could only have a positive effect on African Americans' self-image, and in the opportunities that would be available to them.

The passage of the Reconstruction Acts spurred a big increase in membership in political organizations that worked to promote black causes. Most prominent of these was the Union League, an organization closely allied with the Republican Party that soon had chapters—both segregated and interracial—throughout the South. The Union League and other groups were already involved in such efforts as building schools and churches, caring for the sick, and helping workers achieve fair wages and better working conditions. Now the focus turned to registering voters for the first elections, which would choose delegates for the states' constitutional conventions.

A major push began to educate black people about the issues facing them and convince them that they could affect change through responsible choices on election day, as well as practical matters like voting procedures. Schools and churches became centers for speeches and discussions as black leaders traveled through the South, urging people who had previously had no voice at all in public life to exercise their new rights. These efforts were remarkably successful, for by fall nearly 1.5 million voters had been registered; more than 700,000 of them African Americans. In Alabama, Florida, Louisiana, Mississippi, and South Carolina, blacks formed the majority of the voters. (Because of the restrictions laid out in the legislation, about 150,000 whites who had supported the Confederacy were barred from voting; in addition, many whites chose to boycott the elections.)

The Union League: Helping Blacks to Mobilize

The Union League was a political organization that gave many African Americans their first exposure to the mechanics of politics and voting. Spawned during the Civil War as a Northern white organization supporting the Union war effort, the Union League originally comprised both the elite Union League Clubs as well as gatherings with more diverse membership. Meetings tended to be secret, an aspect its leaders considered a benefit when they decided to extend the Union League into the South during the Reconstruction era.

Whites who had supported the Union during the war (especially those living in the mountains or upcountry regions of the South) were the first Southerners to join the Union League. As the Reconstruction program engineered by the Radicals in Congress got underway, the Republicans realized they could use the Union League to enable the political mobilization of the nearly four million former slaves living in the South. They organized a campaign employing paid speakers, both black and white, who traveled through the South giving speeches and informal talks about the importance of voting and of exercising political rights.

Agents of the Freedmen's Bureau, the federal agency set up to assist the freed people, and other government officials encouraged blacks to join the Union League, and hundreds of thousands of them did. The organization played a key role in registering about a million and a half voters for the elections that took place after the for-mation of the new Southern governments. Nearly seven hundred thousand of those voters were African Americans.

The Union League also had a lasting impact on the socioeconomic system of the South. The dismay felt by blacks as they realized, immediately following the end of the war, that the plantation owners wanted to recreate the labor and social conditions that had existed under slavery led many of them to join the Union League. Their successful mobilization showed them that they could influence what happened in their society, with the result that they were able to resist to some extent the efforts of white Southerners to control them. Thus the sharecropping system which, despite some serious drawbacks, was preferred by blacks because it offered them a measure of control over their labor and families, came to replace the gang-labor system that had existed before the war.

Like all the institutions and people that supported black advancement, the Union League was targeted for attacks by the Ku Klux Klan during the campaign of violence that helped to replace the Reconstruction governments with white supremacists (those who believe that whites are superior and should be in charge). The organization was eventually disbanded by the Republicans, who had become increasingly conservative and friendly toward the former Confederates who now dominated Southern politics and society.

The Southern states form new governments

So it came to be that in each state of the former Confederacy, voters elected delegates to multiracial conventions, where constitutions that provided for black suffrage and equality before the law would be drafted. Convention delegates were a mixed lot. Taking the lead, for the most part, were the white Northerners known as carpetbaggers, a deliberately offensive nickname given to them by resentful Southerners who felt they had come to take advantage of the devastated, demoralized South. (The name implied that these were disreputable people who could carry all their belongings in flimsy fabric suitcases known as carpetbags.) In fact, the carpetbaggers had come South for a variety of reasons: Some were hoping to make money, but others had more noble motivations, such as participating in the formation of a more just, prosperous Southern society. Most were well educated, and their number included many Union army veterans, teachers, Freedmen's Bureau agents, and investors.

Also participating were a relatively small number of white Southerners who, despite scorn from many of their neighbors and from members of the Democratic Party (which most Southerners supported), belonged to the Northern-dominated Republican Party. They were known as scalawags, a term that denotes an unreliable person. Some of these—like Mississippi plantation owner James L. Alcorn (1816–1894)—mainly wanted to ensure that, while blacks would receive civil and political rights, governments would remain dominated by whites. Others sought real social and political change in the South and also hoped to attract Northern investors to bolster the Southern economy; North Carolina politician Thomas Settle (1831–1888) was one of these. In addition, many scalawags—especially those from the mountainous areas of states like Tennessee, Arkansas, and North Carolina—had been Unionists (supporters of the Union, not the Confederacy) during the war. They were more motivated by their resentment of the wealthy class of plantation owners and by their interest in helping small farmers than by a concern for blacks.

Also present among the 1,000 convention delegates were 265 blacks; 107 of these were former slaves and the rest

African American schoolchildren from New Bern, North Carolina, during the Civil War.
© Corbis.

were free blacks. Fewer than 30 of them were from the North, and 40 had served in the Union army during the war. In the years to come, 147 of these delegates would be elected to state legislatures, and 9 to the U.S. Congress.

The old traditions are shaken up

Within a year of the passage of the Reconstruction Acts, eight Southern states had formed governments; by 1870, all of them had. Although they differed in their ideas of how much change was needed or desirable, the South's traditional political and social systems clearly had been shaken up. In most states, the Radicals had managed to dominate over the moderates, pushing through not only a guarantee of civil and political rights for blacks but provisions for state-funded public schools and social services (such as prisons, orphanages, insane asylums, and poor relief). These were no doubt the fairest state governments that had yet been seen in the South.

Among the most controversial issues that had been discussed at the conventions were the integration of schools, the disenfranchisement (removal of voting rights) of former Confederates, and the possibility of land distribution. As it turned out, separate schools for blacks and whites were forbidden only in Louisiana and South Carolina. The fact that none of the states *required* segregated schools, however, was enough to satisfy most blacks, many of whom wanted their children to be taught by black teachers anyway (because they believed white teachers would be prejudiced against them). On the disenfranchisement issue, many Republicans were uncomfortable about stripping anyone of the right to vote; thus, in several states (such as Georgia, Florida, and Texas), few former Confederates were disenfranchised. The land issue was discussed, but no major steps were taken toward realizing the dream of many African Americans that the plantations would be broken up and the land redistributed to those who had provided over two centuries of unpaid labor on it.

In the elections held in the fall of 1867, 90 percent of the African Americans who had registered to vote turned out, helping to give the Republicans a major victory in the South. In the North, however, the Democrats ran a campaign that played on racist fears and hatred, and they made gains in some states. In Ohio, Minnesota, and Kansas, in fact, voters rejected black suffrage. It seemed that despite its victories in the South, the main part of the Republican Party was shifting back toward moderate or even conservative views.

Johnson's impeachment

Meanwhile, in Washington, D.C., President Johnson had continued to clash with the Republican-dominated Congress and was still hoping to weaken its Reconstruction program. There was now only one Radical sympathizer left in the president's Cabinet (made up of the heads of the various federal departments) from those appointed while Lincoln was still in office: Secretary of War Edwin M. Stanton (1814–1869). Seeking to replace Stanton with someone whose political views agreed with his own, Johnson dismissed him in August 1867. At the same time, he replaced several high-ranking military commanders who were sympathetic to the Republicans, including General Philip Sheridan (1831–1888), who had recently taken steps to halt gang violence against blacks in Louisiana.

In early 1868, Congress reacted to Johnson's action by reinstating Stanton, based on the newly passed Tenure of Office Act. This legislation barred the removal, without Senate approval, of Cabinet members during the term of the president who had appointed them (technically, Johnson was still serving out Lincoln's term). In effect, this prevented the president from removing officials who did not share his political views. Johnson chose to challenge the constitutionality of the act, however, by firing Stanton a second time.

This was the final straw in what most members of Congress saw as a series of hostile moves (and general incompetence) by Johnson, including an 1866 speaking tour during

Political cartoon showing President Andrew Johnson as a parrot repeating the word "Constitution," referring to his frequent references to the Constitution during his presidency. © *Bettmann/Corbis.*

THE PAROQUET OF THE WH—E HO—E.

which he had referred to his congressional opponents as traitors. On February 24, 1868, the U.S. House of Representatives passed a resolution of impeachment, meaning that the president would be tried for "high crimes and misdemeanors" which could result in his being removed from office. Johnson was specifically charged with violating the Tenure of Office Act and with bringing the office of the president into "contempt, ridicule, and disgrace."

The impeachment trial lasted eight weeks. Even though it was generally clear from the beginning that the lawyers defending the president had the stronger case (there had been no really clear violation of law on Johnson's part), Johnson let it be known that if he was acquitted, he would go along quietly with the Radical Republicans' programs in the future. A vote was taken on May 26 and the results came up one vote short of the two-thirds majority required to remove the president from office. Even some Republicans had voted not to dismiss the president, based on worries that the impeachment process might someday be misused. Thus Johnson was allowed to finish his term, which came to an end on March 4, 1869.

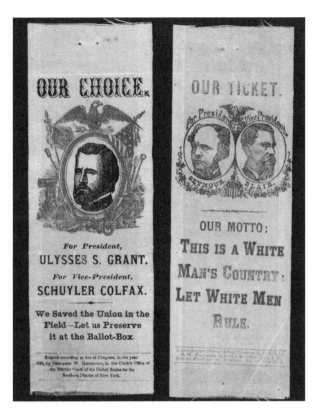

Grant is elected president

The 1868 presidential election would be the first in which African Americans would participate, and they would play an important role in the election of the next president, Ulysses S. Grant (1822–1885; served 1869–77). A career army officer and a hero of the Civil War, during which he had helped carry out such presidential orders as the Emancipation Proclamation, Grant had shown no previous interest in politics. His stance as a moderate made him an attractive candidate for the Republican Party, which wanted to put forth an individual who would represent stability during a troubled period in the nation's history. To oppose Grant, the Democrats nominated a rather colorless figure, former New York governor Horatio Seymour (1810–1886). Their campaign centered on the theme of maintaining white supremacy at a time when, racists maintained, blacks were threatening to take over the country.

The sight of black people voting in the 1867 elections to choose convention delegates had been difficult for many

Campaign ribbons from the 1868 election. Left, ribbon for Republican presidential and vice presidential candidates Ulysses S. Grant and Schuyler Colfax. Right, ribbon for Democratic candidates Horatio Seymour and Francis Preston Blair Jr. *© David J. & Janice L. Frent Collection/Corbis.*

Ulysses S. Grant: War Hero and President

Propelled into the presidency by the popularity he gained as the skilled commander of Union forces during the Civil War, Ulysses S. Grant presided over the latter part of the Reconstruction era. During the final years of his presidency, government support for Reconstruction ran out of steam, and scandals plagued Grant's administration.

The son of an Ohio producer of leather products, Grant was born in 1822 and raised in the small town of Georgetown. He grew up with a love for horses and developed great skill in handling them. Although Grant was not an outstanding student, his father got him an appointment to the U.S. Military Academy at West Point, New York. There he achieved a respectable, though not impressive, degree of academic success, finishing first in his class in horsemanship.

Grant graduated in 1843. He hoped to become a cavalry officer, but these coveted assignments went to the top students, and instead he was assigned to the infantry. He served at posts in Missouri, Louisiana, and Texas. While assigned to the barracks at St. Louis, Missouri, Grant met Julia Dent (1826–1902), the sister of his West Point roommate. They were married in 1848, and subsequently had four children.

After performing well in the Mexican-American War (1846–48), Grant served in a variety of posts from the upper Midwest to California. He had to leave his family behind, though, and his loneliness finally caused him to resign his military commission and return to Missouri. After an unsuccessful stint as a farmer, Grant was forced to accept a job as a clerk in his father's leather store in Galena, Illinois. He was working there when the Civil War began.

Grant's military experience led to his taking a prominent role in recruiting and organizing the men of his town who were volunteering to serve in the Union army. In June 1861, he was made a colonel in the Twenty-first Voluntary Infantry Regiment. Two months later, Grant was promoted to the rank of brigadier general and given command of the army's southeastern Missouri division, which was based in Cairo, Illinois.

Grant proved to be a fine military leader as he led his troops in battles at Fort Donelson and Shiloh, Tennessee, in 1862. His superiors were especially impressed with his later performance at Vicksburg, Mississippi, where he led the eight-week siege that resulted in an important Union victory on July 4, 1863. President Abraham Lincoln, in turn, made Grant a major general and put him in charge of the Mississippi division.

After pushing deeper into the Confederacy, Grant was given overall command

Major General Ulysses S. Grant. *The Library of Congress.*

of the Union army in March 1864. Over the next month, Grant moved closer to the Confederate capital of Richmond, Virginia, which he captured on April 2. A week later, he accepted the surrender of Confederate general Robert E. Lee (1807–1870) at Appomattox Courthouse, Virginia.

As the war ended, Grant was one of the most popular men in the United States. Congress recognized his status the next year by making him a General of the Army of the United States, a rank held only once before, by George Washington (1732–1799). Grant's popularity—especially among the new black voters of the South—helped propel Grant to the presidency in the election of 1868; four years later he was reelected.

During his two terms as president, Grant oversaw the implementation of the Reconstruction plan created by the Radical Republicans in Congress. He was instrumental in passing a series of Enforcement Acts designed to protect the voting rights of Southern blacks, who were under attack by such white terrorist groups as the Ku Klux Klan. Yet Grant also presided over the beginning of Reconstruction's downfall, as Northern interest in the plight of African Americans and in the South in general began to wane.

The final years of Grant's presidency were also marred by financial scandal. Though considered honest himself, he was politically inexperienced and surrounded himself with untrustworthy people, including his vice presidents and personal secretary. Grant was not personally involved, but his administration's reputation was tarnished.

With the election of Rutherford B. Hayes in 1876, Grant set out with his wife on a two-year world tour. His latter years were plagued by money problems, especially after a banking firm he had invested in went bankrupt. At the same time, he learned that he had throat cancer. Anxious to raise money to support his wife after his death, Grant began writing his memoirs. He finished writing in July 1885, a week before his death. His book was a great success and provided his family with nearly $500,000.

An editorial cartoon suggests that the election of Horatio Seymour and Francis Preston Blair Jr. in the presidential election of 1868 will turn the Confederate States of 1864 into a South led by the Ku Klux Klan in 1868.
© Bettmann/Corbis.

white Southerners to accept. Armed with the racist view that blacks were not mentally or morally competent of either choosing or becoming leaders, they predicted a number of dire consequences, from a coming race war to land confiscation and redistribution to incompetent and corrupt governments. To enforce these views, whites used not just words but actions—often very brutal actions. Black voters were threatened and beaten, and black leaders were assassinated. Republican candidates, both black and white, were intimidated and meetings disrupted.

The 1868 presidential campaign was ugly all around. Republicans referred to Democrats as "rebels under the skin." In the South, the white terrorist organization known as the Ku Klux Klan—which had been founded in Tennessee two years earlier—used murder and arson to scare blacks away from the polls. The new Republican state governments could do little to stem the violence. Blacks voted anyway, in huge numbers, proving their belief in the democratic process by their presence at the polls in spite of threatened or actual violence and the loss of jobs.

Grant won the election, though by a close margin. Seymour took the most votes in Georgia and Louisiana, where the "reign of terror" by the Klan and other groups had been the most intense. A Republican president was in the White House, but there were still many U.S. citizens who opposed the values for which he stood. Across the South, Republican governments were in power, put there by an electorate that for the first time included both black and white voters. It remained to be seen how these governments would perform, and even how long they would be allowed to exist. A forbidding tone is evident in the warning given by a Democratic newspaper writer, quoted in *A Short History of Reconstruction*: "These constitutions and governments will last just as long as the bayonets which ushered them into being, shall keep them in existence, and not one day longer."

For More Information

Books

Ayers, Edward L. *The Promise of the New South: Life After Reconstruction.* New York: Oxford University Press, 1992.

Benedict, Michael Les. *A Compromise of Principle: Congressional Republicans and Reconstruction, 1863–1869.* New York: Norton, 1974.

Cox, LaWanda C., and Cox, John H., eds. *Reconstruction, the Negro, and the New South.* New York: Harper & Row, 1973.

Foner, Eric. *A Short History of Reconstruction.* New York: Harper & Row, 1990.

Golay, Michael. *Reconstruction and Reaction: The Emancipation of Slaves, 1861–1913.* New York: Facts on File, 1996.

Jenkins, Wilbert L. *Climbing Up to Glory: A Short History of African Americans During the Civil War and Reconstruction.* Wilmington, DE: Scholarly Resources, 2002.

Litwack, Leon F. *Been in the Storm So Long: The Aftermath of Slavery.* New York: Vintage Books, 1979.

McFeely, William S. *Grant: A Biography.* New York: Norton, 1981.

McPherson, James M. *The Struggle for Equality: Abolitionists and the Negro in the Civil War and Reconstruction.* Princeton, NJ: Princeton University Press, 1965.

Murphy, Richard W. *The Nation Reunited: War's Aftermath.* Alexandria, VA: Time-Life Books, 1987.

Perman, Michael. *The Road to Redemption: Southern Politics, 1869–1879.* Chapel Hill: University of North Carolina Press, 1984.

Smith, John David. *Black Voices from Reconstruction, 1865–1877.* Gainesville: University of Florida Press, 1997.

Stampp, Kenneth M. *The Era of Reconstruction: 1865–1877.* New York: Vintage Books, 1965.

Wagner, Margaret E., Gary W. Gallagher, and Paul Finkelman, eds. *Civil War Desk Reference.* New York: Simon & Schuster, 2002.

Web Sites

Louisiana State University. *The United States Civil War Center.* http://www.cwc.lsu.edu/ (accessed on August 31, 2004).

"Reconstruction." *African American History.* http://afroamhistory.about.com/od/reconstruction/ (accessed on August 31, 2004).

"Reference Resources: Civil War." *Kidinfo.* http://www.kidinfo.com/American_History/Civil_War.html (accessed on August 31, 2004).

"US Civil War." *Internet Modern History Sourcebook.* http://www.fordham.edu/halsall/mod/modsbook27.html (accessed on August 31, 2004).

The Reconstruction Governments

7

The passage of the Reconstruction Acts by the U.S. Congress in 1867 set in motion a remarkable experiment. Because this legislation (passed over the objections of President Andrew Johnson [1808–1875; served 1865–69] and many white Southerners) guaranteed participation by *all* the citizens of the South—whether black or white—this experiment was truly revolutionary. For the first time in the nation's history, the state governments of the South (including the eleven that had formed the Confederacy, which had in 1861 seceded or broken away from the rest of the United States, sparking the Civil War [1861–65]) would take the form of multiracial democracies.

In a region that had once been the setting for the enslavement of four million blacks (brought from Africa since the seventeenth century and forced to work without pay on white farms, plantations, and households), people of both African and white European heritage were participating in government and in civil life. For the first time, black people were voting in elections, serving on juries, and attending

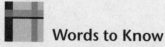

Words to Know

Carpetbaggers: The intentionally offensive nickname for Northerners who went to the South after the Civil War to participate in Reconstruction. Although many white Southerners felt they had come to take advantage of the devastated, demoralized South (and later, racist accounts of Reconstruction reinforced this view), most were actually educated, middle-class men with good intentions. Among their number were Union army veterans, teachers, and investors.

Democratic Party: The political party that had been dominant in the South before the Civil War and which regained control at the end of Reconstruction. Generally, Democrats were conservatives who opposed the kinds of changes advocated by the Republicans, especially those that, they felt, gave the federal government too much power.

Enforcement Acts: Legislation passed in 1871 that was designed to help protect African Americans' right to vote.

Fifteenth Amendment: A constitutional amendment, passed in early 1870, that barred state governments from denying or abridging voting rights "on account of race, color, or previous condition of servitude."

Integration: The intermixing of people or groups previously segregated (separated).

Ku Klux Klan: The most prominent of several white supremacist groups that used violence—in the form of beatings, whippings, murder, rape, and arson—to control black people and their sympathizers through fear and intimidation.

Racism: The belief that there are characteristics or qualities specific to each race, which often results in discrimination (treating people differently based on race).

Reconstruction era: The period stretching roughly from the end of the Civil War in April 1865 to the inauguration of President Rutherford B. Hayes in 1877. Dur-

school. Eventually, they would also be holding political offices at the local, state, and even national levels.

These great changes in Southern life—and in U.S. society in general—had come about through a chain of events that began even before the Civil War ended. During a period referred to as the Reconstruction era (stretching roughing from the Civil War to the end of the 1870s), blacks and whites took part in an effort to rebuild a South that had been devastated by four years of war. This effort took place in an

ing Reconstruction, representatives of the U.S. government—including the president and Congress—and the military would join with both white and black Southerners to try to reorganize the political and social structure of the devastated, defeated South.

Republican Party: The political party that dominated both the U.S. Congress and the new Southern governments during the Reconstruction era. Before the war, most Republicans had tended to live in the North and had favored protections for business interests, public support for internal improvements (like roads and services), and social reforms. As the Reconstruction era progressed, the Republican Party grew more conservative, and its influence in the South decreased as that of the white Southern Democrats increased.

Scalawags: The intentionally offensive nickname for the white Southerners who joined the Republican Party and took part in the Reconstruction govern-

ments. Some scalawags saw this submission as the best route to gaining white control of the South again, whereas others were sincerely interested in creating a new, more just society.

Segregation: The separation of people or groups which, in the Southern United States, was based on race.

Sharecropping: The system of labor that came to dominate the rural South in the years following the Civil War. Preferred by blacks over the old gang-labor system because it gave them some control over their time, work conditions, and families, sharecropping involved the allotment of plots of land to individual families. At harvest time, they would either give the owner a share of the crop they had raised or pay rent to him.

Unionists: Southerners who opposed secession and continued to support the Union throughout the Civil War.

atmosphere charged on one hand with the jubilation and hope experienced by the newly freed slaves and on the other by the resentment, fear, and hatred expressed by many white Southerners. Although the Reconstruction era ended in disappointment for those who had hoped that a more just society would emerge from it, the era was also marked by some important achievements. Among the most notable of these were the new and remarkably fair state governments that were forged in the South between 1867 and 1870.

The Radicals' plan for Reconstruction

The Reconstruction Acts had been created and passed by a Congress dominated by the Radical Republicans, a group made up of senators and representatives who had first fought to end slavery and then sought to win expanded rights for blacks. In general, members of the Republican political party, most of whom lived in the Northern United States, tended to favor protections for business interests, public support for internal improvements (like roads and services), and social reforms. Making up a tiny opposition party were the Democrats, which had been dominant in the South before the war. Democrats were opposed to the kinds of changes proposed by the Republicans, especially those that, they felt, took away individual freedom and local government control by making the federal government too strong.

Under the rules laid out by the Reconstruction Acts, the Southern states were to hold conventions at which elected delegates would devise new constitutions. The constitutions had to include male suffrage (the right of all male citizens, black or white, to vote). In addition, the states had to approve the Fourteenth Amendment (the constitutional amendment that guaranteed equal protection under the law to all U.S. citizens), and each constitution had to be approved by a majority of eligible voters. The Reconstruction Acts specified that those white Southerners who had given aid to the Confederacy during the war would not be eligible to vote or hold office. When all these steps had been completed, the states could hold elections for local, state, and national offices.

A massive effort to educate and register black voters had been remarkably successful, as over seven hundred thousand of them (as well as about an equal number of whites)—representing over 90 percent of those who had registered to vote—turned out first to elect convention delegates and then to choose officeholders. It was obvious that despite the physical and psychological scars left by slavery, and despite the efforts of some white Southerners to control them and hold them back through violence and other means, African Americans were eager to practice their new and hard-won citizenship.

Thus the new, Republican-led state governments set sail amid an atmosphere of optimism. The challenges they faced, however, were huge. In the aftermath of war, the state treasuries were empty, and much of the South lay in ruins. These new governments would take on major public responsibilities never before provided, and these services would be expensive. In addition, they would face the opposition of much of the public: Whereas blacks saw these multiracial governments as the first fair ones ever to appear in the South, many white Southerners refused to recognize them as legitimate. Still clinging to racist beliefs about the inferiority of black people, they were not willing to share their civil and political rights with those who had so recently been slaves. They resisted the changes to their society in ways both passive (such as refusing to vote) and aggressive (through violent assaults on those who did try to participate).

Carpetbaggers, scalawags, and black leaders

For many years after the Reconstruction era ended, there was a popular belief that the period had been a complete disaster for the South. In this view, opportunistic Northerners called "carpetbaggers" (an intentionally offensive nickname that suggested they could carry everything they owned in fabric bags) had come south to take advantage of the defeated people of the former Confederacy. They were schemers whose only motive was to make money. One early-twentieth-century historian, quoted in the *Civil War Desk Reference*, called them "too depraved, dissolute, dishonest and degraded to get the lowest places in the states they had just left." Meanwhile, Southerners who had joined the Republican Party were ridiculed as "scalawags" (rascals or disreputable characters) who had turned their backs on their own people in favor of white Northerners and blacks.

The historians of the early twentieth century helped to promote this view of Reconstruction. They portrayed this as a period dominated by incompetence and corruption on the part not only of the carpetbaggers and scalawags but of blacks too ignorant, illiterate, and irresponsible to handle the burden of citizenship. Contemporary scholars, however, have created a much different picture. They have shown that while some of the carpetbaggers were motivated by greed, most were well-educated, responsible, ambitious men, and many sincerely wanted to help create a better society in the

South. A considerable number were Union army veterans, whereas others had come to the South as teachers, agents of the Freedmen's Bureau, or investors in plantations.

Among the scalawags were many former Unionists or supporters of the Union during the Civil War, many of whom owned farms in the upcountry or mountainous regions of the South and hoped to shift power away from the wealthy plantation owners who had previously dominated Southern politics. Few were very enthusiastic about the idea of equality between blacks and whites, and their alliance with blacks in the Republican Party was mostly one of convenience. Others had been members of the Whig political party (a conservative group active in Southern politics before the war) who now wished to cast their lot with the Republicans, whom they saw as more likely to promote the modernization of the South.

The African Americans who took leading roles during Reconstruction included both free blacks (those who had either never been slaves or had escaped to freedom in the North) and former slaves, many of whom were now teachers, ministers, Union army veterans, and tradesmen. While it is true that they lacked experience and that some were illiterate, they were passionate in their pursuit of expanded civil rights, education, and economic advancement for their people. Their achievements during the period are especially impressive when their background as slaves and as frequent victims of white brutality and mistreatment are considered.

Republican goals and achievements

Among the Republicans who were now in charge of the South's new state governments, many differences of background and opinion existed. There was tension between the native Southerners and the Northerners, between blacks and whites, and between free blacks and former slaves. There were different views on how much power should be given to blacks, on whether or not the government should confiscate and redistribute land, and on whether or not former Confederates should be allowed to vote.

On certain points, however, most Republicans were in agreement. They wanted to guarantee civil and political rights for African Americans, modify the Southern economy to benefit people at all income levels, and provide expanded public services. The idea that the state had a responsibility to offer such benefits to its citizens was somewhat revolutionary; indeed, before the war the Southern states had offered very few services. Describing prewar conditions in South Carolina, twentieth-century African American leader W. E. B. Du Bois (1868–1963), quoted in *Reconstruction and Reaction: The Emancipation of Slaves, 1861–1913,* wrote: "It is said that the antebellum state was ruled by 180 great landlords. They made the functions of the state just as few as possible, and did by private law on plantations most of the things which in other states were carried on by the local and state governments."

Perhaps the most important of the public services guaranteed through the new state constitutions were the tax-supported public school systems. Before the Civil War, of course, most slaves had been strictly prohibited from getting any education, and during the Reconstruction era African Americans were eagerly pursuing their new right to learn to read and write. But even whites—only about one-eighth of whom had attended school before the war—benefited from the new public school systems. In Texas, for example, almost all children began attending school, while in Mississippi, Florida, and South Carolina, about half were enrolled. In South Carolina, the number of students jumped from 30,000 in 1868 to 123,000 in 1876. This expanded access to education is considered the leading achievement of the Reconstruction governments.

The new constitutions also abolished the Black Codes, which governments formed under President Johnson's Reconstruction plan had put in place as a way to control the black labor force. These laws created a situation very close to slavery by restricting not only the work opportunities and conditions available to blacks but their rights and behavior (sometimes confining them to their plantations, for example, unless their employers gave them permission to leave). New laws also provided protection for debtors and free medical care and legal advice for the poor. They called for hospitals, orphanages, prisons, and other public facilities to be built. Benefits to families included laws protecting married women's property rights, making it illegal to physically abuse children, requiring white fathers to support their biracial (mixed race) offspring, allowing interracial marriage (marriage between people of different races), and expanding the grounds for divorce.

Some snags in the plan

However much they were needed and appreciated by citizens, all these new public responsibilities came with a high price tag to the state governments, causing a dramatic growth in expenditures. (For example, South Carolina's budget doubled between 1860 and 1873.) As a result, the states increased property tax rates to pour money back into their treasuries. That meant that plantation owners—who had previously paid hardly any taxes, despite owning so much property—were now forced to part with a significant sum, which they deeply resented. Many blacks and others hoped that the high taxes would result in a breakup of the plantation system by forcing the planters to sell off pieces of their land. This did not occur, however, and the long-cherished dream of owning land was never realized for most blacks. Only South Carolina put a system of land distribution into place, but the number of families that benefitted (fourteen thousand by 1876) was relatively small.

Another controversial issue was that of equal access to public transportation and accommodation. Racist attitudes about the differences between blacks and whites were prevalent not only in the South but across the United States, and most whites demanded physical separation from blacks. Although laws prohibiting the segregation of railroad cars, hotels, and even such facilities as orphanages and insane asylums were put on the books, they were rarely enforced. In addition, most schools were still segregated. The idea of requiring integrated schools was tried only in Louisiana, and succeeded only in the city of New Orleans. The University of South Carolina was also an exception to the general rule of segregated education. This issue was complicated by the fear of many black parents that integrated schools might expose their children to prejudice and discrimination. They wanted their children to have full access to education, but often preferred that it be delivered by black teachers in a welcoming atmosphere.

Blacks take an active role

One of the most significant achievements of the Reconstruction era involved the number of blacks who, for the first time in U.S. history, took an active role in politics and government. White Southerners complained, both during the period and later, that their homeland was unfairly sub-

jected to "Negro rule," but this was not really true. In fact, whites took the most prominent roles in the new governments, especially at the beginning, when it was thought that blacks should stay in the background in order to avoid causing alarm. Gradually, however, a significant number of African Americans were elected to offices.

Prominent officeholders included two men who served in the U.S. Senate, Blanche K. Bruce (1841–1898) and Hiram Revels (1822–1901), both of Mississippi, and fourteen who were elected to the U.S. House of Representatives, including John Roy Lynch (1847–1939) of Mississippi, Jefferson Long (1836–1901) of Georgia, and Joseph Rainey (1832–1887) and Robert Smalls (1839–1915), both of South Carolina. At various times during the Reconstruction era, blacks held the state offices of lieutenant governor, treasurer, superintendent of education, and secretary of state. In addition, six hundred served as state legislators. On the local level, there were several black mayors (including Robert H.

John Roy Lynch: African American Legislator

Born into slavery, John Roy Lynch became a very successful Mississippi politician during the Reconstruction era. After the Reconstruction governments were overthrown by white supremacist "Redeemers," Lynch moved to the North.

Lynch was the son of the Irish overseer of a Louisiana plantation and his slave wife. After his father's death, Lynch and his mother were sold to another planter. They were living in Natchez, Mississippi, when, in 1863, the Union army liberated them. By 1866, Lynch had learned the photography trade and was managing a business, while also attending evening school to acquire an education. He added to his studies by reading books and newspapers and listening to the students and teachers he could hear from the white school across the alley from his photography studio.

Lynch became politically active in 1868, when he began writing and speaking in favor of the new state constitution (written in accordance with the program created by the Radical Republicans in the U.S. Congress). He also took part in Republican Party activities. Lynch gained the attention and approval of Mississippi governor Adelbert Ames (1835–1933), who made him a justice of the peace in 1869. Later that year, he was elected to Mississippi's House of Representatives, where he served until 1873, eloquently speaking out on such causes as federal aid to education and civil rights. During his last term, Lynch was speaker of the house.

In 1872, Lynch was elected to the U.S. House of Representatives. Reelected in 1874, he was defeated in 1876, but ran again in 1880. His Democratic opponent was initially declared the winner of the election, but Lynch successfully contested the results and took his seat in Congress. After losing the 1882 election, he went back to managing the plantation he had recently purchased, though remaining ac-

Wood, who headed the city government of Natchez, Mississippi) and members of city and town councils, as well as county supervisors, tax collectors, and judges. The cities of Tallahassee, Florida, and Little Rock, Arkansas, had black police chiefs, and there were thirty-four black sheriffs in Louisiana and Mississippi. P. B. S. Pinchback (1837–1921) served briefly as governor of Louisiana.

African Americans could not be said to have dominated Southern politics during this period. Their only major-

John Roy Lynch. *Fisk University Library. Reproduced by permission.*

fers from Democratic administrations. Lynch turned to law in 1896, acquiring a license in Washington, D.C., and opening an office there. After working to get President William McKinley (1843–1901; served 1897–1901) elected, he was encouraged by the president to join the U.S. Army. Thus he became paymaster of volunteers for the army, with the rank of major. In 1901, Lynch received his commission in the regular Army, serving in posts in Nebraska and California as well as in Cuba and the Philippines.

tive in Republican politics. Between 1872 and 1900, he served as a delegate to various Republican national conventions.

In 1889, President Benjamin Harrison (1833–1901; served 1889–93) gave Lynch a position at the Navy Department. He subsequently turned down two job of-

Lynch retired from the Army in 1911 and settled in Chicago, where he practiced law for twenty-five years. In 1913, he wrote a book entitled *The Facts of Reconstruction,* in which he refuted the inaccurate portrayals of Reconstruction that had become common. Lynch died in Chicago in 1939 and was buried with military honors at Arlington National Cemetery.

ity was in South Carolina's House of Representatives, which elected the first black Speaker of the House in 1872. Still, the election of six hundred blacks as state legislators represented a huge change and historic milestone in the life of both the South and the nation in general.

Charges of corruption

One of the major charges leveled against the leaders of the Reconstruction era was that they were corrupt, using

Robert Smalls: A Daring Deed, and a Stellar Career

Born a South Carolina slave, Robert Smalls gained fame when he managed to pilot a Confederate ship into the custody of the Union army. He later became one of the most successful black politicians of the Reconstruction era.

Smalls was born near Beaufort, South Carolina. After moving with his master to Charleston, he was allowed to hire himself out as a boatman by paying his master $15 a month. He learned piloting skills and became very familiar with the area's coastal waterways. In 1862, Smalls was forced to join the Confederate Navy as a "wheelsman" (the title of pilot was considered too elevated for a slave) on the steamboat *Planter*. He learned the signals needed to safely pass the Confederate forts and the locations of land mines.

By the spring of 1862, the Union had blockaded the harbors of the main forts along the Atlantic coasts of the Confederate states. On May 12, with the white crew on shore, Smalls took the opportunity to steer the *Planter* out of Charleston harbor to the Union lines. This daring exploit earned Smalls instant celebrity and became a symbol of what slaves—assumed by many whites to be obedient and happy with their enslaved status—were willing and able to do.

Smalls received an award of $1,500 and was made a second lieutenant in the Navy. In December 1863, Smalls was promoted to the rank of captain and was made the pilot of the *Planter*. He took part in seventeen battles. After the war, Smalls's good-humored personality, intelligence, and speaking skills helped him gain influence as a leader. Through his investments in real estate and local companies, he also gained wealth and was able to contribute to and raise funds for such causes as building schools.

Smalls helped write South Carolina's 1868 constitution and subsequently

their positions and power to gain financial and material benefits for themselves. These charges called the integrity of the Reconstruction governments into question and also scared off the investors that they had hoped to attract to the South. Although in some cases the charges were true, contemporary historians have noted that this was a period of widespread corruption in the United States as a whole, a time when the social disorganization wrought by the Civil War combined with fast-paced economic growth and untrustworthy business leaders created conditions ripe for corruption. In the North, in fact, these years were marked by several great cor-

Robert Smalls. *The Library of Congress.*

ported free public education and the interests of the former slaves, including cheaper land, continuing eligibility for military service, enforcement of the Civil Rights Acts, health care for the poor, and equal accommodations on public transportation.

After violence and fixed elections had finally pushed all African Americans out of Southern politics, Smalls served as Beaufort's customs collector from 1890 to 1913, while remaining active in the Republican Party. Despite his own frequent protests against corruption in government, Smalls was himself convicted of bribery, but he received a pardon from South Carolina's governor. In 1896, Smalls was one of six black members of the state constitutional convention, where he made an eloquent but vain attempt to prevent the disenfranchisement (removal of voting rights) of the state's African Americans. He died in 1915.

became a state legislator and senator. He served as a member of the U.S. House of Representatives from 1874 to 1886, although by the end of that period, white supremacists had taken control of the Southern state governments. During his political career, Smalls consistently sup-

ruption scandals, including those perpetrated by groups known as the Whiskey Ring and the Tweed Ring.

Republican officials were not immune to the "get rich quick" mentality that dominated U.S. society, especially those who were not landowners and faced uncertain futures when they left office. This created something called the "politics of livelihood," which referred to politicians who had to rely solely on their offices for income. It affected not only poor blacks but scalawags, some of whom were harshly condemned for serving in the Republican governments. As quoted in *Reconstruction and Reaction: The Emancipation of Slaves,*

1861–1913, a New Orleans man who lost his job as a weights-and-measures inspector lamented, "I do not know what I shall do. My own relatives have turned their backs and it will be impossible for me to get any employment."

Under these conditions, it is perhaps less surprising that some officials took part in corruption, which included such practices as accepting bribes (payments) for voting a certain way, selling property to the government at inflated rates, or buying shares in property for less than the market value. Some of the most notable cheaters of the period included scalawag Franklin J. Moses (1838–1906), who served as both a legislator and governor in South Carolina, and Governor Robert K. Scott (1826–1900), a carpetbagger, also from South Carolina. Members of the Democratic Party were also involved, however; in fact, after Reconstruction had ended, a Democratic treasurer of Mississippi stole $316,000 from the state government, which was more than anyone ever had before.

In the South, a factor that helped open the door to corruption was railroad development, which many states got involved with in pursuit of economic growth and recovery. Hoping that railroads would open their states to expanded trade and glorious profits, they offered either direct grants or laws endorsing bonds to finance them. However, railroad construction and operation were extremely expensive processes and put too much financial burden on the states. Only a few (including Georgia, Alabama, Arkansas, and Texas) actually benefitted.

A new labor system

In addition to the political developments occurring in the South, a new system of labor and class organization was developing. Although plantation owners continued to occupy the top social rung of Southern society, the disenfranchisement (removal of voting rights) of former Confederates had diminished their political influence. The overproduction of cotton led to a decrease in its profitability. Other changes included a shift in prosperity from the previously thriving coastal towns to those further inland, which were now linked to the North and West by the new railroads. Cities like Atlanta and Macon in Georgia; Selma, Alabama; and St. Louis, Missouri, were humming as merchants, bankers, and railroad promoters carried on their trades.

Meanwhile, most rural blacks in the South were working as sharecroppers, a system that to them represented a kind of compromise as their hopes of landownership faded. Under this arrangement, individual families were given specific plots of land to farm. At each harvest, they would either give the owner a share (usually one-half) of the crop they had raised or pay rent to the landowner. Blacks preferred this

African Americans pick cotton on a plantation in Georgia in 1870.
Getty Images.

system because it allowed them to live apart from other families and gave them control of their own time and labor.

By contrast, plantation owners disliked sharecropping because it gave them less control over their labor force; they went along with it only grudgingly. They managed to increase their influence, however, through a credit system by which workers would purchase needed supplies on credit, usually at very high interest rates. This system effectively trapped laborers by forcing them to carry credit over from year to year, never allowing them to pay off their debts.

By the end of the Reconstruction era, sharecropping dominated most areas of the South where cotton and tobacco were grown. In the Louisiana sugar industry, however (where Northern investors had made it possible for production to resume quickly after the war), workers still labored in the gangs typical of the slavery system but were also given individual plots in which to raise some crops of their own. In the rice-growing regions of South Carolina and Georgia, plantation owners had been unable to replace the irrigation systems and equipment destroyed during the war. Most of the large plantations here did break up into small farms, some of which were purchased by black farmers. Generally, the African Americans who lived in these areas grew their own food and earned cash through day labor.

Blacks who lived in the towns and cities of the South had more opportunities for employment, but most were still restricted to jobs as low-paid, unskilled manual laborers or servants with no chance of advancement. The number of black professionals and craftsmen was still very small, and businesses owned by blacks—such as grocery stores, restaurants, and funeral parlors—tended to be the kind that provided only a small number of jobs. Still, urban life offered blacks access to the schools, churches, newspapers, and fraternal societies that were at the heart of the African American community. In addition, such black educational institutions as Fisk University began, in the 1870s, to turn out graduates who offered an example of achievement and the promise of advancement.

White terrorists resist the changes

Even before the end of the Civil War, white Southerners had begun to resist the changes occurring in the society and culture they cherished. The familiar world they had known, in which black people existed as inferior beings fit only to serve whites, was falling down around them, and they fought back. They did so through violent attacks that included arson, beatings, rape, and murder. These attacks were focused not only on the former slaves but on anyone who tried to help them or seemed sympathetic to the idea of freedom, civil rights, and equality, including teachers, soldiers, and white Unionists.

During the period of President Johnson's Reconstruction program, race riots had occurred in two major Southern cities—Memphis, Tennessee, where forty-six blacks were killed, and New Orleans, Louisiana, where thirty-four blacks and three whites died. These riots had underscored the link between white resentment and violence. With the triumph of the Radical Republicans' plan for Reconstruction, the violence increased. Secret terrorist societies, most of whose members covered their identities with masks and long robes, began a widespread campaign to try to control through fear what they had not been able to control any other way. They wanted to prevent blacks from exercising their new rights, and they also wanted to ensure that plantation owners had the same kind of disciplined labor force they had enjoyed during the days of slavery.

The Ku Klux Klan

These terrorist groups included the Knights of the White Camellia in Louisiana, the Knights of the Rising Sun in Texas, and the White Line in Mississippi. The most notorious of all was the Ku Klux Klan. Begun as a kind of social club in Pulaski, Tennessee, in 1865, the Klan quickly grew into a full-fledged terrorist organization with members and sympathizers across the South. By 1867, it was under the leadership of Nathan Bedford Forrest (1821–1877), a former slave trader and plantation owner who had served as a general in the Confederate army. Forrest bore the title of Grand Wizard.

Although it was never tightly or centrally organized, the main goal of the Ku Klux Klan was clear to all: to restore white supremacy by destroying the power of the Republican Party in the South. Klan groups were locally formed and operated, with a diverse membership that ranged from poor whites

Ku Klux Klan leader Nathan Bedford Forrest. *Hulton Archive/Getty Images.*

to plantation owners to doctors and lawyers. The months leading up to the 1868 elections were particularly bloody. Blacks were threatened not only with violence but with the loss of jobs, credit, or homes if they voted for Republican candidates. The Klan targeted black schools, churches, and homes for destruction. Most of the victims were black, but white Republicans were also threatened, beaten, and killed.

The bloodshed continued even after 1869, when Forrest ordered the breakup of the Klan. The victims included individuals both prominent, including a member of Congress from Arkansas, three South Carolina state legislators, and three scalawag members of the Georgia legislature, and ordinary, like Irish-born William Luke, a teacher in a black school. Former slave Washington Eager was killed, his brother said, because he could read and write. In Jackson County, Florida, the 150 individuals murdered by the Klan included a Jewish merchant who was considered to be sympathetic to blacks.

The new state governments found it hard to fight the violence, as law enforcement officers refused to become involved, witnesses were afraid to testify in court, and courts refused to convict suspected terrorists. In three states—Tennessee, Arkansas, and Texas—governors who were willing to declare martial law (when a military government takes control, with ordinary law suspended) were able to organize militias that proved somewhat effective in stemming the violence. Suspending constitutional rights and making arrests in this way were not popular, however, owing to the risk of stirring up sympathy for the suspects.

The Enforcement Acts

Finally, the U.S. Congress was pushed into action. In early 1870, the Fifteenth Amendment had been ratified, bar-

ring state governments from denying or abridging voting
rights "on account of race, color, or previous condition of
servitude." (It did not, however, specifically prohibit the
kinds of literacy and property requirements that would later
be used to keep blacks away from the polls.) Clearly, allowing
terrorist groups to keep blacks from voting was in violation
of the amendment. In May, Congress passed the first of three
Enforcement Acts designed to help protect the right to vote.
This act mandated fines or prison time for anyone convicted
of preventing voters from casting ballots and made it a
felony (a serious crime) to interfere with the exercising of
constitutional rights. But because of lack of enforcement, this
law proved ineffective.

The second Enforcement Act, passed in February
1871, provided for the appointment of federal election supervisors to oversee voting, and interfering with elections was
made a federal crime. In April 1871, the strong support of
President Ulysses S. Grant (1822–1885; served 1869–77)

Whites in Louisiana work to prevent African Americans from voting. *The Granger Collection, New York. Reproduced by permission.*

helped push through the third Enforcement Act. This law made it a federal crime to prevent someone not only from voting but from holding office, serving on juries, or otherwise denying them equal protection under the law. The act gave the federal government the right to step in if the states failed to ensure these constitutionally guaranteed rights; in fact, the president could suspend habeas corpus (the right to be tried in court) and use military force if necessary.

Despite the somewhat controversial nature of these acts, which some said gave the federal government too much power over the states, Attorney General Amos T. Akerman (1821–1880) made an aggressive effort to enforce them. The results were only marginally effective, though; for example, of six hundred South Carolinians convicted under the Acts, only sixty-five were sent to federal prison. They were, however, thought to have reduced the violence that occurred around the relatively peaceful 1872 election in which Grant was reelected. Nevertheless, the violence had already taken a serious toll on Republican Party organizations and on the morale of black communities.

Developments in the North and the West

Events and trends occurring across the rest of the United States during the Reconstruction era both paralleled and, in some ways, influenced what was happening in the troubled Southern part of the country. In the North, the span of years from 1865 to 1877 was marked by economic growth and political and social reforms, but there were also periods of economic depression, episodes of political corruption, and clashes between the expanding class of wealthy people and professionals and the small farmers and workers who still made up the bulk of the population. Northern state governments, like those in the South, were raising taxes and expanding their budgets in order to pay for new social services and public schools. But the North had not experienced the devastation of the Civil War in the same dramatic way as the South, and its stronger economy meant that it could better afford to finance the changes.

Between 1865 and 1873, industrial production (especially iron and steel manufacturing) increased by 75 percent. The population was expanding—including the addition of three million immigrants—but migration to the open spaces of the West had been eased by the construction of 35,000 miles of railroad routes. In the West were plenty of opportunities for farming as well as lumber harvesting, mining, and ranching.

While African Americans fought for their rights in the South, Native Americans were losing theirs in the West. Before the massive western migration of settlers intensified, the government had signed treaties with various Indian nations, allowing them to maintain—to lesser or greater extents, in specified areas—the hunting-based life patterns they had followed for centuries. But the need for land on which to build railroads and accommodate homesteaders (people who claimed land following the Homestead Act in 1862) led to a major change, as the government began pushing Native Americans onto reservations (areas of land set aside for Indians to live on). In 1871, Congress declared that the Indian nations were no longer sovereign (acting independently, without outside influence) and that there would be no more treaties. Although Native Americans continued to resist this trend through about 1890, most were living on reservations by the end of the Reconstruction era. Meanwhile, Chinese immigrants who had come to the United States to help construct the railroads were also routinely discriminated against.

The growth of the railroad and mining industries, with their dependence on receiving federal land grants, led to closer ties between business and government. This in turn created more opportunities for corruption as, for example, government officials would serve on the governing boards of companies and would receive favors in exchange for arranging government aid. Although President Grant himself appears to have been honest, his administration's reputation was tarnished by the involvement of several high-ranking officials in various scandals. Anxiety about the ties between government and business also spurred the growth of the labor movement: whereas only three labor unions had existed before the Civil War, there were twenty-one by the early 1870s. They campaigned for better working conditions, winning such benefits as the eight-hour work day for government workers in 1868. The unions, however, generally excluded women, African Americans, and people of Chinese heritage from their membership.

Achievements and disappointments

By the early 1870s, the Southern United States had become the setting for a pattern of both accomplishments and dashed hopes. Remarkably, a multiracial democratic government had been established and blacks were, for the first time in U.S. history, eagerly participating in every aspect of public life. Many public facilities had been rebuilt or newly constructed, school systems had been set up, and labor conditions on plantations had improved. As noted in *Reconstruction and Reaction: The Emancipation of Slaves, 1861–1913,* several years after the end of the Reconstruction era, a black legislator from South Carolina, Thomas E. Miller (1849–1938), would recall Republican accomplishments in a speech to the white-supremacist-dominated legislature of South Carolina:

> We were eight years in power. We had built schoolhouses, established charitable institutions, built and maintained the penitentiary [prison] system, provided for the education of the deaf and dumb, rebuilt the jails and courthouses, rebuilt the bridges and reestablished the ferries. In short, we had reconstructed the state and put it on the road to prosperity.

But the days of hope and achievement—darkened, of course, by the shadow of violent resistance—that Miller remembered with pride were almost over. Soon a new movement of conservative politicians would "redeem" the South, reclaiming it for the white supremacists who had previously dominated its society.

For More Information

Books

Ayers, Edward L. *The Promise of the New South: Life After Reconstruction.* New York: Oxford University Press, 1992.

Benedict, Michael Les. *A Compromise of Principle: Congressional Republicans and Reconstruction, 1863–1869*. New York: Norton, 1974.

Cox, LaWanda C., and John H. Cox, eds. *Reconstruction, the Negro, and the New South*. New York: Harper & Row, 1973.

Foner, Eric. *Freedom's Lawmakers: A Directory of Black Officeholders During Reconstruction*. Baton Rouge: Louisiana State University Press, 1996.

Foner, Eric. *A Short History of Reconstruction*. New York: Harper & Row, 1990.

Golay, Michael. *Reconstruction and Reaction: The Emancipation of Slaves, 1861–1913*. New York: Facts on File, 1996.

Jenkins, Wilbert L. *Climbing Up to Glory: A Short History of African Americans During the Civil War and Reconstruction*. Wilmington, DE: Scholarly Resources, 2002.

Litwack, Leon F. *Been in the Storm So Long: The Aftermath of Slavery*. New York: Vintage Books, 1979.

Litwack, Leon F., and August Meier, eds. *Black Leaders of the Nineteenth Century*. Urbana: University of Illinois Press, 1988.

Lynch, John Roy. *Reminiscences of an Active Life*. Chicago: University of Chicago Press, 1970.

Perman, Michael. *The Road to Redemption: Southern Politics, 1869–1879*. Chapel Hill: University of North Carolina Press, 1984.

Smith, John David. *Black Voices from Reconstruction, 1865–1877*. Gainesville: University of Florida Press, 1997.

Stampp, Kenneth M. *The Era of Reconstruction: 1865–1877*. New York: Vintage Books, 1965.

Wagner, Margaret E., Gary W. Gallagher, and Paul Finkelman, eds. *Civil War Desk Reference*. New York: Simon & Schuster, 2002.

Web Sites

Louisiana State University. *The United States Civil War Center*. http://www.cwc.lsu.edu/ (accessed on August 31, 2004).

"Reconstruction." *African American History*. http://afroamhistory.about.com/od/reconstruction/ (accessed on August 31, 2004).

"Reference Resources: Civil War." *Kidinfo*. http://www.kidinfo.com/American_History/Civil_War.html (accessed on August 31, 2004).

"US Civil War." *Internet Modern History Sourcebook*. http://www.fordham.edu/halsall/mod/modsbook27.html (accessed on August 31, 2004).

White Supremacists "Redeem" the South

Chattanooga, Tennessee, was the setting for an incident that became, in the troubled yet hopeful years of the Reconstruction era (stretching from the end of the Civil War in April 1865 to the 1870s), all too common in the Southern United States. The hooded henchmen of the Ku Klux Klan, one of several white terrorist groups that roamed the South during this period, trying to control blacks and their sympathizers through fear, severely beat a black man named Andrew Flowers. The attack was spurred by Flowers's recent election as justice of the peace (a kind of judge who can hear minor cases in towns and counties). One of many victims of such violence, Flowers later recalled that his attackers had "said they had nothing in particular against me, that they didn't dispute I was a very good fellow, but they did not intend any nigger [a derogatory word for African American] to hold office in the United States."

Flowers's only crime was having the nerve to imagine that a black citizen of the United States could become an officeholder. Such a development was unthinkable to many white Southerners, whose lives before the Civil War had been

Words to Know

Amnesty: An official pardon for those convicted of political offenses.

Carpetbaggers: The intentionally offensive nickname for Northerners who went to the South after the Civil War to participate in Reconstruction. Although many white Southerners felt they had come to take advantage of the devastated, demoralized South (and later, racist accounts of Reconstruction reinforced this view), most were actually educated, middle-class men with good intentions. Among their number were Union army veterans, teachers, and investors.

Civil Rights Act of 1875: Legislation that was supposed to reinforce the guarantee of civil and political rights for blacks and also prohibit segregation in public places, especially public schools. It proved ineffective, though, and was struck down by the Supreme Court in 1883.

Compromise of 1877: The agreement that resolved the controversy over the election of Republican Rutherford B. Hayes as president. Democrats agreed to accept Hayes's election in exchange for Home Rule in the South. The agreement allowed for the overthrow of the last three Reconstruction governments.

Democratic Party: The political party that had been dominant in the South before the Civil War and which regained control at the end of Reconstruction. Generally, Democrats were conservatives who opposed the kinds of changes advocated by the Republicans, especially those that, they felt, gave the federal government too much power.

Home Rule: Local self-government, desired by white supremacists in the South as a way to regain control of their state governments.

Liberal Republicans: Members of a reform movement who were against corruption, high taxes, and what they saw as extravagant public spending. They favored free trade, limited government, and basing the allotment of federal government jobs on examinations. They also supported Home Rule for the South as well as amnesty for former Confederates, who they considered the "natural leaders" of the South.

Mississippi plan: The pattern of violent disruptions of elections that would become a blueprint for the "redemption" of Southern states by Democrats and other white supremacists.

New Departure: A brief attempt by members of the Southern Democratic Party to attract black voters by downplaying its true white supremacist views and focusing on such issues as taxes, government spending, and amnesty for former Confederates.

Panic of 1873: A period of serious economic decline that was set off by the bankruptcy of powerful banker Jay Cooke.

Reconstruction era: The period stretching roughly from the end of the Civil War in April 1865 to the inauguration of President Rutherford B. Hayes in 1877. During Reconstruction, representatives of the U.S. government—including the president and Congress—and the military would join with both white and black Southerners to try to reorganize the political and social structure of the devastated, defeated South.

Redemption movement: The successful effort, which took place between 1869 and 1877, to overthrow or "redeem" the Republican governments and replace its leaders with men devoted to white supremacy.

Republican Party: The political party that dominated both the U.S. Congress and the new Southern governments during the Reconstruction era. Before the war, most Republicans had tended to live in the North and had favored protections for business interests, public support for internal improvements (like roads and ser-vices), and social reforms. As the Reconstruction era progressed, the Republican Party grew more conservative, and its influence in the South decreased as that of the white Southern Democrats increased.

Scalawags: The intentionally offensive nickname for the white Southerners who joined the Republican Party and took part in the Reconstruction governments. Some scalawags saw this submission as the best route to gaining white control of the South again, whereas others were sincerely interested in creating a new, more just society.

Slaughterhouse Cases: A series of Supreme Court cases in the 1880s in which the rulings effectively denied blacks the right to use the federal courts to fight unfair state laws, declared that the U.S. Constitution did not "confer the right of suffrage on anyone," and voided parts of the Enforcement Acts (which had guaranteed penalties for those who use violence to interfere with elections).

White supremacists: Those who hold the racist view that people of northern European or white heritage are superior to those of African and other non-white descent and ought to be in control of society.

built around the institution of slavery. Established in the earliest days of white settlement in the United States, this system had involved the capture of blacks in Africa and their transportation to the Southern region of the new nation, where they were forced to become unpaid, often mistreated laborers in the fields and homes.

A new beginning

Slavery had ended with the victory of the Northern Union (the federal government) over the Confederacy, made up of eleven Southern states that had chosen to separate themselves from the rest of the country. The bitterness and resentment of white Southerners, however, had not only survived the war's wake but intensified. Their hopes for a return to the kind of society they had previously known were briefly lifted when President Andrew Johnson (1808–1875; served 1865–69) announced his plans for the Reconstruction of the South, for it seemed that they would be allowed to recreate the conditions of slavery.

The subsequent victory of the Radical Republicans, a group of U.S. senators and representatives fueled both by ambition and idealism, had put an end to such hopes. Through a series of legislative acts, including three important amendments to the U.S. Constitution, the Republicans had laid the groundwork for a Southern society in which blacks enjoyed the same civil and political rights as whites, and in which those who had helped the Confederacy were shut out of power. In the late 1860s, a remarkable experiment in multiracial democracy had taken place, with blacks participating fully in voting for, and even becoming, the new leaders of their states.

Resistance to Reconstruction

This experiment had been carried out not only with the energy generated by four million former slaves eager to make the most of their newfound freedom but with the support of sympathetic whites, most of them Northerners. Some of these Northerners, ridiculed as disreputable "carpetbaggers" by many white Southerners, served in the new state governments, along with the men called "scalawags" (another scornful nickname, this one for white members of the Republican Party) and both free blacks (those who had never been slaves or who had escaped to freedom in the North) and former slaves. Together, these individuals had created the fairest governments yet seen in the South. They had established the first public school systems, set up public services like prisons and orphanages, and provided free medical care and legal advice for the poor.

All these new benefits, however, had come at a high cost to the state treasuries. To pay for them, the governments had raised taxes, which caused widespread dismay among whites, especially the owners of plantations (large estates on which basic crops like cotton and tobacco were grown), who had previously paid very little. As time went on, corruption—a problem that was widespread in government across the United States during this period—caused further hostility toward the Reconstruction governments.

Most of all, though, white Southerners resented the idea that African Americans could enjoy equal rights and take part in public life. Convinced that blacks were inferior to those of European heritage and fit for nothing better than serving white people, the white Southerners could not accept the changes in their society. They fought back through violence, in brutal attacks like the one on Flowers after his election as a justice of the peace. They beat and murdered blacks. They burned down black schools, churches, and homes and intimidated and attacked whites they thought supported black rights. They threatened with future brutality—as well as the loss of jobs and credit—African Americans who dared to take part in activities (especially voting) that might lead to advancement.

The Redemption begins

During the first half of the 1870s, white Southerners would exert a mighty effort to, as they called it, "redeem" their homeland, to return it to the control of white supremacists (those who believe that whites are superior and should be in charge). This effort, referred to as the Redemption, took place against a backdrop of indifference on the part of the federal government and those Northerners who had previously supported the dream of creating a new and more just Southern society. The Republican governments would fall, and the cause of justice and equality for African Americans would be delayed for many, many years.

These grim circumstances would come about through a number of factors, beginning with a shift in the interests and direction of the Republican Party. Historians trace the origins of this shift to the 1868 election of President Ulysses S. Grant (1822–1885; served 1869–77). Instead of choosing a dynamic leader as their candidate, the Republicans nominated a military hero (one of several generals who had led the Union army to victory in the Civil War) with good intentions but little political ability or judgment. (This would result in poor Cabinet and staff choices that would bring dishonor to the Grant administration.) Lacking both a strong leader at its helm and a unifying vision, the Republican Party—which had been a force for change and a supporter of reform movements, from the fight against slavery to the struggle to win equal rights for the freed people, since the birth of the party in the 1850s—lost its commitment to the experiment it had begun in the Southern Reconstruction governments.

A number of factors played into this development. One factor was the death or retirement of the most influential members of the Radical wing of the party—the men who had lent the Reconstruction effort its fire and purpose. U.S. representative Thaddeus Stevens (1792–1868) of Pennsylvania, a longtime, tireless fighter for equal rights, died in August 1868, and former Secretary of War Edwin M. Stanton (1814–1869) soon followed. U.S. senator Charles Sumner (1811–1874) of Massachusetts broke with the party early in the Grant administration, as did U.S. senator Carl Schurz (1829–1906) of Missouri, who had once written an influential report urging federal support for the South (see Chapter 4). Even the leaders of the abolitionist movement, who had worked so hard for so many years toward the goal of freeing the slaves, seemed now to feel that black people's problems were solved.

The Liberal Republicans

In place of the small but influential group of Radicals in Congress, there was now a group called the "stalwarts," extremely conservative men with close ties to business interests, who were in favor not of change or reform but of keeping things the way they were. In reaction to this group, as well as to the political corruption that was plaguing the nation, arose a new group called the Liberal Republicans. Members of this reform movement were disgusted not only by the bribery and other forms of misbehavior in which public officials were involved but also by high taxes and what they saw as extravagant public spending. Liberal Republicans were in favor of free trade and limited government; their strongest belief, though, was that the civil service (the network of federal government jobs) must be changed. Whereas in the past, government jobs had been used as rewards for supporting whoever had been elected, the Liberals thought they should be based on intelligence and ability, which could be proved by passing an examination.

The Liberals still accepted the Fourteenth and Fifteenth Amendments, which guaranteed civil and political rights to African Americans. They had been disillusioned, however, by the Reconstruction governments, which they saw as riddled by corruption, incompetence, and overspending. Thus they favored "Home Rule" (local self-government) for the South and asserted that the former Confederates who had previously ruled the region should be offered amnesty (a pardon for their previous disloyalty to the Union). These white men were put forth as the "natural leaders" of the South and the only people capable of restoring order and stability to the region, which was necessary to attract the Northern investors who could pump money into the Southern economy.

A curious turnaround was now taking place, as Northern journalists warned of the dangers of allowing unworthy, ignorant, uneducated people (whether they were blacks in the South, Irish immigrants in the Northeast, or Chinese on the West Coast) to vote. Southern whites were now being portrayed as the victims of injustice, while blacks were seen as undeserving of equal citizenship and carpetbaggers as thieves out for all they could steal from the South. As for the resentment and hatred that white Southerners had shown for African Americans, it was up to black people themselves to alter those feelings: "The removal of white prejudice against the negro depends almost entirely on the negro himself," declared the *Nation* magazine, as noted in *A Short History of Reconstruction*.

Indeed, even respectable, intellectual journals like the *Nation* were now joining their voices to those who had claimed that black people were fundamentally different from and inferior to whites, that they had perhaps been better off under slavery, that only white Southerners could really understand them, and that it was pointless to try to educate them. These new attitudes created new alliances between Northern Republicans and Democrats (the conservative party that had dominated the South before the war and now based its platform on white supremacy) of both regions.

Deepening divisions in the South

Meanwhile, in the South, the resentment against blacks of lower-class whites, who dominated but by no means monopolized the ranks of the Ku Klux Klan and other terrorist groups, grew with the perception that blacks were not only economic competitors in a time of economic hardship but threats to the very self-esteem of poor whites. Denying blacks an equal place in society, in this view, meant more room there for those at the bottom rungs of white society. Those on the top rung, however, viewed blacks more as a potential labor force than as social or economic competitors, so they did not have as much difficulty in allowing them some civil and political equality. In fact, the "New Departure" faction of the Southern Democratic Party even tried to attract black voters by focusing on such issues as taxes, government spending, and amnesty rather than on racial matters.

As the 1872 elections approached, however, a much more common stance for Democratic candidates was that of white supremacy. Candidates would try to gain support by stirring fears of rape of white women by black men, of miscegenation (sexual relationships between blacks and whites, which some believed would weaken or mar the purity of the white race), and the "Africanization" of the South, through which the concerns, rights, and privileges of blacks would overshadow those of whites.

Whereas there had once been a considerable (if never large) number of white Southerners in the Republican Party, a strict racial dividing line was now developing: blacks were Republicans, and whites were Democrats. Scalawags gave in to the scorn, ridicule, and sometimes mistreatment to which they and their families were subjected by dropping out of the Republican Party in large numbers.

Grant is reelected

As the 1872 presidential election loomed, the Republicans, of course, rallied behind the incumbent president, Ulysses S. Grant. The Democrats united with the Liberal Republicans in nominating a somewhat unlikely candidate, the popular *New York Tribune* newspaper editor Horace Greeley (1811–1872). The only issue that all of Greeley's supporters seemed to have in common was the need for a new policy in the South. Greeley came out in favor of local control of government and of Southern state governments headed by the region's "natural leaders," with blacks told to fend for themselves and not expect special favors.

Grant won a solid majority of the votes, carrying all of the states in the North, while Greeley won only in the ex-Confederate states of Georgia, Tennessee, and Texas and the border states of Kentucky, Maryland, and Missouri. Thanks to the passage during the two previous years of the Enforcement Acts, which had been somewhat successful in closing down the Ku Klux Klan and curbing racial violence, this was a fairly peaceful election in which Southern blacks were allowed to cast their votes freely. Sadly, the next major elections, held in 1874, would present a much different picture.

Horace Greeley, editor of the *New York Tribune* and the 1872 Democratic presidential nominee. *The Library of Congress.*

The Panic of 1873

Before those elections, though, the nation was plunged into a period of major economic decline called the Panic of 1873. The crisis was sparked by the bankruptcy of Jay Cooke (1821–1905), one of the most powerful bankers in the nation, who had speculated too wildly in railroad bonds—Cooke bought and sold the bonds, with the assumption that the railroads would be successful and the intention

Officials of the New York Stock Exchange close their doors to members during the Panic of 1873. *Getty Images.*

of making a large profit. This event caused a drastic dip in confidence among the U.S. public. The resulting depression put more than a million people out of work and closed thousands of businesses. Farmers also suffered, for agricultural prices and land values fell. Miners and factory workers reacted to wage cuts with violent strikes, underlining the growing distinction and bad blood between the country's working and upper classes, each of whom frantically defended its own interests first and felt ill will and distrust toward the other.

In the South, which had already been suffering from a poor economy, the effects of the depression were felt even more strongly. The prices of cotton, tobacco, rice, and sugar all declined dramatically, leading to widespread bankruptcy and more families living in poverty. The prosperity that so many had hoped for in the years following the Civil War now seemed even farther out of reach than ever before. Abandoning their feeble attempts at a "New Departure," Southern Democrats focused on lowering taxes and controlling the plantation labor force as their main objectives, with the overriding theme of white supremacy as the way to accomplish these goals.

Using violence and intimidation as weapons

White Southerners were now determined to reclaim or "redeem" their state governments, and once again, they turned to violence and intimidation as weapons. These tactics had already worked well in the four states that had seen the earliest redemptions—Virginia, North Carolina, Tennessee, and Georgia, where the Republican governments had been overthrown between 1869 and 1871. In Georgia, for example, the success of the terrorist groups in keeping blacks from the polls had resulted in the Democrats capturing the state legislature in 1870, and the governorship the next year. When he took office, Redeemer governor James M. Smith (1823–1890) advised blacks to forget about politics and "get down to honest hard work." The state had quickly put a poll tax and strict residency and registration rules (designed to make it nearly impossible for poor blacks to vote) on the books.

In Mississippi, a newspaper writer frankly announced the Democrats' intentions for the upcoming elections, as quoted in *The Era of Reconstruction: 1865–1877:* "All other means having been exhausted to abate the horrible condition of things, the thieves and robbers, and scoundrels, white and black, deserve death and ought to be killed.... [They] ought to be compelled to leave the state or abide [by] the consequences.... [We will] carry the election peaceably if we can, forcibly if we must." Thus began the pattern of violence that would come to be known as the "Mississippi plan," which would become a blueprint for the other six states yet to be redeemed.

The Mississippi Plan

Mississippi Democrats known as White Liners (white supremacists) organized rifle clubs and militia groups and began drilling and parading through black communities. They broke up Republican meetings and provoked bloody riots. For example, in Vicksburg in December 1874, the White Liners demanded the resignation of the town's black sheriff, Peter Crosby (1846–1884). When an unarmed group of blacks showed up to support Crosby, a white mob attacked them, then went on a rampage through the countryside, killing over three hundred blacks. At the polls, armed guards prevented blacks from voting or forced them to vote for Democrats. Economic forms of coercion were also used, as blacks were threatened with the loss of their jobs—or even the denial of medical treatment—if they voted for Republicans.

Mississippi governor Adelbert Ames (1835–1933) was shocked by these developments, but felt powerless to stop them. He issued a proclamation ordering the private militias to disband, but it was ignored. Ames appealed to President Grant to send federal troops to help stem the violence, but the

Mississippi governor Adelbert Ames. *The Library of Congress.*

request was refused. As noted in *The Era of Reconstruction: 1865–1877,* Attorney General Edwards Pierrepont (1817–1892) informed Ames that people were "tired of these annual autumnal outbreaks in the South." This was yet another indication that Northern interest in the South and the problems of Southern blacks was waning.

On election day, scores of Mississippi blacks were either too scared to show up at the polls or driven away as soon as they arrived. In Aberdeen, the White Liners set up a cannon and sent armed thugs through the crowds of waiting voters, and the town's Republican sheriff actually locked himself in his own jail for safety. The town's election results typify what happened throughout the state: The Democrats won with a majority of 1,175 votes, even though in 1871 the Republicans had had a majority of 648.

Mississippi had now been redeemed. Thoroughly disgusted, Governor Ames wrote to his wife, as quoted in *Reconstruction and Reaction: The Emancipation of Slaves, 1861–1913:* "Yes, a revolution has taken place— by force of arms—and a race disenfranchised—they are to be returned to a condition of serfdom—an era of second slavery." The following March, the Democrats invented outrageously false charges against Ames in order to threaten him with impeachment (an attempt to remove him from office), so Ames left the state. Within a year, Mississippi's Republican Party had dissolved.

The downfall of Reconstruction begins

Another outcome of the 1874 elections was that the Republicans lost control of the U.S. House of Representatives, which they had dominated for so many years. Responding to both the nationwide economic depression and the corruption of the Grant administration, voters turned against the

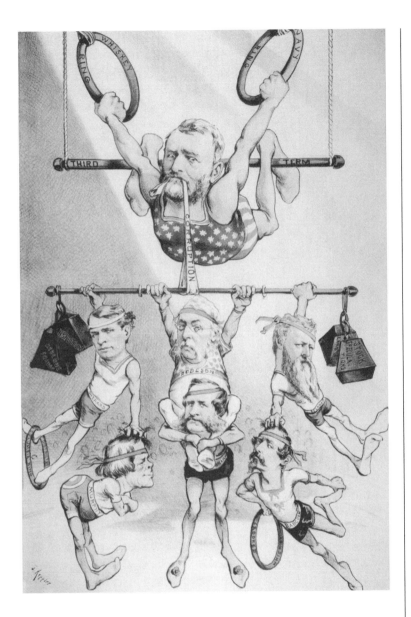

A political cartoon by Joseph Keppler in an 1880 issue of *Puck* magazine looks back at the corrupt administration of Ulysses S. Grant, while attacking the prospect of a reelection bid by the former president.
The Granger Collection, New York. Reproduced by permission.

ruling party. Before the election, the Republicans had had a 110-vote majority in the House, and now the Democrats had a majority of 60. With the South now holding half of the committee chairs in Congress, the prospect of continued federal intervention in Southern affairs seemed unlikely.

Thus during his second term as president, Grant presided over a retreat from the Reconstruction policies so carefully crafted by the Radical Republicans. As he lay dying

The cover of a booklet of campaign songs promoting Democratic presidential candidate Samuel Tilden, who received more popular votes than his opponent, Republican Rutherford B. Hayes, but who lost the presidency by one electoral vote. © *Bettmann/Corbis.*

in March 1874, one of these old Radicals, Charles Sumner, had urged his colleagues to push through one more piece of legislation to try to safeguard equality for all U.S. citizens. In Sumner's honor, Congress passed this legislation, the Civil Rights Act of 1875, which guaranteed civil and political rights and also prohibited segregation (separation of people by race) in public places and, most notably, in public schools. The act, however, laid the burden of enforcement at the door of black litigants (those involved in a lawsuit) and was not effective.

In addition, during the next decade the Supreme Court would undo many of the gains of the early 1870s in a series of decisions known collectively as the Slaughterhouse Cases. In effect, these rulings denied blacks the right to use the federal courts to fight unfair state laws. In 1875, a ruling on women's suffrage that the U.S. Constitution did not "confer the right of suffrage on anyone" had a negative impact on blacks. The next year, in the *United States v. Cruikshank* case (which arose out of a bloody racial incident known as the Colfax Massacre), the Court voided parts of the Enforcement Acts. Finally, in 1883, the Supreme Court struck down the Civil Rights Act of 1875, ruling it unconstitutional.

The 1876 elections

The Southern state elections of 1876 were as bloody as those held during the previous two years. In South Carolina, Florida, and Louisiana, the Mississippi Plan was again put into effect, with similar results. On the national level, the results of the presidential election gave blacks and those concerned about justice in the South more reason to despair.

Hoping to counteract the negative feelings created by Grant's crooked administration, the Republicans chose a

White supremacists beat a North Carolina freedwoman. *The Granger Collection, New York. Reproduced by permission.*

morally upright but rather bland candidate, Ohio governor Rutherford B. Hayes (1822–1893), whose campaign promises included support for local self-government in the South. The Democratic nominee was New York governor Samuel Tilden (1814–1896). The election was extremely close, and the results set off a political crisis: while Tilden won more popular votes, Hayes had a one-vote lead in the Electoral College (a body of people representing each state, who formally cast votes for the election of the president and vice president). The Republicans immediately proclaimed many Southern votes invalid because of the widespread violence and intimidation used there, while the Democrats contested these charges.

Meanwhile, other crises stemming from Southern election results were brewing. In Louisiana, federal troops surrounded the state capitol, keeping Republican governor William P. Kellogg (1830–1918) in office as a huge mob of White Liners gathered outside, demanding his removal. In South Carolina, Democratic candidate Wade Hampton

Rutherford B. Hayes: An Unthreatening Choice

Chosen as the Republican nominee because of his moderate views and integrity, Ohio governor Rutherford B. Hayes won a close presidential election that ended with a compromise. Its terms meant that he would preside over the end of Reconstruction.

Hayes was born in Delaware, Ohio, in 1822. His parents had earlier migrated from Vermont. His father died before his birth, and he and his sister were raised by their mother. Weak and sickly as a child, Hayes received a good early education. After graduating from Kenyon College in 1842, he entered Harvard Law School and earned his law degree three years later. From 1845 to 1849, he practiced law in Upper Sandusky, Ohio. Then he moved his practice to Cincinnati.

In 1852, Hayes married Lucy Ware Webb (1831–1889), who was involved in various types of reform, such as the temperance movement (which tried to curb people's use of alcohol; when he became president, no alcoholic beverages were served in the White House) and abolitionism. His wife's activism inspired Hayes's own interest in such causes. He began defending runaway slaves for free, and he helped to found the Republican Party in Ohio.

Hayes became city solicitor of Cincinnati in 1858, and he was still in this position in 1861 when the Civil War began. Hayes started organizing local volunteers to serve in the Union army, and in June he was commissioned a major in the Twenty-third Ohio Volunteer Infantry. He served throughout the whole war and was wounded four times. By the end of the war, Hayes had been promoted to major general. Before the war was over, he was elected to the U.S. House of Representatives. Hayes served in Congress for two years, coming out in strong support of the measures proposed by the Radical Republicans for the Reconstruction of the South. His pet project, however, was developing the Library of Congress.

Hayes resigned from Congress in 1867 in order to run for governor of Ohio. He won the election and was reelected in 1869. As governor, he oversaw his state's ratification of the Fifteenth Amendment and the establishment of Ohio State University.

In 1872, Hayes returned to his home in Cincinnati. After an unsuccessful run for Congress, he retired from politics. But when the Republican Party urged him to become its candidate for governor again in 1875, he reluctantly agreed. Hayes was elected, and began serving his third term. The next year, however, facing a presidential election in a period of widespread corruption and public distrust, the national Republican Party chose him as its candidate for president. He was considered a dignified, honest, moderate alternative to the other choices, all of whom seemed to be either too corrupt or too radical. His De-

Rutherford B. Hayes. *The Library of Congress.*

mocratic opponent was New York governor Samuel Tilden.

When the November election results came in, it initially appeared that Hayes had lost. Tilden had won the popular vote, but the Republicans alleged that twenty electoral votes from Florida, Louisiana, South Carolina, and Oregon were invalid owing to election fraud. When Hayes thus won the Electoral College count by a single vote, the Democrats objected. A stalemate that would last into the first months of 1877 began, with neither side willing to concede the election. It was resolved only after a somewhat mysterious series of negotiations resulted in a compromise: the Democrats would accept Hayes's election, and the Republicans agreed to allow "self-government" in the South.

The compromise signaled the end of Reconstruction and the triumph of the so-called Redeemers, who would restore rule by white supremacists (those who believed that whites were superior and should be in charge) in the South. In April, Hayes withdrew federal troops from the state capitols of Louisiana and South Carolina, allowing the Democratic winners of the suspect elections in these states to take office. The new Southern leaders assured Hayes that black civil and political rights would be protected, and the new president thereafter pursued a "let alone" policy toward the South. Meanwhile, the Democratic governments not only broke their promises to Hayes but eventually established the "Jim Crow" system (separation of people by race) of legalized and restricted rights that would dominate the South well into the twentieth century.

Hayes had resolved to serve only one term as president, and he was true to his word. His successor was a fellow Ohioan and Republican, James A. Garfield (1831–1881; served 1881). After leaving office, Hayes set out on a nearly three-month tour of the West, during which he traveled by a colorful variety of vehicles that ranged from a train to a stagecoach to a ferry boat. He enjoyed a very active retirement that included work on such causes as black education and prison reform as well as organizing veterans' reunions. Hayes died in Fremont, Ohio, in 1893.

Prominent Redeemer Wade Hampton

Wade Hampton was a Confederate war hero who sat out most of the Reconstruction era but became the governor of South Carolina once the "Redeemer" movement restored white supremacist rule in the Southern states.

Born into a wealthy family that was a well-established part of the Southern aristocracy, Hampton grew up on the Millwood plantation in South Carolina. His father raised cotton and thoroughbred horses and owned hundreds of slaves. Hampton graduated from South Carolina College in 1836 and—despite having studied law—returned to manage his family's plantations, including several in Mississippi.

He was elected to the South Carolina state legislature in 1852 and reelected twice before becoming a senator in 1856. He resigned that position in 1861. Although Hampton had not approved of the idea of secession (separation from the Union), once it occurred he gave his full support to the Confederacy, offering both money and military service to the cause. As an infantry officer, he was wounded at the battle of Manassas. His military skills were noticed by his superiors and he was promoted to brigadier general in May 1862. After being wounded again in the battle of Seven Pines, Hampton became second in command of a cavalry unit and took part in several major battles. At Gettysburg, he was wounded a third time. He took command of all Confederate cavalry forces in May 1864.

After the war, Hampton returned to South Carolina. Most of his fortune had been lost during the war, and he spent the Reconstruction years tending to his plantations. By the mid-1870s, the white Democrats of the South had determined to restore their power by whatever means necessary. Nominated for governor in 1876, Hampton entered into the campaign with gusto. He took what was known as a "cooperationist" approach, attempting to attract the African American vote by supporting some limited rights for

(1818–1902)—while calling for racial peace and referring to blacks as his "true friends"—had won the gubernatorial election through a program of violence carried out by supporters called the Red Shirts, who appeared on horseback wearing shirts that were intentionally the color of blood. Republicans refused to accept the election results, and Governor Daniel Chamberlain (1835–1907) remained in office. As in Louisiana, the South Carolina state capitol was surrounded by federal troops.

Wade Hampton. *The Library of Congress.*

groups like the Ku Klux Klan had used to keep blacks away from the polls as through his popularity. When Republican governor Daniel Chamberlain and his supporters refused to concede the election to Hampton, a standoff began at the state capitol, with Chamberlain kept in office only through the presence of Union troops. It ended with the compromise by which Democrats agreed to accept the election of Republican presidential candidate Rutherford B. Hayes and the Hayes administration agreed to leave the South alone to manage its own affairs. The troops were withdrawn from South Carolina, and Hampton took office.

blacks and emphasizing racial peace. At the same time, however, he was always accompanied by an imposing band of mounted supporters called "Red Shirts," whose clothing was intended to mimic the color of blood.

When Hampton won the very close election, it was as much through the organized campaign of terror that white

Reelected in 1878, Hampton subsequently became a U.S. senator, serving in that office until 1891 when he was defeated by Benjamin R. Tillman (1847–1918), the candidate of the Populist Party (a group made up of small farmers and craftsmen). Hampton later served as commissioner of Pacific railroads for nine years. He died in 1902.

A compromise is reached

In Washington, D.C., a series of somewhat mysterious meetings took place at which Republicans and Democrats worked out a deal in which the Democrats would accept Hayes's election in exchange for allowing the Southern states to govern using Home Rule. Thus, they would be empowered to complete the process of Redemption. On April 10, 1877, Hayes ordered the federal troops to leave South Carolina's capitol, and Hampton took power. Two weeks later, federal troops also marched away from Louisiana's state house in Baton Rouge, leaving Democrats in control of that state.

For most historians and students of history, these events signaled the end of the Reconstruction era. As noted by black Louisiana citizen Henry Adams and quoted in *Reconstruction and Reaction: The Emancipation of Slaves, 1861–1913,* "The whole South—every state in the South—had got into the hands of the very men that held us as slaves." In the North, as reported in *A Short History of Reconstruction,* the magazine the *Nation* predicted that "the negro will disappear from the field of national politics. Henceforth, the nation, as a nation, will have nothing more to do with him."

Indeed, it seemed that the nation as a whole had completely forsaken its black citizens. For the rest of Hayes's administration, he would follow a "let alone" policy toward the South. The Southern states would be overtaken by white supremacy, and blacks would be pushed out of politics and public life. Within the next few decades, the oppressive laws known as the Jim Crow system—which made segregation a legal fact of life in the South—would be put in place. (The name "Jim Crow" came from the black minstrel shows popular during the era, which featured exaggerated, stereotypical black characters.) During the earlier years of the Reconstruction era, the federal government had felt a responsibility to protect the fundamental rights of all U.S. citizens. It would be many years before it would again take up that responsibility. Meanwhile, African Americans would continue to hope, work, and struggle for expanded educational opportunities, for civil and political rights, and for the equality promised in both the Declaration of Independence and the U.S. Constitution.

For More Information

Books

Ayers, Edward L. *The Promise of the New South: Life After Reconstruction.* New York: Oxford University Press, 1992.

Benedict, Michael Les. *A Compromise of Principle: Congressional Republicans and Reconstruction, 1863–1869.* New York: Norton, 1974.

Cox, LaWanda C., and Cox, John H., eds. *Reconstruction, the Negro, and the New South.* New York: Harper & Row, 1973.

Foner, Eric. *Freedom's Lawmakers: A Directory of Black Officeholders During Reconstruction.* Baton Rouge: Louisiana State University Press, 1996.

Foner, Eric. *A Short History of Reconstruction.* New York: Harper & Row, 1990.

Golay, Michael. *Reconstruction and Reaction: The Emancipation of Slaves, 1861–1913.* New York: Facts on File, 1996.

Litwack, Leon, and August Meier, eds. *Black Leaders of the Nineteenth Century.* Urbana: University of Illinois Press, 1988.

Perman, Michael. *The Road to Redemption: Southern Politics, 1869–1879.* Chapel Hill: University of North Carolina Press, 1984.

Smith, John David. *Black Voices from Reconstruction, 1865–1877.* Gainesville: University of Florida Press, 1997.

Stampp, Kenneth M. *The Era of Reconstruction: 1865–1877.* New York: Vintage Books, 1965.

Wagner, Margaret E., Gary W. Gallagher, and Paul Finkelman, eds. *Civil War Desk Reference.* New York: Simon & Schuster, 2002.

Wharton, Vernon L. *The Negro in Mississippi, 1865–1900.* New York: Harper & Row, 1965.

Williams, Lou Faulkner. *The Great South Carolina Ku Klux Klan Trials, 1871–1872.* Athens: University of Georgia Press, 1996.

Web Sites

Louisiana State University. *The United States Civil War Center.* http://www.cwc.lsu.edu/ (accessed on August 31, 2004).

"Reconstruction." *African American History.* http://afroamhistory.about.com/od/reconstruction/ (accessed on August 31, 2004).

"Reference Resources: Civil War." *Kidinfo.* http://www.kidinfo.com/American_History/Civil_War.html (accessed on August 31, 2004).

"US Civil War." *Internet Modern History Sourcebook.* http://www.fordham.edu/halsall/mod/modsbook27.html (accessed on August 31, 2004).

The Mixed Legacy of the Reconstruction Era

Union army general Rufus Saxton (1824–1908) had long been a friend to African Americans. He had been on hand in the Sea Islands (located off the coasts of South Carolina and Georgia) in the summer of 1865, just after the end of the Civil War (1861–65). For a brief period, it appeared that the federal government would soon be distributing free land to the newly freed slaves, in recognition of the many years of unpaid labor they had provided and in compensation for the crime of slavery. The collapse of that promise was just one of many disappointments that African Americans had endured, and Saxton had shared in that disappointment.

In a letter written many years later to black South Carolina politician Robert Smalls (1839–1915), Saxton remembered a happier day: January 1, 1863, when the Emancipation Proclamation (a document issued by President Abraham Lincoln [1809–1865] that declared most slaves free) was signed. Describing the celebration of that event in Beaufort, South Carolina, Saxton, quoted in *Reconstruction and Reaction: The Emancipation of Slaves, 1861–1913*, wrote: "Never in

Civil rights movement: A political, civil, and social struggle that took place in the middle of the twentieth century. Seeking full citizenship and equality for African Americans, the movement challenged segregation and discrimination through such activities as protest marches, boycotts, and refusals to go along with racist laws.

Exoduster movement: A migration made up of African Americans who, following the overthrow of the multiracial Reconstruction governments in the South by white supremacist "Redeemers," migrated to the new western state of Kansas. They sought a greater degree of political

equality, expanded educational and economic opportunities, and an escape from racial violence.

Jim Crow: The system of legalized segregation found in the South beginning in the 1890s that mandated the segregation of schools and other public facilities.

Lynch law: A brutal system of justice by which blacks accused of crimes but usually not formally charged or tried would be hanged by mobs of whites.

Plessy v. Ferguson: A U.S. Supreme Court case regarding segregation of the railroads. Asserting that the Fourteenth

all his round did a glad sun shine upon a scene of more dramatic power. What a day of promise that was!"

Promises broken

Unfortunately, that promise went mostly unfulfilled. Black and white citizens of the regions known as the North and the South had just completed a bloody war to determine both if the United States would remain one country and if slavery would continue to exist in the nation. During the Reconstruction era, the period stretching roughly from the end of the Civil War in 1865 to the inauguration of President Rutherford B. Hayes (1822–1893; served 1877–81) in 1877, the black and white citizens of both the North and the South had participated in a great effort. They had attempted to remake a Southern society that had been devastated, both materially and socially, by four years of war. The outcome of that war had dramatically changed the ways in which both the Southern economy (which had been dependent on the

Amendment was never intended to prevent "social" segregation, the court found that segregation was acceptable as long as black passengers were provided with "equal" accommodations.

Reconstruction era: The period stretching roughly from the end of the Civil War in April 1865 to the inauguration of President Rutherford B. Hayes in 1877. During Reconstruction, representatives of the U.S. government—including the president and Congress—and the military would join with both white and black Southerners to try to reorganize the political and social structure of the devastated, defeated South.

Redemption movement: The successful effort, which took place between 1869 and 1877, to overthrow or "redeem" the Republican governments and replace its leaders with men devoted to white supremacy.

Second Mississippi Plan: A concerted effort by the Redeemer governments to prevent blacks from voting. Whereas the first Mississippi Plan had used terror to accomplish this goal, the second featured the inclusion of new voting laws or "suppression clauses" in state constitutions that restricted voting through literacy and property requirements, poll taxes, and "understanding clauses."

unpaid labor of four million black slaves) and relationships between its people were ordered.

In the late 1860s and early 1870s, owing to some landmark legislation that a group called the Radical Republicans had pushed through Congress, the governments of the eleven Southern states that had previously seceded (separated themselves) from the Union were reformed in a shape never before seen in the United States, and not to be repeated for many decades after their downfall. They were multiracial democracies in which both blacks and whites were full participants. Whereas most African Americans had previously existed as noncitizens with no rights at all, they were now guaranteed by the U.S. Constitution the same civil and political rights long enjoyed by whites.

These revolutionary circumstances created a climate of hope, in which black Southerners dared to believe that they would one day achieve full equality with whites.

Through a combination of factors, though, most of their hopes were dashed. Economic hardships and complexities proved a formidable obstacle to advancement, as did the waning interest of those powerful Northern supporters who had lent their energies and concern to the South. What proved most devastating, however, was the opposition of white Southerners, who simply could not envision or tolerate a world in which blacks and whites were equals. This resistance took the form of a loosely organized but deadly campaign of terror that involved attacks—including arson, beatings, whippings, rape, and murder—on blacks and their sympathizers. The central purpose of this brutality was to scare blacks into submission, to keep them from exercising their hard-won rights—especially the right to vote.

Reconstruction is dismantled, and the "Redemption" begins

One by one, beginning as early as 1869, the Southern states were "redeemed": they were taken back into control by the white supremacists (those who believe that people of northern European descent are inherently superior to others and ought to be in charge) who had ruled the South before the Civil War. Having previously taken an activist role in guiding Southern developments and trying to ensure justice for blacks, the federal government now turned away. The contested 1876 election of Republican Rutherford B. Hayes was resolved with a promise that, if the Democrats would accept Hayes's election, the government would leave the South alone to govern itself as it wished. The election, marked in the South by violence and election fraud, also sealed the fate of the last three states to be redeemed.

In later years, the story of this period told by white Southerners—and even by the Northern historians who shared their racist views of blacks as inferior to whites in intelligence and morality—would depict the Reconstruction era governments as hopelessly corrupt and incompetent. They would imply that a gang of dishonest, inept, illiterate (unable to read and write) blacks, aided by the Northern participants scornfully referred to as "carpetbaggers" (an offensive term for Northerners who came to the South after the Civil War to participate in Reconstruction), had been in charge of the South. They would insist that whites had been victimized by blacks, carpetbaggers, and scalawags (an offensive term for white Republicans who took part in Reconstruction) who had tried to get away with as much as they could.

Black achievements are reversed

By the later part of the twentieth century, revisionist historians had marshaled the facts to suggest a different scenario. They proved that in fact, most scalawags and carpetbaggers were well intentioned and competent, while many Democrats (the political party that had dominated the prewar years in the South) were also involved in corruption. Perhaps most significantly, they also showed that blacks actually held relatively few major offices in the Reconstruction governments. There had been no black governors, for instance, and only a few who had held such high offices as lieutenant governor or state treasurer; only two had been elected to the U.S. Senate, while fourteen had served in the U.S. House of Representatives, and blacks had held a majority only in the South Carolina state legislature.

Nevertheless, the achievements of blacks during this era had been remarkable, especially considering that so many of them had so recently been slaves with no access to education or political training. About six hundred served in state legislatures, and many more held local offices (such as sheriff and justice of the peace). For a few brief years, the Southern states had been the nearest thing to multiracial democracies ever seen in the nation, and such governments were not to be seen again for many, many years. As noted in *A Short History of Reconstruction*, "The tide of change rose and then receded, but it left behind an altered landscape."

Many of the changes that now occurred, as the Redeemer governments took control, happened very gradually. The new leaders were a loose group of Democrats and Unionists (supporters of the Union during the Civil War) who came both from the wealthy class of professionals and owners of plantations (large estates on which basic crops like cotton, tobacco, rice, and sugar were grown) and the middle or working classes of small farmers, many of whom lived in the up-country regions of the South. Although some tensions existed between these groups, all were united in their determination to remove every trace of Reconstruction. They especially wanted to take political power away from blacks and to ensure white control over the black labor force.

New governments lower taxes, cut services

One of the biggest complaints against the Reconstruction governments was that they had raised taxes in order to pay for new public services such as school systems, prisons, and medical care for the poor. Before the war, plantation owners had paid few taxes on their property, and they resented their new obligations. So one of the first goals of the Redeemer governments was to slash property taxes and reduce state expenses. They put more of a burden on sharecroppers (farmers who produced crops on land rented from large landowners, with whom they shared their proceeds) and small farmers and laborers, who now had to pay taxes on many items, including tools. Meanwhile, in a regressive tax system (in which those who own the least property bear the biggest burden), people who owned large quantities of land paid little.

Not surprisingly, the new governments also backed away from the idea that the state should take on social responsibilities. Some now claimed they could not afford to fund public schools, and the gap between spending on schools for black and white students began to widen. Florida closed its state prison and stopped construction on the state's first agricultural college, while Alabama shut down its public hospitals. All across the South, governments showed that they felt no obligation to educate or provide free care for its citizens.

Black options narrow

Long considered the champion of black equality, the Republican Party began to disappear from the South as the campaign of violence and election fraud waged against those who dared to vote the Republican ticket took its toll. As the years passed, blacks held fewer and fewer seats in state legislatures and local governments, while those who remained in office faced strong hostility and opposition from the Democrats who dominated politics. This showed how successful the white supremacists had been in keeping blacks from the polls; for example, in Mississippi's Amite County, 1,093 blacks had voted in 1873, but three years later only 73 cast ballots.

Although the system of segregation known as "Jim Crow" (the name came from the black minstrel shows popular during the era, which featured exaggerated, stereotypical black characters) was not formalized until the 1890s, black people's political, economic, and social options were already being narrowed. New laws reminiscent of the very strict Black Codes (in which laws were put in place by the Southern governments during the administration of President Andrew Johnson [1808–1875; served 1865–69] that returned power to the former leaders of the Confederacy) reinforced plantation owners' control over their labor force. Vagrancy laws, for example, once again made joblessness illegal, and workers could be arrested for leaving a job before a contract had expired.

Most black Southerners were now working as sharecroppers, in a system that they preferred to the kind of gang-labor that had prevailed during slavery because it gave them more control over their time, work conditions, and families. But sharecropping also confined many blacks to a cycle of poverty and debt, for they were often forced to carry credit (incurred because they had to buy supplies before their crops were harvested) over from year to year, with no hope of ever catching up. Now the Redeemer governments increased the plantation owners' control over credit and property. The Landlord and Tenant Act of 1877, for example, made the entire crop the planters' property until rent was paid, and left it to the planter to decide when the tenant had fulfilled his obligations. Meanwhile, all efforts to organize workers into unions were quickly crushed.

A harsher criminal code

The Reconstruction governments had changed the penal code (the system of penalties for crimes), which had allowed for harsh penalties that were more often given to black defendants. The Redeemers now reversed that action. Those convicted of theft, for instance, faced a very high penalty.

Arson was a capital offense, and a conviction for burglary could bring a life sentence. Under Mississippi's "pig law," someone who stole a pig or a cow (or any property worth more than $10) was automatically sentenced to five years in prison.

Throughout the South, the convict lease system was expanded. This allowed states to hire out prison inmates as laborers, often to do the most backbreaking, least desirable jobs that were otherwise hard to fill. The railroad, mining, and lumber industries all benefitted from this practice. Among these workers (most of whom were blacks imprisoned for minor crimes), death rates were very high; in a group of 204 convicts, for example, 20 died and 23 were returned to prison either ill or disabled, all within a 6-month period.

During Reconstruction, a considerable number of Southern cities and towns had had African American sheriffs and police officers, which had been a positive development in the eyes of blacks, who had often been treated unfairly by white law enforcement officers. Now there were few blacks on police forces or in state militias (a military force raised from a civilian population, to supplement regular army forces in an emergency).

A new kind of society takes shape

All these changes created an unusual economic situation in the South, where a small upper class of planters, merchants, and manufacturers prospered but the majority of citizens—both black and white—lived in poverty. By 1880, in fact, Southerners' average income level was only 40 percent of that of the North. Blacks were, not surprisingly, hardest hit by the South's economic woes, for many of them still suffered from such problems as illiteracy, malnutrition, and inadequate housing.

In some ways, however, blacks benefitted from the necessity of turning their focus inward. People with talent and ambition who might have gone into politics, if such an avenue had been open to them, turned their energies to education, business (opening stores, restaurants, barbershops, and funeral homes, for instance, that catered to black customers), the church, and the professions. Black educational

institutions like Fisk, Howard, and Alcorn universities survived, and their graduates' accomplishments enriched black life. Thus strong black communities were built in many towns and cities, providing what would be a solid springboard for the civil rights movement of the 1950s and 1960s.

Not all African Americans, however, were willing to passively accept their diminished status and opportunities. The triumph of the Redeemers led some blacks to consider migration, with a few training their sights on Africa but more focusing on the wide open grasslands of Kansas. Members of what was called the "Exoduster" movement believed that they would find a greater degree of political equality and an escape from the violence that plagued the South. There they would enjoy expanded educational and economic opportunities and—perhaps most attractive of all—they would no longer live side by side with the white Southerners who despised them. Even though black leaders like Frederick Douglass (c. 1817–1895) opposed the idea of migration because it

Four scenes show the coming and going of Exoduster migrants in St. Louis, Missouri. Top, the travelers leave St. Louis for Kansas. Bottom left, arrival by steamboat in St. Louis; center, members of a black church provide food and rest; and right, representatives of St. Louis's African American community greet arriving migrants.
© *Bettmann/Corbis.*

seemed like an abandonment of the struggle for equality in the South, a significant number of ordinary blacks joined what came to be known as the Exodus. For the vast majority, however, moving away from South—whether to Africa or the West—was simply not a practical option.

A grim time for African Americans

As noted in *Reconstruction and Reaction: The Emancipation of Slaves, 1861–1913*, the great black intellectual W. E. B. Du Bois (1868–1963), commenting on the period that followed Reconstruction, wrote that enslaved blacks "went free, stood a brief moment in the sun; then moved back again toward slavery." Du Bois would come to lead a new wave of activism in the early twentieth century. The waning years of the nineteenth century were grim ones for African Americans. An inhumane, illegal system of punishment called "lynch law" was practiced, by which blacks accused of crimes but usually not formally charged or tried would be brutally hanged by mobs of whites. During the 1890s, more than 150 such lynchings occurred, and the practice continued well into the twentieth century.

In 1887, Florida passed the first of the Jim Crow laws that would, as they spread across the South, make the segregation of schools and public facilities absolute. From now on, in addition to the traditional separation of black and white churches and schools, hospitals, prisons, hotels, restaurants, parks, and drinking fountains would be segregated. There would be separate waiting rooms, elevators, and cemeteries for blacks. Nearly every aspect of life would be divided to maintain a physical distance between black and white Southerners.

Plessy v. Ferguson

The controversial issue of segregation on the railroads, which was encoded into law in nine states, resulted in a Supreme Court ruling that would stand for more than fifty years. After several lower courts had ruled that segregation of the railroads was acceptable as long as black passengers were provided with "equal" accommodations, the case of *Plessy v. Ferguson* came before the Supreme Court. After purchasing a first-class ticket, a black Louisiana resident named Adolph Plessy (1862–1925) had refused to leave a whites-only railroad car. In his defense, he cited the Fourteenth Amendment, which supposedly outlawed discrimination on the basis of skin color.

The Court disagreed. It ruled against Plessy and in favor of the "separate but equal" doctrine, claiming, as quoted in *Reconstruction and Reaction: The Emancipation of Slaves, 1861–1913*, that the Fourteenth Amendment "could not have been intended to abolish distinctions based upon color, or to enforce social, as distinguished from political, equality." Thus the legality of the "separate but equal" concept was reinforced, even though it was widely known that separate most assuredly did *not* mean equal. The idea and its application would survive until 1954, when the Supreme Court struck it down in the landmark *Brown v. Board of Education* decision.

The Second Mississippi Plan

Keeping blacks under control required, more than anything else, preventing them from voting. When violence and election fraud became too much of a burden, the Redeemer governments turned to legal restrictions to keep blacks away from the ballot box. The state of Mississippi took the lead in an effort known as the "Second Mississippi Plan" (the first had been the campaign of terror that prevented blacks from voting in the elections of the mid-1870s; see Chapter 8). The state constitution was rewritten with new voting laws that, while still technically meeting the requirements of the U.S. Constitution, put on the books a number of "suppression clauses" designed to deny blacks—the majority of whom were poor and uneducated—the right to vote.

Examples include education and property qualifications, a poll tax (money to be paid before voting), and finally an "understanding clause" that required a voter to prove that he could read and understand a part of the state constitution. Blacks doubted that many white voters (a large number of whom were as little educated as blacks) would really have been able to pass this test. As it turned out, only 10 percent of blacks qualified to vote under the new laws, while two-thirds of whites did. The total number of voters in Mississippi was thus reduced from 257,000 to 76,000, almost all of them white.

Booker T. Washington: Dynamic Leader or Accommodationist?

The most prominent and respected black leader of the late nineteenth century, Booker T. Washington promoted a philosophy of advancement through self-sufficiency and accommodation to segregation. Although this approach initially held great appeal for both blacks and whites, the African American intellectuals of a later generation came to reject it.

Washington was born in 1856, the son of a slave mother who worked as a cook on a Virginia plantation. The identity of his white father is not known. After the Civil War, Washington moved with his family to Malden, West Virginia, where he worked for a short period in the area's salt furnaces and coal mines before becoming a house servant. He was able to attend school, and in 1872 he entered Hampton Institute, which was one of the first major educational institutions established for blacks.

Hampton Institute had been founded by Samuel Chapman Armstrong (1839–1893), whose belief in education based on practical skills would be carried on by Washington. After graduating in 1875, Washington returned to Malden to work as a teacher, but he soon came back to Hampton Institute as an instructor and was put in charge of some Native American students who had been sent to the school to learn about white farming methods.

In 1881, Washington was chosen by Armstrong to be the principal of a new, as yet unbuilt school in Tuskegee, Alabama. Washington supervised the school's construction, and by 1888 there were four hundred students studying such trades as farming, carpentry, shoemaking, and cooking on a campus of 400 acres. At the Tuskegee Institute, students were taught that self-respect, practical skills, strict discipline, cleanliness, and thrift would bring them economic independence and success. Segregation was seen as a fact of life that was not worth fighting.

As the leader of what soon became the most influential of African American institutions, Washington wielded considerable power; it was said that the "Tuskegee machine" could make or break careers. He was in great demand as a public speaker. One of Washington's most famous appearances was at the Cotton States and International Exposition, held in Atlanta, Georgia, in 1895. In a speech referred to as the "Atlanta Compromise," Washington told a white audience that economic equality was more important to blacks than social equality.

This message appealed to many whites, and it probably helped him maintain the valuable connections he established with rich, socially conscientious white men like Andrew Carnegie (1835–1919), George Eastman (1854–1932), and

Booker T. Washington. *The Library of Congress.*

Julius Rosenwald (1862–1932), who contributed money to Washington's cause. One of these causes was the National Negro Business League, which Washington founded in 1900 in order to help African Americans achieve success in business. The next year marked the appearance of Washington's autobiography, *Up from Slavery,* which inspired both black and white readers with the story of a slave boy who grew up to achieve remarkable things.

Yet Washington's voice was notably silent about the injustices that were everyday realities in the lives of blacks, especially those living in the South, where Jim Crow laws restricted both behavior and rights. Later researchers discovered that Washington did, in fact, take part in some secret activism; for example, he provided funding for lawsuits to challenge some of the Jim Crow laws.

As hate crimes against blacks increased, a new generation of black thinkers and leaders emerged, equipped with an outlook decidedly different from Washington's. They thought that blacks should pursue education for its own sake and not just to learn a trade. They also believed that African Americans should demand the rights they were owed as U.S. citizens. The most prominent of these leaders, W. E. B. Du Bois, founded the Niagara Movement (which eventually became the National Association for the Advancement of Colored People, or NAACP) in 1905. The movement called for unqualified equality for blacks, and even approved of violence as a means to achieve it.

The African American community was now split into two groups, with the new generation criticizing Washington and his followers for quietly putting up with segregation, racism, and injustice. They also alleged that Washington had overlooked the growing population of urban African Americans, focusing instead on rural blacks. Nevertheless, Washington remained active as a speaker and public figure until his death in 1915. By that time, the student population at Tuskegee Institute had grown to fifteen hundred students.

W. E. B. Du Bois: A More Militant Form of Activism

An important figure in the African American community for many decades of the twentieth century, W. E. B. Du Bois called for militant activism and an immediate end to inequality and injustice. Born in predominantly white Great Barrington, Massachusetts, in 1868, Du Bois grew up mostly sheltered from racism. An excellent and industrious student, he attended Fisk University in Tennessee in the 1880s, where he experienced for the first time the harsh realities of the Jim Crow system of legalized segregation of blacks and whites and discrimination against African Americans.

After three years at Fisk, Du Bois transferred to Harvard University. He earned a bachelor's degree in 1888 and a master's degree in 1891, then set out on two years of travel and study overseas. On his return, he entered Harvard again, and in 1895 became the first black to earn a doctorate of philosophy (Ph.D.) from that university. Du Bois spent the next fifteen years teaching economics and history at Atlanta University. In 1896, he wed Nina Gomer (1872–1950); the marriage would last until her death in 1950.

In 1903, Du Bois published *The Souls of Black Folk,* which would become one of the most influential works documenting the injustices committed against African Americans since the Civil War. Du Bois hoped the book would educate and influence white audiences and thus somehow stem the violence that was occurring across the South in the late nineteenth and early twentieth centuries. Instead, the violence continued and even intensified.

Increasingly convinced that only protest would bring about change, Du Bois founded the Niagara Movement in 1905. Its members demanded immediate and total equality—that is, not only political and civil rights but an end to segregation and other forms of social discrimination—a stance that put them in opposition to the accommodationist approach taken by Booker T. Washington and his followers. Eventually the Niagara Movement became the National Association for the Advance-

Meanwhile, a new political movement called Populism was gathering steam across the nation, but in the South, at least, it was not one that favored expanded rights for blacks. Made up mostly of small farmers and poor whites, the Populist movement was opposed to the political dominance of the wealthy, conservative class of planters and professionals. Although they supported improved schools, tax reform, and other progressive actions, their devotion to a more democratic society did not extend to African Ameri-

W. E. B. Du Bois. *The Library of Congress.*

ment of Colored People (NAACP). Du Bois served as the editor of the organization's publication *The Crisis* for twenty-four years.

Du Bois viewed black advancement as an international issue, and in 1919 he helped organize the first of several Pan African Congresses. Participants called for an end to the European dominance of African countries, which had been colo-

nized by such countries as Great Britain, Portugal, and Germany for several centuries. Du Bois's increasingly radical positions led to his being forced to resign from his *Crisis* post in 1934. He returned to Atlanta University and taught for ten years.

During the course of the 1940s and 1950s, Du Bois grew more and more sympathetic to the aims of communism (a system of government in which a nation's leaders are selected by a single political party that controls all aspects of society), which made him a target of suspicion to the democratic U.S. government. In 1951, the now eighty-three-year-old Du Bois was arrested and tried as an agent of the Soviet Union. Although the charges were eventually dropped, Du Bois continued to be harassed by the government and had his passport taken away for six years. In 1961, he officially joined the Communist Party USA (CPUSA). Almost immediately he was invited by Kwame Nkrumah (1909–1972), the president of Ghana, to make his home in that West African nation. Du Bois died in Ghana's capital, Accra, in 1963.

cans. In fact, one of the most famous and respected Populist leaders, Benjamin R. Tillman (1847–1918), had actually written South Carolina's "understanding clause."

Two new black leaders emerge

Toward the end of the nineteenth century, a new African American leader emerged in the South. Born a slave in Virginia in 1856, Booker T. Washington (1856–1915) grad-

W. E. B. DuBois (seated) with, from left to right, F. H. M. Murray, Lafayette M. Hershaw, and William Monroe Trotter at a Niagara Movement meeting in Harpers Ferry, West Virginia, 1906.

uated from Hampton Institute (a black college) in 1875. Six years later, he became principal of Tuskegee Institute in Alabama, which would become a leading center for black education and activism. Washington urged blacks to acquire vocational training (in the skilled trades, for example) rather than formal education as the best route toward progress. In his famous Atlanta Compromise speech in 1895, he told a white audience that blacks were more interested in economic advancement than in political and social equality. Washington urged African Americans to practice the values of patience and hard work while waiting and preparing for full citizenship, and he accepted segregation as inevitable given the hostility between the races.

Impressed by Washington's dynamic leadership and practical advice, many blacks became his followers. His views offended some, however, especially up-and-coming black intellectuals like W. E. B. Du Bois, who became Washington's harshest critic. Educated at Fisk and Harvard universities, Du Bois helped to spark a new trend in black activism. His belief that blacks should seek liberal education and not vocational training and that they should actively pursue equality, not wait for whites to grant it, caused a split with Washington and his followers. Du Bois's beliefs were the basis for the Niagara Movement which, as he wrote in his autobiography, demanded for African Americans "every single right that belongs to the freeborn American, political, civil, and social."

The Jubilee, and hard years ahead

The year 1913 marked the fiftieth anniversary of the Emancipation Proclamation, and African Americans across the nation honored the occasion with numerous "Jubilee" celebrations. This was a time to take stock of black achievements and advancements, which included an illiteracy rate that was down from 90 percent in 1865 to 70 percent in 1913. Blacks now owned 128,557 farms, 550,000 homes, and 38,000 businesses. Yet the black middle class was still tiny, with most African Americans still living under distressing conditions of poverty, racism, and limited opportunities.

Just as some members of an earlier generation had viewed departure as a solution to these ills, Southern blacks living in the early years of the twentieth century began a migration that would continue for several decades. In search of greater freedom and more options, they began moving first to the larger Southern cities (the black populations of which increased by 32 percent in the 1890s and 36 percent between 1900 and 1910) and then to the North. The entry of the United States into World War I (1914–18) created a demand for workers, and blacks answered the call, with an estimated two million migrating to Northern cities by 1920. There they lived in densely packed, segregated communities, in which they began to develop a strong sense both of their distinct African American identity and their potential power.

The period of economic downturn known as the Great Depression (1929–41)—sparked by the stock market crash of 1929—caused widespread unemployment, poverty, and suffering for millions of U.S. citizens of all races. But it also gave a boost to the fledgling labor movement, which led the struggle to expand and protect the rights of workers. This, in turn, helped to nurture the civil rights movements, as radical labor organizers from the North went south to try to help black farm workers form unions. Although they did not succeed in their main goal, they did foreshadow the civil rights workers who would spread across the South in the 1950s and 1960s, working to register voters and to overturn the white supremacy that kept African Americans from reaching their full potential.

Evaluating the Reconstruction era

Clearly, the end of the Reconstruction era would usher in a long stretch of years full of hardships, struggle, and accumulating anger and resistance. These years would finally result in the gains of the late twentieth century, as racism—the kind that had been encoded in law, anyway, if

The Twentieth-Century Civil Rights Movement

By the middle of the twentieth century, public outrage over the injustices endured by African Americans since their liberation from slavery, along with the emergence of dynamic black leaders like Dr. Martin Luther King Jr. (1929–1968), helped to create a new wave of momentum. The result was a modern civil rights movement that would dramatically change not only the lives of African Americans but the face of U.S. society itself.

In 1954, in a series of landmark cases known collectively as *Brown v. Board of Education,* the U.S. Supreme Court struck down the policy of "separate but equal" that had been used to justify the segregation of public schools in the South. But it was the 1955 Montgomery Bus Boycott that is more often cited as the spark that set off the civil rights movement. The boycott began when a work-weary black woman named Rosa Parks (1913–) was arrested after refusing to give up her seat to a white passenger on one of the segregated city buses in Montgomery, Alabama. The city's black community quickly mobilized to organize a boycott, which lasted for thirteen months and resulted in the integration of the buses.

Because of the activism of King, whose philosophy of nonviolent resistance struck a chord with many thousands of supporters, and other dedicated opponents (both black and white) of racism and discrimination, the following decade was one of great change. It resulted in the passage of some important pieces of legislation in the mid-1960s, especially the Civil Rights Act and the Voting Rights Act. These acts affirmed the federal government's commitment to protecting the civil and political rights of all the nation's citizens.

As the 1960s progressed, however, black dissatisfaction with their continuing low economic status and limited opportunities mounted. This was especially true within the growing African American communities in the crowded, crime-ridden, inner-city ghettoes of the North and West. In contrast to King's nonviolent approach, leaders like Malcolm X (1925–1965) and the Black Panthers called for strong, even armed resistance to oppression.

Beginning in the Harlem section of New York City in the summer of 1964, a series of bloody riots erupted across the nation, resulting in devastating losses of

not always the kind that resided in people's hearts—would be vanquished and African Americans would begin to take their rightful places at all levels of U.S. society. In looking back on Reconstruction, many commentators have labeled this period a failed experiment.

Civil rights activists Ralph Bunche (far left), Dr. Martin Luther King Jr., and his wife Coretta Scott King are seen walking in the march from Selma to Montgomery, Alabama, to protest the segregation of Montgomery's city buses.
© Corbis.

life and property. Racial disturbances rocked the Watts neighborhood of Los Angeles in 1965 and a number of other cities in 1967 (including Detroit, Michigan; Washington, D.C.; Chicago, Illinois; and Atlanta, Georgia).

President Lyndon B. Johnson (1908–1973; served 1963–69) soon ap-pointed a special commission to investi-gate the causes of the riots. The report of the Kerner Commission found that a com-plex mix of factors that included poverty, frustration, and police misbehavior had created explosive conditions in the inner-city ghettoes. The report could not, how-ever, suggest an easy solution to these problems. Meanwhile, more riots broke out in 1968 after the assassination of King, but this time the government responded quickly and strongly.

As the end of the twentieth centu-ry approached, it was clear that African Americans had made great strides in polit-ical, economic, educational, and other areas, becoming fuller members of main-stream U.S. society than ever before. Yet social segregation was still a reality, as were ongoing outbreaks of violence (the Ku Klux Klan, for instance, continued its reign of terror well into the twentieth cen-tury), and the poverty and hopelessness endured by many blacks still presented great obstacles to African American ad-vancement.

In the immediate aftermath of Reconstruction, white supremacists went to work to characterize it as a disaster dur-ing which blacks and carpetbaggers had run amuck through the South, victimizing the white Southerners who should have remained in charge all along. Influential historian

In this scene from D. W. Griffith's *The Birth of a Nation,* Klansmen ride into a Southern town and attack a group of soldiers. *AP/Wide World Photos. Reproduced by permission.*

William A. Dunning (1857–1922) and his followers perpetuated this myth and shaped public thinking dramatically. Thus in the famous and wildly popular 1915 film *The Birth of a Nation* by D. W. Griffith (1875–1948), the white Southerners' cause and even the Ku Klux Klan were glorified and blacks portrayed negatively. The national bestseller *The Tragic Era* by Claude G. Bowers (1878–1958) portrayed blacks and carpetbaggers as villains and whites as their victims.

Meanwhile, the more complex and favorable realities of the Reconstruction governments—which black congressman John Roy Lynch (1847–1939), a lone voice of praise, called "the best those states ever had" in his 1913 book *The Facts of Reconstruction*—faded from the wider public memory. In a scholarly sense, these realities would not be uncovered until the revisionist historians (those who presented revised views of a long-standing opinion of a historical event) who emerged in the latter half of the twentieth century began to publish their research. But within the black community itself, both the achievements and the disappointments of Reconstruction would be long and well remembered.

"Perhaps the remarkable thing about Reconstruction," writes one of the leading revisionists, Eric Foner, "was not its failure but that it was attempted at all and survived as long as it did." Yes, the Redeemers had succeeded in achieving through terror what they could not through legal means. Yes, the rights so briefly enjoyed by African Americans had been swept away, their leaders expelled from public life. (Although South Carolina political boss Robert Smalls had been elected to Congress as late as 1884, many others had died in poverty, like former lieutenant governor Alonzo J. Ransier [1834–1882], also of South Carolina, who ended his life as a Charleston street sweeper.) Still, six hundred blacks had been elected to state legislatures, and many more had served at the state and local levels. Most importantly, three amendments had been added to the U.S. Constitution. The vast importance of these pieces of legislation would come to light again in later years, when they would provide the legal basis for sweeping changes in U.S. society.

Meanwhile, in the scrapbooks and memories of black families would remain the faded pictures of Reconstruction heroes in whom they would, for generations to come, take quiet pride. Along with that pride would exist sadness and even outrage at the way this important period was portrayed. During the Great Depression, interviewers funded by the federal Works Progress Administration traveled through the South, recording their conversations with former slaves. Reflecting on the difference between black impressions of Reconstruction and the popular view of it, one eighty-eight-year-old African American, quoted in *A Short History of Reconstruction,* said, "I know folks think books tell the truth, but they shore don't."

For More Information

Books
Ayers, Edward L. *The Promise of the New South: Life After Reconstruction.* New York: Oxford University Press, 1992.

Cox, LaWanda C., and John H. Cox, eds. *Reconstruction, the Negro, and the New South.* New York: Harper & Row, 1973.

Foner, Eric. *A Short History of Reconstruction.* New York: Harper & Row, 1990.

Golay, Michael. *Reconstruction and Reaction: The Emancipation of Slaves, 1861–1913.* New York: Facts on File, 1996.

Kirchberger, Joe H. *The Civil War and Reconstruction.* New York: Facts on File, 1991.

Litwack, Leon, and August Meier, eds. *Black Leaders of the Nineteenth Century.* Urbana: University of Illinois Press, 1988.

Lynch, John Roy. *Reminiscences of an Active Life.* Chicago: University of Chicago Press, 1970.

Perman, Michael. *The Road to Redemption: Southern Politics, 1869–1879.* Chapel Hill: University of North Carolina Press, 1984.

Smith, John David. *Black Voices from Reconstruction, 1865–1877.* Gainesville: University of Florida Press, 1997.

Stampp, Kenneth M. *The Era of Reconstruction: 1865–1877.* New York: Vintage Books, 1965.

Wagner, Margaret E., Gary W. Gallagher, and Paul Finkelman, eds. *Civil War Desk Reference.* New York: Simon & Schuster, 2002.

Wharton, Vernon L. *The Negro in Mississippi, 1865–1900.* New York: Harper & Row, 1965.

Web Sites

Louisiana State University. *The United States Civil War Center.* http://www.cwc.lsu.edu/ (accessed on August 31, 2004).

"Reconstruction." *African American History.* http://afroamhistory.about.com/od/reconstruction/ (accessed on August 31, 2004).

"Reference Resources: Civil War." *Kidinfo.* http://www.kidinfo.com/American_History/Civil_War.html (accessed on August 31, 2004).

"US Civil War." *Internet Modern History Sourcebook.* http://www.fordham.edu/halsall/mod/modsbook27.html (accessed on August 31, 2004).

Where to Learn More

Books

Anthony, Susan B., Elizabeth Cady Stanton, and Matilda Joslyn Gage, eds. *History of Woman Suffrage.* New York: Fowler & Wells, 1881–1922. Reprint, Salem, NH: Ayer Co., 1985.

Appiah, Kwame Anthony, and Henry Louis Gates Jr., eds. *Africana: The Encyclopedia of the African and African American Experience.* New York: Basic Civitas Books, 1999.

Archer, Jules. *A House Divided: The Lives of Ulysses S. Grant and Robert E. Lee.* New York: Scholastic, 1995.

Ayers, Edward L. *The Promise of the New South: Life After Reconstruction.* New York: Oxford University Press, 1992.

Barney, William L. *The Civil War and Reconstruction: A Student Companion.* New York: Oxford University Press, 2001.

Benedict, Michael Les. *A Compromise of Principle: Congressional Republicans and Reconstruction, 1863–1869.* New York: Norton, 1974.

Berlin, Ira A., et al., eds. *Freedmen: A Documentary History of Emancipation, 1861–1867.* New York: Cambridge University Press, 1982.

Blassingame, John W., ed. *Slave Testimony.* Baton Rouge: Louisiana State University Press, 1977.

Cox, LaWanda C., and John H. Cox, eds. *Reconstruction, the Negro, and the New South.* New York: Harper & Row, 1973.

Crook, William H. *Through Five Administrations: Reminiscences of Colonel William H. Crook*. New York: Harper & Brothers, 1910.

Cruden, Robert. *The Negro in Reconstruction*. Englewood Cliffs, NJ: Prentice Hall, 1969.

Davis, Jefferson. *The Rise and Fall of the Confederate Government*. New York: D. Appleton, 1881. Reprint, New York: Da Capo Press, 1990.

Douglass, Frederick. *Escape from Slavery*. Edited by Michael McCurdy. New York: Knopf, 1994.

Douglass, Frederick. *My Bondage and My Freedom*. New York: Miller, Orton and Mulligan, 1855. Reprint, Urbana: University of Illinois Press, 1987.

Foner, Eric. *Reconstruction: America's Unfinished Revolution, 1863–1877*. New York: Harper & Row, 1988.

Foner, Eric. *A Short History of Reconstruction*. New York: Harper & Row, 1990.

Franklin, John Hope. *Reconstruction After the Civil War*. Chicago: University of Chicago Press, 1961.

Golay, Michael. *Reconstruction and Reaction: The Emancipation of Slaves, 1861–1913*. New York: Facts on File, 1996.

Jenkins, Wilbert L. *Climbing Up to Glory: A Short History of African Americans During the Civil War and Reconstruction*. Wilmington, DE: Scholarly Resources, 2002.

Josephson, Matthew. *The Robber Barons: The Great American Capitalists, 1861–1901*. New York: Harcourt, Brace and Company, 1934. Reprint, 1995.

Kirchberger, Joe H. *The Civil War and Reconstruction*. New York: Facts on File, 1991.

Litwack, Leon F. *Been in the Storm So Long: The Aftermath of Slavery*. New York: Vintage Books, 1979.

Litwack, Leon F., and August Meier, eds. *Black Leaders of the Nineteenth Century*. Urbana: University of Illinois Press, 1988.

Lynch, John Roy. *The Facts of Reconstruction*. New York: Neale Publishing Co., 1913. Reprint, Indianapolis: Bobbs-Merrill, 1970.

Mantell, Martin E. *Johnson, Grant and the Politics of Reconstruction*. New York: Columbia University Press, 1973.

McCulloch, Hugh. *Men and Measures of Half a Century: Sketches and Comments*. New York: C. Scribner's Sons, 1888. Reprint, New York: Da Capo Press, 1970.

McFarlin, Annjennette Sophie, ed. *Black Congressional Reconstruction Orators and Their Orations, 1869–1879*. Metuchen, NJ: Scarecrow Press, 1976.

McKittrick, Eric. L. *Andrew Johnson and Reconstruction*. Chicago: University of Chicago Press, 1960. Reprint, New York: Oxford University Press, 1988.

McPherson, James M. *The Struggle for Equality: Abolitionists and the Negro in the Civil War and Reconstruction*. Princeton, NJ: Princeton University Press, 1965.

Morris, Roy, Jr. *Fraud of the Century: Rutherford B. Hayes, Samuel Tilden, and the Stolen Election of 1876*. New York: Simon & Schuster, 2003.

Murphy, Richard W. *The Nation Reunited: War's Aftermath*. Alexandria, VA: Time-Life Books, 1987.

Oubre, Claude F. *Forty Acres and a Mule: The Freedmen's Bureau and Black Land Ownership*. Baton Rouge: Louisiana State University Press, 1978.

Patrick, Rembert W. *Reconstruction of the Nation*. New York: Oxford University Press, 1967.

Perman, Michael. *The Road to Redemption: Southern Politics, 1869–1879*. Chapel Hill: University of North Carolina Press, 1984.

Rehnquist, William H. *Centennial Crisis: The Disputed Election of 1876*. New York: Alfred A. Knopf, 2004.

Simpson, Brooks D. *The Reconstruction Presidents*. Lawrence: University Press of Kansas, 1998.

Smith, John David. *Black Voices from Reconstruction, 1865–1877*. Gainesville: University of Florida Press, 1997.

Stampp, Kenneth M. *The Era of Reconstruction: 1865–1877*. New York: Vintage Books, 1965.

Stephens, Alexander Hamilton. *Recollections of Alexander H. Stephens: His Diary Kept When a Prisoner at Fort Warren, Boston Harbour, 1865*. New York: Doubleday, 1910. Reprint, Baton Rouge: Louisiana State University Press, 1998.

Trefousse, Hans Louis. *Impeachment of a President: Andrew Johnson, the Blacks, and Reconstruction*. Knoxville: University of Tennessee Press, 1975. Reprint, New York: Fordham University Press, 1999.

Wagner, Margaret E., Gary W. Gallagher, and Paul Finkelman, eds. *Civil War Desk Reference*. New York: Simon & Schuster, 2002.

Wharton, Vernon L. *The Negro in Mississippi, 1865–1900*. New York: Harper & Row, 1965.

Woodward, C. Vann. *Reunion and Reaction: The Compromise of 1877 and the End of Reconstruction*. Boston: Little, Brown, 1951. Reprint, New York: Oxford University Press, 1991.

Web Sites

Civil War Archive. http://www.civilwararchive.com/intro.htm (accessed on September 13, 2004).

The Civil War Homepage. http://www.civil-war.net/ (accessed on September 13, 2004).

Douglass, Frederick. "Reconstruction." *The Atlantic Online*. http://www.theatlantic.com/unbound/flashbks/black/douglas.htm (accessed on July 19, 2004).

"Famous American Trials: The Andrew Johnson Impeachment Trial." *University of Missouri–Kansas City.* http://www.law.umkc.edu/faculty/projects/ftrials/impeach/impeachmt.htm (accessed on July 26, 2004).

Hoemann, George A. *Civil War Homepage.* http://sunsite.utk.edu/civil-war/ (accessed on September 13, 2004).

Library of Congress. "African American Odyssey." *American Memory.* http://memory.loc.gov/ammem/aaohtml/aohome.html (accessed on September 13, 2004).

Louisiana State University. *The United States Civil War Center.* http://www.cwc.lsu.edu/ (accessed on August 31, 2004).

Osborn, Tracey. "Civil War Reconstruction, Racism, the KKK, & the Confederate Lost Cause." *Teacher Oz's Kingdom of History.* http://www.teacheroz.com/reconstruction.htm (accessed on September 13, 2004).

"Reconstruction." *African American History.* http://afroamhistory.about.com/od/reconstruction/ (accessed on August 31, 2004).

"Reference Resources: Civil War." *Kidinfo.* http://www.kidinfo.com/American_History/Civil_War.html (accessed on August 31, 2004).

"US Civil War." *Internet Modern History Sourcebook.* http://www.fordham.edu/halsall/mod/modsbook27.html (accessed on August 31, 2004).

Index

A

Abolitionism, 2
Abolitionists, 13–14
    Douglass, Frederick, 22–23
    Garrison, William Lloyd, 14, 14
        (ill.)
    Johnson, Andrew, and, 35
    Sumner, Charles, 106–7
    Ten Per Cent Plan and, 43
    women's suffrage and, 113, 114
Accommodationists, 200–201
Accommodations, equal access
    to, 150
Activism, African American, 204,
    206–7
Adams, Henry, 186
Advertisements, newspaper, 59
African American churches,
    60–61, 61 (ill.), 62–63
African American ministers, 61,
    63
African American schools, 64, 65
    (ill.)
    churches and, 63
    Freedmen's Bureau and, 87, 109

Southern United States and, 92
African American suffrage, 37, 38,
    44, 71, 130–31. See also Vot-
    ing rights
    becoming reality, 117–18
    Douglass, Frederick, and, 23
    in elections of 1867, 135
    Fourteenth Amendment and,
        112–13
    Johnson, Andrew, and, 94
    Lincoln, Abraham, and, 48
    racial riots and, 115
    Radical Republicans and, 104,
        108
    Republican Party and, 105
African Americans. See also Free
    African Americans; Redemp-
    tion movement; Slavery
    activism of, 204, 206–7
    Black Codes and, 91–94, 93 (ill.)
    celebrate war's end, 47
    citizenship responsibilities and,
        118, 146
    cotton and, 33 (ill.), 40, 42
        (ill.), 157 (ill.)
    courts and, 70

demands of, 130
disenfranchisement of, 140–41,
    160, 161, 162 (ill.), 176–78,
    194–95, 199
education and, 1–2, 46 (ill.),
    64–65, 65 (ill.), 69–70, 92,
    149, 158
educational institutions of, 87,
    196–97, 200–201, 202, 204
in elections of 1867, 135, 137
in elections of 1868, 137,
    140–41, 160
Emancipation Proclamation of
    1863 and, 30–31, 31 (ill.)
employment, 158
equality and, 9, 14, 37
Freedmen's Conventions and,
    127–30
freedom's effects on, 56–65
in Georgia, 39 (ill.)
Howard, Oliver Otis, and, 69,
    86–87
identity questions of, 131
integration and, 5, 134, 150
Johnson, Andrew, and, 81–82,
    94, 105, 109
labor system and, 67, 68,
    156–58
landownership and, 45–47,
    67–68, 83–85, 103, 119–20,
    134–35, 150
in law enforcement, 152, 196
Lincoln, Abraham, and, 48
migrations of, 56–57, 82–83,
    197 (ill.), 197–98, 205
obstacles faced by, 127
at political conventions, 133–34
political rights and, 37–38, 134,
    170
in politics and government, 61,
    63, 150–53
Populism and, 202–3
Reconstruction era and south-
    ern, 9
Redemption criminal code and,
    195–96
school children, 134 (ill.)
Sea Islands and, 39–40
as sharecroppers, 157–58, 195
as soldiers, 2, 20–25, 36, 37 (ill.)
in Southern Reconstruction
    governments, 170–71, 193
strong Southern communities
    of, 196–97

taking leading roles in Recon-
    struction, 148
Union League and, 131, 132
violence against southern, 58,
    70, 89, 129, 140, 159, 160,
    171, 181 (ill.)
Africans, 12, 13
Akerman, Amos T., 162
Alabama, Selma to Montgomery
    march, 207 (ill.)
Alcorn, James L., 133
Alcorn University, 197
American Civil War, 1, 4–5, 27–49
    African American school chil-
        dren during, 134 (ill.)
    beginning, 16–18
    Grant, Ulysses S., and, 138–39
    Hampton, Wade, in, 184
    Hayes, Rutherford B., in, 182
    Howard, Oliver Otis, and, 86
    Lincoln, Abraham, and, 2, 4, 5,
        7
    Radical Republicans and, 108
    Schurz, Carl, and, 90
    slavery and, 4–5, 17, 18–20, 30,
        51
    Smalls, Robert, in, 154
    Stevens, Thaddeus, and, 102
    Sumner, Charles, and, 107
American Indians. See Native
    Americans
Ames, Adelbert, 152, 177–78, 178
    (ill.)
Ames, Mary, 1–2
Amnesty, 74, 80, 88, 168. See also
    Pardons
Anderson, Jourdon, 54–55
Anthony, Susan B., 111 (ill.), 114
Antislavery newspapers, 14, 15
    (ill.)
Antiwar protests, 20
Aristocracy, plantation, 12, 85–88
Arkansas, 152, 160
Armstrong, Samuel Chapman,
    200
Ashley, James M., 104
Atlanta Compromise, 200, 204

B

Banks, Nathaniel B., 37, 41
Bingham, John A., 105

The Birth of a Nation (Griffith), 208, 208 (ill.)

Black Codes, 68, 74, 91–94, 93 (ill.), 100, 195
  Civil Rights Bill and, 109–10
  Reconstruction governments and, 149

Black Panthers, 206

Blacks. *See* African Americans

Blaine, James G., 105

Blair, Francis Preston, Jr., 137 (ill.), 140 (ill.)

Booth, John Wilkes, 48

Border states, 2. *See also* specific border states

Bowers, Claude G., 208

Boycotts, Montgomery bus, 206

Brooks, Preston, 106

Brown v. Board of Education, 199, 206

Bruce, Blanche K., 151, 151 (ill.)

Bunche, Ralph, 207 (ill.)

Bureau of Refugees, Freedmen, and Abandoned Lands. *See* Freedmen's Bureau

Bus segregation, 206

Butler, Benjamin, 17–18, 36

C

Campbell, John, 161 (ill.)

Campbell, Tunis G., 128

Cardozo, Francis L., 128

Carnegie, Andrew, 200

Carpetbaggers, 8–9, 133, 147–48, 170–71, 192–93

Chamberlain, Daniel, 184, 185

Chandler, Zachariah, 77, 80

Chinese immigrants, 163

Churches, 60–61, 61 (ill.), 62–63

Cincinnati Commercial, 54

Cities, blacks in, 56–57, 82–83, 158, 205

Citizenship, African Americans and responsibilities of, 118, 146

Civil rights
  Creoles, 37
  Douglass, Frederick, and, 22–23
  Johnson, Andrew, and, 71, 77, 110

  Reconstruction era and, 9, 70–71, 134
  Republicans and, 105, 110, 111

Civil Rights Act of 1867, 98, 124

Civil Rights Act of 1875, 168, 180

Civil Rights Act of 1964, 113, 206

Civil Rights Bill, 109–10, 110 (ill.), 111

Civil rights movement, 190, 205, 206–7

Civil service, 173

Civil War. *See* American Civil War

Colfax, Schuyler, 137 (ill.)

Colleges and universities, African American, 87, 196–97, 200–201, 202, 204

Colonialism, 203

Colored Tennessean, 59

Communism, 203

Communist Party USA (CPUSA), 203

Compromise of 1877, 168, 183, 185–86

Confederacy. *See also* Southern United States
  African American soldiers and, 25
  amnesty and, 80, 88
  formation of, 7, 16
  Fourteenth Amendment and, 113–14
  Johnson, Andrew, and, 77, 80, 88–89
  landownership and, 83–84
  pardons and, 88–89
  Tennessee and, 78–79

Confederate States of America. *See* Confederacy

Congress. *See* U.S. Congress

Constitutional amendments, 209. *See also* specific amendments

Contraband, 28, 32

Contracts. *See* Labor contracts

Convict lease system, 196

Cooke, Jay, 175–76

Corruption
  Grant, Ulysses S., and, 163–64, 179 (ill.)
  in Reconstruction governments, 153–56, 171, 192–93

Cotton
  African Americans and, 33 (ill.), 40, 42 (ill.), 157 (ill.)
  Northerners and, 94–95

overproduction of, 156
Cotton States and International
    Exposition (1895), 200
Courts
    Freedmen's Bureau and, 70
    white terrorists and, 160
CPUSA (Communist Party USA),
    203
Creoles, 36, 37
Criminal code, of Redemption
    government, 195–96
The Crisis, 203
Crosby, Peter, 177

D

Davis Bend, Mississippi, 28,
    41–42
Davis, Henry Winter, 44
Davis, Jefferson, 16, 28, 41, 88
Davis, Joseph, 41, 42
Declaration of Independence, 13
Declaration of Sentiments, 112
Delany, Martin R., 128
Delaware, 2, 16, 34
Democratic Party, 15–16, 101. *See
    also* Southern Democrats
    in elections of 1866, 117
    in elections of 1867, 135
    in elections of 1868, 137
    in elections of 1874, 178–80
    Radical Republicans and, 105,
        108, 146
DeYoung, John, 69
Disenfranchisement. *See* Voting
    rights
District of Columbia, African
    American suffrage in, 117
Douglas, Stephen, 6
Douglass, Frederick, 14, 19,
    22–23, 23 (ill.), 97–98, 151
    (ill.)
    on African American migra-
        tion, 197–98
    African American soldiers and,
        21, 24
    Johnson, Andrew, and, 94
Du Bois, W. E. B., 149, 202–3, 203
    (ill.), 204, 204 (ill.)
    on post-Reconstruction period,
        198
    vs. Washington, Booker T., 201

Dubuclet, Antoine, 36
Dunning, William A., 208

E

Eager, Washington, 160
Eastman, George, 200
Economy
    based on slave labor, 12–13
    in Northern United States, 4,
        162–63
    in Reconstruction era South,
        66–67, 104, 156, 171, 174,
        176, 196
    in Southern United States, 4,
        13
Edisto Island, 1
Editorial cartoons. *See* Political
    cartoons
Education
    African American institutions,
        158, 196–97, 200–201, 202,
        204
    African Americans and, 1–2, 3,
        46 (ill.), 64–65, 65 (ill.),
        69–70, 92, 149, 158
    integration in, 134, 150
    in Reconstruction era South,
        149
    in Redemption government,
        194
    vocational, 200–201, 204
Elections
    African American voters in, 146
    of 1865, 88
    of 1866, 117
    of 1867, 135, 137
    of 1868, 137 (ill.), 137–41, 140
        (ill.), 160
    of 1872, 162, 174
    of 1874, 177–80
    of 1876, 180 (ill.), 180–85
    Enforcement Acts and, 160–62
    fraud in, 183
    violence and intimidation in,
        140–41, 160, 162 (ill.),
        176–78, 194–95
Emancipation, 18–20, 19 (ill.). *See
    also* Freedom
    American Civil War and, 30–31
    rejoicing over, 31 (ill.), 52–54,
        189–90

Emancipation Proclamation of 1863, 7, 18–20, 30–31, 51, 204–5
Enforcement Acts, 139, 144, 160–62, 175
Equal Pay Act of 1963, 113
Equality, 4, 9, 71
  Creoles and, 37
  disagreement over, 14
  Fourteenth Amendment and, 114–15
  Radical Republicans and, 105, 108, 126
Etheridge, Emerson, 93–94
Exoduster movement, 190, 197 (ill.), 197–98

F

Family reunions, 59–60
Feminist leaders, Fourteenth Amendment and, 112–13, 114
Fessenden, William Pitt, 105
Fifteenth Amendment, 23, 52, 144, 160–61
Fifty-fourth Massachusetts regiment, 2, 23, 24, 47
Films, African American regiment in, 24
Financial scandals, Grant, Ulysses S., and, 139
First South Carolina Volunteers, 2, 24, 84 (ill.)
Fisk University, 197, 202, 204
Florida, 93, 149, 152
Flowers, Andrew, 167, 170
Former slaves. *See also* Free African Americans; Slavery
  behavior of, 58–59
  education and, 1–2, 3
  freedom's effects on, 56–65
  interviews with, 209
  as leaders, 148
  letters of, 54–55
  of Sea Islands, 39–40
Forrest, Nathan Bedford, 159, 160 (ill.)
"Forty Acres and a Mule," 28, 46–47, 52, 68
Fourteenth Amendment, 111–15
  Plessy v. Ferguson on, 199

Reconstruction Acts and, 126, 131
Free African Americans, 35–38. *See also* African Americans; Former slaves
  Freedmen's Conventions and, 128–29
  in Southern governments, 171
Free Soil Party, 106
Freedmen's Bureau, 45, 45 (ill.), 57, 68–70, 108–9
  Howard, Oliver Otis, and, 86–87
  land distribution and, 83–84, 120
  violence and, 57 (ill.), 70
Freedmen's Bureau Bill, 108–9
Freedmen's Conventions, 124, 127–30
Freedom, 1–26, 19 (ill.), 51–72
  abolitionists, 13–14
  African American soldiers and, 20–25
  American Civil War begins, 16–18
  effects of, 56–65
  Emancipation Proclamation, 18–20
  free African Americans and, 36
  Lincoln, Abraham, 6–7
  North vs. South, 4, 9, 12, 15–16
  obstacles in, 127
  plantation aristocracy, 12
  Reconstruction era, 5, 8–9
  rejoicing over, 52–54, 189–90
  responsibilities of, 118
  slavery conditions before, 10–11, 13
Fugitive Slave Law, 102

G

Garfield, James A., 183
Garrison, William Lloyd, 14, 14 (ill.), 22
Georgia
  African American village in, 39 (ill.)
  African Americans picking cotton in, 157 (ill.)
  black landownership in, 29, 45–47, 53, 68, 83–85, 120

elections of 1868 and, 141
plantation break ups in, 158
violence against African Americans in, 177
Ghettoes, 206–7
Gideon's Band, 28, 29, 40
Glory, 24
Governors, provisional, 80
Grant, Ulysses S., 18, 47, 79, 89, 138–39, 139 (ill.)
corruption and, 163–64
election of 1868, 137 (ill.), 137–41
end of Reconstruction and, 179–80
Enforcement Acts and, 161–62
political cartoon, 179 (ill.)
reelection, 175
shift in Republican Party with, 172
Sumner, Charles, and, 107
Great Depression, 205
"The Great Leveler." *See* Stevens, Thaddeus
Greeley, Horace, 175, 175 (ill.)
Grey, William H., 123
Griffith, D. W., 208

H

Hampton Institute, 200, 204
Hampton, Wade, 184–85, 185 (ill.)
Harper's Weekly, 57 (ill.), 91, 110 (ill.)
Harrison, Benjamin, 153
Harvard University, 202, 204
Hayes, Lucy, 182
Hayes, Rutherford B., 91, 139, 181, 182–83, 183 (ill.), 185–86, 192
Hershaw, Lafayette M., 204 (ill.)
Historians
on African American suffrage, 130
on corruption in Reconstruction era, 154
Johnson, Andrew, and, 88
Radical Republicans and, 108
Reconstruction era and, 8–9, 147–48
Holloway, Houston, 53–54
Home Rule, 168
Greeley, Horace, and, 175

Hayes, Rutherford B., and, 183, 185–86
Liberal Republicans and, 173
Homestead Act of 1862, 78
Hood, James, 118
Howard, Oliver Otis, 69, 84, 86–87, 87 (ill.)
Howard University, 87, 197
Humphreys, Benjamin, 92

I

Immigrants, Chinese, 163
Impeachment of Andrew Johnson, 79, 103, 107, 124, 135–37
Integration, 5, 124, 134, 144, 150
Intimidation of voters, 176–78, 184–85
Ironclad Oath, 44

J

Jackson, Andrew, 78
Jackson, Thomas "Stonewall," 18
Jim Crow laws, 183, 186, 190, 195, 198, 201
Johnson, Andrew, 35, 78–79, 79 (ill.), 170
civil rights and, 71, 110
disastrous speaking tour, 116–17
elections of 1866 and, 117
Fourteenth Amendment and, 115
impeachment, 79, 103, 107, 124, 135–37
political cartoons of, 101 (ill.), 136 (ill.)
Reconstruction and, 76, 77, 79, 80–82, 85–95, 100, 105, 111, 126
U.S. Congress and, 78, 80, 95, 103, 105, 109, 110, 111, 135–37
Johnson, Lyndon B., 207
Joint Committee on Reconstruction, 108, 110–11
Jubilee of Emancipation Proclamation, 204–5
Julian, George W., 104

K

Kansas, African American migration to, 197–98
Kansas-Nebraska Act of 1854, 6
Kansas-Nebraska Bill, 106
Kellogg, William P., 181, 184
Kentucky, 2, 16, 34
Keppler, Joseph, 179 (ill.)
Kerner Commission, 207
King, Coretta Scott, 207 (ill.)
King, Martin Luther, Jr., 206, 207 (ill.)
Knights of the Rising Sun, 159
Knights of the White Camellia, 159
Ku Klux Klan, 159–60
  African American voters and, 140, 141
  Campbell, John, and, 161 (ill.)
  Flowers, Andrew, and, 167
  in late 20th century, 207
  Union League and, 132

L

Labor
  land and, 67–68, 82–83
  in Reconstruction era South, 38–42, 66–68, 74–75, 82–83, 156–58
  slave, 10, 11, 12
Labor contracts, 41, 68, 92, 93
Labor movement, 164, 205
Labor unions, 164
Land
  labor and, 67–68, 82–83
  redistribution of, 45–47, 67–68, 83–85, 103, 119–20, 134–35, 150
Landlord and Tenant Act of 1877, 195
Law enforcement
  African Americans in, 152, 196
  white terrorists and, 160
Laws. *See also* Black Codes
  of Reconstruction governments, 149
  segregation, 150
  vagrancy, 57, 195
Lee, Robert E., 18, 47, 139
Legislation. *See* specific legislation

Legislators. *See* Southern legislators
Letters, former slave, 54–55
Liberal Republicans, 168, 172–74
Liberator, 14, 15 (ill.)
The Life and Times of Frederick Douglass (Douglass), 23
Lincoln, Abraham, 6–7, 7 (ill.)
  African American soldiers and, 2, 21
  African Americans and, 48
  American Civil War and, 4, 5, 7
  black suffrage and, 71
  Douglass, Frederick, and, 23
  Emancipation Proclamation of 1863, 18–19, 31 (ill.)
  Grant, Ulysses S., and, 138
  Johnson, Andrew, and, 79
  political cartoon, 101 (ill.)
  Reconstruction and, 7, 28, 34, 42–43, 44, 76
  in Richmond, Virginia, 47
  Schurz, Carl, and, 90
  slavery and, 6–7, 16, 18–19, 20, 30
  Wade-Davis Bill and, 29, 44
Living conditions, slave, 10–11, 11 (ill.), 13
Long, Jefferson, 151
Long, Thomas, 24
Louisiana
  African American suffrage in, 44
  African Americans in law enforcement, 152
  Black Codes in, 93
  elections of 1868 and, 141
  elections of 1876 in, 181, 184
  integrated schools and, 150
  labor experiments in, 40–41, 158
  racial riots in, 115, 116 (ill.)
  reconstruction of, 35–38
  voter intimidation in, 162 (ill.)
Louisiana Purchase, 15
Luke, William, 160
Lynch, John Roy, 151, 152–53, 153 (ill.), 208
Lynch law, 190, 198

M

Malcolm X, 206
Marriage, slavery and, 11, 59

Martial law, 65–66
Maryland, 2, 16, 34–35
Massachusetts Anti-Slavery Society, 22
Massachusetts regiment, Fifty-fourth, 2, 23, 24
McClellan, George, 18, 20, 79
McKinley, William, 153
Memphis, Tennessee, racial riots in, 115, 159
Mexican-American War, 15
Middle Passage, 12
Migration, African American
    to Kansas, 197 (ill.), 197–98
    to North, 205
    urban, 56–57, 82–83, 205
Migration, western, 163
Militia Act of 1862, 2, 21
Miller, Thomas E., 164
Ministers, African American, 61, 63
Miscegenation, 59, 82
Mississippi
    African American–run community in, 28, 41–42
    African Americans in law enforcement, 152
    Black Codes in, 93
    corruption by government officials, 156
    education, 149
    Mississippi Plan, 168, 177–78, 180
    pig law in, 196
    Second Mississippi Plan, 191, 199, 202–3
Mississippi Plan, 168, 177–78, 180
Missouri, 2, 16, 34
Missouri Compromise of 1820, 6, 8 (ill.)
Moderate Republicans
    Johnson, Andrew, and, 111
    Reconstruction debate and, 104–5
    in Thirty-ninth Congress, 101
Montgomery bus boycott (1955), 206
Morton, Oliver P., 117
Moses, Franklin J., 156
Mott, Lucretia, 112
Movies, African American regiment in, 24
Mulattoes, 36, 124, 128–29

Multiracial democracy, 143–44, 147, 150–53, 170–71, 191–92, 193
Multiracial political conventions, 133–35
Murray, F. H. M., 204 (ill.)
Mutual benefit societies, 53, 61, 64

N

NAACP (National Association for the Advancement of Colored People), 201, 202
Names, African Americans and, 59–60
Nast, Thomas, illustrations by, 19 (ill.)
Nation magazine, 173–74, 186
National Association for the Advancement of Colored People (NAACP), 201, 202
National Negro Business League, 201
Native Americans, 87, 91, 163
New Departure, 168–69, 174
New Orleans, Louisiana, 35–37
    integrated schools and, 150
    racial riots in, 115, 116 (ill.), 159
New York Stock Exchange, 176 (ill.)
New York Tribune, 54, 175
Newspapers. *See also* specific newspapers
    advertisements, 59
    antislavery, 14, 15 (ill.)
Niagara Movement, 201, 202, 204, 204 (ill.)
Nineteenth Amendment, 113
Nkrumah, Kwame, 203
North Carolina, 93
North Star, 22
Northern United States
    African American migration to, 205
    corruption in, 154–55
    Reconstruction era developments in, 162–63
    vs. Southern United States, 4, 9, 12, 15–16

O

Oath of allegiance, by First South
     Carolina Volunteers, 84 (ill.)
107th Colored Infantry, 37 (ill.)
Overseers, 10

P

Pan African Congresses, 203
Panic of 1873, 169, 175–76, 176
     (ill.)
Pardons, 43, 68, 80, 88
Parks, Rosa, 206
Patrollers, 10
"Pattyrollers." *See* Patrollers
Penal code, of Redemption gov-
     ernment, 195–96
Philbrick, Edward S., 40
Phillips, Wendell, 117
Pierrepont, Edwards, 178
"Pig law," 196
Pinchback, P. B. S., 37–38, 38 (ill.)
Plantation aristocracy, 12, 85–88
Plantation owners
     Civil War effects on, 66
     property taxes and, 150
     in Redemption era South, 195
     sharecropping and, 158
     wealth and, 12
Plantations
     breakup of, 119
     labor experiments on, 41–42
     slaves on, 10, 11, 11 (ill.)
Planter, 154
Planter aristocracy, 12, 85–88
Plessy, Adolph, 199
Plessy v. Ferguson, 190–91, 198–99
Pocket-veto, of Wade-Davis Bill,
     44
Political cartoons, 45 (ill.), 101
     (ill.), 110 (ill.), 136 (ill.), 140
     (ill.), 179 (ill.)
Political conventions, multiracial,
     133–35
Political corruption
     Grant, Ulysses S., and, 163–64,
          179 (ill.)
     in Reconstruction govern-
          ments, 153–56, 171, 192–93
Political organizations, 131, 132

Political parties. *See* specific par-
     ties
Political rights. *See also* Voting
     rights
     disagreement over, 37–38
     Douglass, Frederick, and, 23
     Radical Republicans and, 134,
          170
"Politics of livelihood," 155
Poll tax, 177, 199
Populism, 202–3
Poverty. *See also* Economy
     African Americans and, 62–63,
          195
     in Redemption era South, 196
Preachers, African American, 61
Preliminary Emancipation Procla-
     mation, 18–19
Presidential elections. *See* Elec-
     tions
Presidents. *See* specific presidents
President's Reconstruction plan,
     73–96
     Johnson, Andrew, and, 76, 77,
          79, 80–82, 85–95, 100, 105,
          111, 126
     land and labor, 82–85
     Lincoln, Abraham, and, 7, 28,
          34, 42–43, 76
     opposition to, 94–95
     Radical Republicans and,
          76–77, 81
Proclamation of Amnesty, 74, 80,
     84
Proclamation of Amnesty and Re-
     construction, 7, 28, 34,
     42–43, 76, 103
Property taxes, 150, 194
Protests, war, 20
Public facilities' segregation, 198
Public school systems, 69–70, 149
Public services, Reconstruction
     governments and, 148–49
Public transportation, equal ac-
     cess to, 150
Puck magazine, 179 (ill.)
Punishment, of slaves, 10

R

Racial riots, 98, 115, 116 (ill.),
     159, 206–7

Racism, 55–56
  segregation and, 150
  slaveholders and, 67
  slavery and, 4, 13–14
  Union Army and, 32
  white Southerners and, 140
Radical Republicans, 43–44, 71,
    170
  Civil Rights Bill and, 109–10
  elections of 1866 and, 117
  end of, 172
  Freedmen's Bureau Bill and,
    108–9
  Johnson, Andrew, and, 77, 81,
    95, 117, 135, 137
  optimism of, 76–77
  prominent, 101–4, 106–7
  Reconstruction Acts of 1867
    and, 118–19
  Reconstruction plan of, 81,
    97–121, 123–42, 146
  Southern governments and,
    191
  Union League and, 132
Railroads
  Reconstruction era corruption
    and, 156
  segregation of, 198–99
  western migration and, 163
Rainey, Joseph, 151
Ransier, Alonzo J., 209
Ratification of Fourteenth
    Amendment, 115
Reconstruction
  African American churches dur-
    ing, 60–61
  challenges of, 5, 8, 98–99
  changing view of, 8–9
  end of, 178–80, 183
  evaluation of, 205–9
  failures of, 190–92
  Johnson, Andrew, and, 76, 77,
    79, 80–82, 85–95, 100, 105,
    111, 126
  labor and, 66–68
  legacy of, 189–210
  Lincoln, Abraham, and, 7, 28,
    34, 42–43, 44, 76
  overview, 3–4, 51–52, 143–45
  President's plan in, 73–96, 126
  Radical Republicans and, 81,
    97–121, 123–42, 146
  rehearsals for, 33–40
  Stevens, Thaddeus, and, 102–3

successes of, 209
  U.S. Congress struggles with
    plan for, 118
  Wade-Davis Bill and, 43–44
Reconstruction Acts of 1867,
    118–19, 126, 146
  political activity grows with,
    130–31
  revolutionary effects of, 120,
    143
Reconstruction governments
  achievements and disappoint-
    ments, 143–65
  corruption and, 153–56
  disagreements and tensions in,
    148
  forming of, 133–35
  multiracial democracy, 143–44,
    147, 150–53, 170–71,
    191–92, 193
  Radical Republican's plan for,
    146–47
  Republican goals and achieve-
    ments in, 148–49
  white terrorists and, 159–62
Red Shirts, 184, 185
Redemption movement, 167–87,
    191, 192–99
  African American disenfran-
    chisement in, 176–77
  beginnings of, 171–72
  Compromise of 1877 and, 183
  elections and, 176–85
  Hampton, Wade, in, 184–85
  Hayes, Rutherford B., and,
    185–86
Regiments, African American, 2,
    23, 24, 36
Regressive tax system, 194
Regulations, labor, 41
Republican Party, 15–16, 169. See
    also Moderate Republicans;
    Radical Republicans
  debate over Reconstruction in,
    104–5
  in elections of 1866, 117
  in elections of 1867, 135
  in elections of 1868, 137, 140,
    141
  in elections of 1874, 178–80
  freed African Americans and,
    43–44
  Johnson, Andrew, and, 35, 77,
    79

Liberal Republicans, 168, 172–74
  Lincoln, Abraham, and, 6
  in Mississippi, 178
  shifting direction of, 172
  in Southern Redemption gov-
    ernments, 194–95
  in U.S. Congress, 100–101,
    104–5, 108
Reunions, family, 59–60
Revels, Hiram, 151, 151 (ill.)
Richmond, Virginia, 47
Riots, 20. *See also* Racial riots
Rivers, Prince, 128
Rosenwald, Julius, 201
Runaway slaves, 14, 16–18

S

St. Louis, Missouri, 197 (ill.)
Saxton, Rufus, 83, 84 (ill.), 85, 85
    (ill.), 189–90
Scalawags, 133, 147, 148, 170–71,
    193
  historians and, 8–9
  "politics of livelihood" and, 155
  Republican Party and, 174
Scandals. *See also* Corruption
  Grant, Ulysses S., and, 139,
    163–64
  in Northern United States,
    154–55
Schools. *See* Education
Schurz, Carl, 89–91, 91 (ill.), 108,
    172
Scott, Robert K., 156
Sea Islands, 29, 38–40, 46
Secession
  American Civil War and, 16
  Johnson, Andrew, and, 77
  map of, 17 (ill.)
  Sumner, Charles on, 107
Second Mississippi Plan, 191, 199,
    202–3
Segregation, 53, 58–59, 150. *See
    also Plessy v. Ferguson*
  accommodation to, 200–201
  Jim Crow laws, 195, 198
  in schools, 134
Selling, of slaves, 10–11
Selma to Montgomery, Alabama,
    march, 207 (ill.)
Separate but equal, 206
Settle, Thomas, 133

Sexual violence, 59
Seymour, Horatio, 137, 137 (ill.),
    140 (ill.), 141
Sharecropping, 132, 145, 157–58,
    194, 195
Shaw, Robert Gould, 24
Sheridan, Philip, 115, 135
Sherman, John, 105
"Sherman land," 46, 53, 68
Sherman, William T., 30, 41–42
  on Freedmen's Bureau, 69
  Howard, Oliver Otis, and, 86
  Special Field Order #15 and, 29,
    45–47, 53, 68, 83, 120
Slaughterhouse Cases, 169, 180
Slaveholders, 36, 54–56, 67
Slavery, 170. *See also* Emancipa-
    tion; Former slaves
  American Civil War and, 4–5,
    17, 18–20, 30, 51
  conditions under, 13
  division over, 4–5, 15–16
  economy based on, 12–13
  education of slaves, 64
  end of, 30–31, 44, 51–72, 97
  expansion of, 6, 8 (ill.), 15
  Johnson, Andrew, and, 35, 78,
    81–82
  Lincoln, Abraham, and, 6–7,
    16, 18–19, 20, 30
  living conditions of slaves,
    10–11, 11 (ill.), 13
  Louisiana and, 36–37
  marriage and, 11, 59
  Maryland and, 34
  racism and, 4, 13–14
  runaway slaves, 14, 16–18
  slaves in Union Army, 17–18,
    28, 32, 82–83
  Stevens, Thaddeus, and, 102
  Sumner, Charles, and, 106–7
Smalls, Robert, 128, 151, 154–55,
    155 (ill.), 189, 209
Smith, James M., 177
Social services
  of African American churches,
    63
  Freedmen's Bureau and, 87
  in multiracial democratic
    South, 171
  Reconstruction governments
    and, 134
Soldiers, African American, 2,
    20–25, 36, 37 (ill.)

The Souls of Black Folk (Du Bois),
202
South Carolina, 47
  African American landowner-
    ship in, 29, 46–47, 53, 68,
    83–85, 120, 150
  African Americans in politics,
    152–53
  Black Codes in, 93
  education in, 149
  elections of 1876 in, 184–85
  plantation breakups, 158
  prewar conditions, 149
  Reconstruction government's
    budget, 150
South Carolina Volunteers, First,
  2, 24, 84 (ill.)
Southern Democrats, 193–95. *See
  also* Democratic Party
  corruption by, 156
  economy and, 171, 176
  in elections of 1872, 174
  vs. Radical Republicans, 146
Southern legislators
  federal government participa-
    tion by, 111
  Thirty-ninth Congress and, 105
Southern United States. *See also*
    Confederacy; Reconstruc-
    tion; Redemption movement
  African American landowner-
    ship in, 45–47, 67–68, 83–85,
    103, 119–20, 134–35, 150
  African Americans in politics
    and government, 61, 63,
    150–53, 155
  Black Codes in, 91–94
  as a changed society, 73–76
  desolation in, 66, 73–74
  economy of, 4, 13, 66–67, 104,
    156, 171, 174, 176, 196
  elections in, 88, 135, 140–41,
    174, 176–85
  federal government participa-
    tion and, 111
  Fourteenth Amendment and,
    112–13, 115
  Freedmen's Conventions in,
    127–30
  labor and, 4, 38–42, 66–68,
    74–75, 156–58
  Lincoln, Abraham, and, 6–7
  mistreatment of African Ameri-
    cans in, 129, 140

multiracial democracy in,
  170–71, 191–92, 193
vs. Northern United States, 4,
  9, 12, 15–16
public school system in, 69–70
Reconstruction challenges in, 5
Reconstruction governments
  in, 133–35, 141, 143–65
reports on conditions in,
  89–92, 108, 110–11
Republican Reconstruction
  plan for, 118–19, 126
slaves in, 10–11, 12, 13
Union League and, 132
Union's African American soldiers and, 25
violence against African Americans in, 58, 70, 89, 129, 140,
  159, 160, 171, 181 (ill.)
wealth in, 12
white terrorists in, 158–60
Sparks, Eliza, 27
Special Field Order #15, 29,
  45–47, 53, 68, 83, 120
Stalwarts, 172–73
Stanton, Edwin M., 46, 119, 135,
  172
Stanton, Elizabeth Cady, 111
  (ill.), 112, 113, 114
State constitutions, Reconstruc-
  tion era South and, 119, 126,
  146
Stephens, Alexander H., 88
Stevens, Thaddeus, 76, 102–3,
  103 (ill.), 104, 172
  Johnson, Andrew, and, 103, 117
  Southern land redistribution
    and, 120
Suffrage. *See* African American
  suffrage
Sumner, Charles, 76, 104, 106–7,
  107 (ill.), 172, 180
Suppression clauses, of Second
  Mississippi Plan, 199
"Swing around the circle," 116

T

Taxes
  poll tax, 177, 199
  in Reconstruction, 150, 194
  for social services, 171

Ten Per Cent Plan. *See* Proclamation of Amnesty and Reconstruction
Tennessee, 35
  Confederacy and, 78–79
  Fourteenth Amendment and, 115
  racial riots, 115
  white terrorists, 159, 160
Tenure of Office Act, 135, 136
Texas, 93, 149, 159, 160
Thirteenth Amendment, 7, 44, 75, 109
Thirty-ninth Congress, 95, 100–101, 104–6, 117–18
Tilden, Samuel, 180 (ill.), 181, 183
Tillman, Benjamin R., 185, 203
"To Thine Own Self Be True," 110 (ill.)
The Tragic Era (Bowers), 208
Trotter, William Monroe, 204 (ill.)
Trumbull, Lyman, 105, 108
Tuskegee Institute, 200, 201, 204

U

Underground Railroad, 14
Understanding clauses, 199
Union army. *See also* American Civil War; specific regiments
  African Americans in, 2, 20–25
  slaves and, 17–18, 28, 32, 82–83
  Smalls, Robert, and, 154
Union League, 125, 131, 132
Unionists, 193–94
  Johnson, Andrew as, 81–82
  in Louisiana, 36–37
  in Maryland, 34
Unions, labor, 164
United States. *See also* Southern United States
  border states, 2
  secession from, 17 (ill.)
United States v. Cruikshank, 180
Universities. *See* Colleges and universities, African American
Up from Slavery (Washington), 201
Urban migration, 56–57, 82–83, 205
U.S. Congress
  African Americans and, 71

Freedmen's Conventions and, 130
Johnson, Andrew, and, 78, 80, 95, 103, 105, 109, 110, 111, 135–37
Republican majority in, 100–101, 104–5, 108
runaway slaves and, 18
Stevens, Thaddeus, in, 102–3
struggle with Reconstruction plan, 118
U.S. Constitution. *See* specific amendments
U.S. Supreme Court
  Brown v. Board of Education, 199, 206
  Plessy v. Ferguson, 190–91, 198–99
  Slaughterhouse Cases, 169, 180

V

Vagrancy, 53, 57, 93, 195
Veto
  of Civil Rights Bill, 110
  of Freedmen's Bureau Bill, 109
Violence
  in elections, 176–78
  Freedmen's Bureau and, 57 (ill.), 70
  in late 20th century, 207
  sexual, 59
  against Southern African Americans, 58, 70, 89, 129, 140, 159, 160, 171, 181 (ill.)
  by white terrorists, 159–60
Vocational education, 200–201, 204
Voting rights, 5, 23, 194–95. *See also* African American suffrage
  in District of Columbia, 117
  in elections of 1872, 175
  in elections of 1874, 177–78
  Enforcement Acts and, 160–62
  of former Confederates, 134, 146
  Grant, Ulysses S., and, 139
  in Redemption era South, 176–77
  Second Mississippi Plan and, 199
Voting Rights Act, 206

W

Wade, Benjamin F., 44, 104
Wade-Davis Bill, 29, 43–44
Washington, Booker T., 200–201, 201 (ill.), 202, 203–4
Washington, George, 139
Watts riots, 207
West
  black suffrage in, 118
  migration to, 163
  Reconstruction era developments in, 163
  slavery and, 6, 8 (ill.), 18
West Virginia, 34
Whig Party, 148
White churches, 60, 62
White Liners, 159, 177–78, 184
White Southerners
  African American voters and, 137, 140
  African Americans in politics and government, 150–51
  amnesty for, 80
  emancipation and, 32–33, 54–56
  free labor system and, 68
  Freedmen's Bureau and, 108
  Johnson, Andrew, and, 105
  Lincoln, Abraham, and, 7
  mistreatment of African Americans by, 129, 140

multiracial governments and, 147
in multiracial political conventions, 133
new African American behavior and, 58–59
plantation aristocracy and, 86–87
Reconstruction Acts and, 146
Reconstruction era and, 9
resentment of, 73, 74
resistance to change, 89, 158–60
White supremacists, 181 (ill.)
  elections of 1868 and, 137
  Ku Klux Klan as, 159
  Reconstruction evaluation by, 207–8
  Redemption movement and, 167–87
White terrorists, 5, 158–60
  African American voters and, 140
  black churches and, 63
  Enforcement Acts and, 139, 160–62
Wilson, Henry, 104
Women's rights, 112–13
Women's suffrage, 113, 114, 114 (ill.)
Wood, Robert H., 151–52
Woodhull, Victoria, 114 (ill.)
World War I, 205